SHAKESPEARE AND
THE MEDIEVAL TRADITION

GARLAND REFERENCE LIBRARY
OF THE HUMANITIES
(VOL. 603)

SHAKESPEARE AND
THE MEDIEVAL TRADITION
An Annotated Bibliography

J. Paul McRoberts

GARLAND PUBLISHING INC. · NEW YORK & LONDON
1985

Library of Congress Cataloging in Publication Data

McRoberts, J. Paul, 1938–
Shakespeare and the medieval tradition.

(Garland reference library of the humanities ; v. 603)
Includes indexes.
1. Shakespeare, William, 1564–1616—Bibliography.
2. Shakespeare, William, 1564–1616—Sources—Bibliography.
3. Middle Ages in literature—Bibliography. 4. Civiliza-
tion, Medieval, in literature—Bibliography. 5. Drama,
Medieval—History and criticism—Bibliography. I. Title.
II. Series.
Z8813.M34 1985 [PR2953.M54] 016.8223′3 85-6925
ISBN 0-8240-8716-X (alk. paper)

Printed on acid-free, 250-year-life paper
Manufactured in the United States of America

This Book is for
Wanda, Michele, and Chad

CONTENTS

Indexes

PREFACE

The Scope, Definitions,
Limitations, Format, and Sources

This bibliography, *Shakespeare and the Medieval Tradition*, annotates books, articles, notes, chapters, letters to editors, and (in some cases) introductions to individual plays which concern the criticism of Medieval elements in Shakespearean drama. Including cross-references, the book lists over 1200 entries and contains only those works published in English between 1900 and 1980. Studies published in languages other than English were not included unless, of course, they were later translated to English. Generally, I have tried not to pronounce judgments on the critical commentary, and I do not claim that my annotations will satisfy everyone or that I have not overlooked some titles. Indeed, I invite suggestions and criticisms so that if in the future the bibliography is revised and expanded to cover commentary published since 1980, scholars and students will have a better research guide.

I have interpreted the term "Medieval" to include all critical commentary referring to Shakespeare and aspects of his Medieval heritage. At times the term is related to philosophical or religious concepts exposed by Augustine, Aquinas, Dante or Boethuis; but for the most part, the term is associated with English authors and English literature during the Medieval period. In addition, I have interpreted "tradition" to include folklore, ballads, homiletic material, astrological studies, stage construction, rhetorical studies, grammar school textbooks, analogues, source studies, and themes and conventions of Medieval literature.

In compiling my bibliography, I am indebted to the bibliographical research of Walther Ebisch and Levin L. Schücking, Gordon Ross Smith, and the editors of the *Shakespeare Bibliography*, especially Harrison T. Meserole. Ebisch and Schücking's *A Shakespeare Bibliography* is highly selective and does not include materials published since 1935. Furthermore, less than a score of works are listed which concern Shakespeare and Medievalism. Gordon Ross Smith's definitive bibliography on Shakespeare contains published material from 1936 to 1958, but finding relevant materials is difficult as John Velz has pointed out (*English Studies*,

45 (1964), 189-191). Further, Smith lists slightly more than
100 entries, and some of these are not annotated. In recent
years, of course, the *Shakespeare Quarterly Bibliography* has
provided extensive listings and annotations of Shakespearean
criticism. Indeed, the success of the editors in gathering
information (often over 2,000 entries per year) points to the
need of focusing upon specific areas of Shakespearean
scholarship. Hence, my bibliography of Shakespeare's
Medieval heritage provides a comprehensive compilation of
scholarship in an important area of Shakespearean criticism.

In arranging my bibliography, I have followed the recent
organizational structure of the *Shakespeare Quarterly Bibliography*; therefore, my text is categorized into three areas:
general Shakespearean studies, studies of particular play
groups, studies relating to individual plays. The guiding
principle has been to put background material into the category
of general studies. Hence, books like the following would be
found in the first category: Glynne Wickham's *Early English
Stages 1300 to 1600*, G. R. Owst's *Literature and the Pulpit in
Medieval England*, and C. S. Lewis' *Allegory of Love*. The
second category, works dealing with particular genres, includes
those studies which primarily deal with the tragedies, comedies,
histories, and romances. Thus works such as Willard Farnham's
The Medieval Heritage of Shakespearean Tragedy and R. G.
Hunter's *Shakespeare and the Comedy of Forgiveness* are in this
section. Finally, the third division references those works
commenting upon a single play. Thelma Greenfield's "The
Clothing Motif in *King Lear*," and E. C. Pettet's "*Timon of
Athens*: The Disruption of Feudal Morality" are examples of
works in this section.

Each book or essay is fully listed once only in the category where I believe scholars would look for such information.
When the content of a reference would seem to be helpful to
other areas, I cross-referenced it to other sections of the
bibliography as a "see" with the entry number immediately
following. In addition, the reference is identified by title.
One of the distinct features of this bibliography is the
manner in which references are accessible. Scholars can approach
the bibliography through its four indexes: (1) names of authors,
editors, and contributors to the publications listed in the
bibliography; (2) a complete list of all Shakespearean plays
and works referred to in the text; (3) names of Medieval writers,
characters, people, books, songs, and poems; (4) a list of subjects including themes, ideas, motifs, religious concepts,
philosophies, and literary conventions. Numbers appearing
after a listing refer to item numbers in the bibliography.

Entry format is essentially that of the *MLA Handbook*. But

I have simplified this bibliographical system when I felt it
was beneficial. For the abbreviations of titles of the plays,
poems, journals, and other source materials, I am indebted to
the *Shakespeare Quarterly Bibliography*. Entries are arranged
alphabetically by author in each section with an annotation
provided for each entry unless the material was unavailable for
examination. Unpublished doctoral dissertations which are not
listed in *Dissertation Abstracts International* are typical of
those entries without annotation.

In many instances I was led to sources from notes in
numerous books and articles dealing with the surviving Medieval
culture and Shakespeare. In addition, I have used the following
bibliographic sources:

Dissertation Abstacts. Ann Arbor, Mich.: University
Microfilms (1938-1980).
Ebisch, Walther, and Levin L. Schücking. *A Shakespeare
Bibliography*. Oxford: Clarendon Press, 1931.
————. *A Shakespeare Bibliography*: *Supplement for the
Years 1930-1935*. Oxford: Clarendon Press, 1937.
Jaggard, William. *Shakespeare Bibliography*. New York:
F. Ungar, 1959.
Microfilm Abstracts (1938-1950).
Modern Humanities Research Association: *Annual Bibliography
of English Language and Literature* (1905-1980).
MLA International Bibliography (1929-1980).
Review of English Studies (1925-1980).
Shakespeare Association Bulletin (1924-1949).
Shakespeare-Jahrbuch (1896-1980)--Heidelberg.
Shakespeare-Jahrbuch (1896-1980)--Weimar.
Shakespeare Newsletter (1951-1980).
Shakespeare Quarterly (1950-1980).
Shakespeare Survey (1948-1980).
Smith, Gordon Ross. *A Classified Shakespeare Bibliography
1936-1958*. University Park, Pa.: Pennsylvania State
University Press, 1963.
Studies in Philology (1922-1900).
Velz, John W. *Shakespeare and the Classical Tradition*: *A
Critical Guide to Commentary*, (1660-1960). Minneapolis:
University of Minnesota Press, 1968.
Year's Work in English Studies (1938-1980).

I am grateful to Professor John Velz of the University of
Texas who pointed to the need of a bibliography on Shakespeare
and his surviving Medieval culture. In some ways my own work
parallels Professor Velz' book *Shakespeare and the Classical
Tradition*. In addition, I am appreciative of Professor
Johnstone Parr of Kent State University who first encouraged

me to pursue this bibliography. To Professor Harrison T. Meserole of The Pennsylvania State University I am indebted for various suggestions which helped to improve my manuscript. Professor Meserole's keen advice gave me direction both in the early and later stages of the manuscript. A grant from The Pennsylvania State University enabled me to do some of the research and provided some of the funds for clerical assistance. A special acknowledgment goes to the staff of the Library of the Beaver Campus of The Pennsylvania State University, especially June Gradisek and Linda DiSanti who attended to my requests for inter-library loan material. June Golletti and Michele McRoberts faithfully typed and photocopied the manuscript, and my sincerest thanks goes to them. Finally, Dr. Dan S. Green, Director of Academic Affairs, assigned me to teaching schedules which provided an opportunity to complete this bibliography. To all of these people I am very grateful.

J. P. McRoberts
The Pennsylvania State University
Beaver Campus

LIST OF SOURCES AND ABBREVIATIONS

AJP	*American Journal of Philology*
AM	*Atlantic Monthly*
AN&Q	*American Notes and Queries*
Anglia	*Anglia: Zeitschrift für Englische Philologie*
APSR	*American Political Science Review*
AR	*Antioch Review*
Archiv	*Archiv für das Studium de Neueren Sprachen und Literature*
BCAH	*Bulletin of the Canadian Association of Humanities*
BDECU	*Bulletin of the Department of English* (Calcutta Univ.)
BJRL	*Bulletin of John Rylands Library*
BM	*Burlington Magazine*
BSUF	*Ball State University Forum*
CahiersE	*Cahiers Elisabéthains*
CE	*College English*
CentR	*The Centennial Review*
Cithara	
CJ	*Classical Journal*
CL	*Comparative Literature*
CLAJ	*College Language Association Journal*
CompD	*Comparative Drama*
ContempR	*Contemporary Review*
CP	*Concerning Poetry*
CritQ	*Critical Quarterly*
CUC	*California University Chronicle*
CUF	*Columbia University Forum*
DAI	*Dissertation Abstracts International*
DR	*Dalhousie Review*
DS	*Dante Studies*
DUJ	*Durham University Journal*
EA	*Etudes Anglaises*
E&S	*Essays and Studies by Members of the English Association*
EAEL	*Essays in American and English Literature*
EHR	*English Historical Review* (London)
EIC	*Essays in Criticism* (Oxford)
EIE	*English Institute Essays*
EJ	*English Journal*
ELH	*Journal of English Literary History*

ELN	*English Language Notes*
ELR	*English Literary Renaissance*
EM	*English Miscellany*
EMQ	*Emory University Quarterly*
Encounter	
ES	*English Studies*
ESA	*English Studies in Africa (Johannesburg)*
EStud	*Englische Studien*
ETJ	*Educational Theater Journal*
FMLS	*Forum for Modern Language Studies*
Folklore	
Genre	
HAB	*Humanities Association Bulletin* (Canada)
HT	*History Today*
JAF	*Journal of American Folklore*
JEGP	*Journal of English and Germanic Philology*
JMRS	*Journal of Medieval and Renaissance Studies*
HLQ	*Huntington Library Quarterly*
IEY	*Iowa English Yearbook*
IUS	*Indiana University Studies*
KR	*Kenyon Review*
LA	*Living Age*
Library	
LM	*The London Mercury*
MichA	*Michigan Academician*
MLN	*Modern Language Notes*
MLR	*Modern Language Review* (London)
MLS	*Modern Language Studies*
MLQ	*Modern Language Quarterly*
Month	
MP	*Modern Philology* (Chicago)
NC	*Nineteenth Century*
N&Q	*Notes and Queries* (London)
NDQ	*North Dakota Quarterly*
NeoPhil	*NeoPhilologus*
NM	*NeuPhilogische Mitteilungen*
ON	*Opera News*
OL	*Orbis Litterarum*
PBA	*Proceedings of the British Academy*
PLL	*Papers on Language and Literature*
PM	*Players Magazine*
PMLA	*Publication of Modern Language Association*
PQ	*Philological Quarterly* (Iowa City)
PULC	*Princeton University Library Chronicle*
QQ	*Queens Quarterly*
QR	*Quarterly Review*
REL	*Review of English Literature*
Renascence	

RenD	*Renaissance Drama* (Northwestern Univ.)
RenQ	*Renaissance Quarterly*
RES	*Review of English Studies* (London)
RIP	*Rice Institute Pamphlet*
RORD	*Research Opportunities in Renaissance Drama*
RP	*Renaissance Papers*
RS	*Research Studies* (Washington State Univ.)
SAB	*Shakespeare Association Bulletin*
SAP	*Studia Anglica Posnaniensia*
SAQ	*South Atlantic Quarterly*
Scrutiny	
SEL	*Studies in English Literature*
SFQ	*Southern Folklore Quarterly*
ShakS	*Shakespeare Studies*
ShN	*Shakespeare Newsletter*
ShS	*Shakespeare Survey*
ShStud	*Shakespeare Studies* (Japan)
SI	*Studies in Iconography*
SJW	*Shakespeare-Jahrbuch* (Weimar)
SM	*Speech Monographs*
SN	*Studia NeoPhilologica*
SP	*Studies in Philology*
Speculum	
SQ	*Shakespeare Quarterly*
SR	*Sewanee Review*
SRen	*Studies in the Renaissance*
SRO	*Shakespeare Research and Opportunities*
TDR	*The Drama Review*
TDReview	*Tulane Drama Review*
ThS	*Theatre Survey*
TLS	*Times Literary Supplement*
TSE	*Tulane Studies in English*
TSL	*Tennessee Studies in Literature*
TSLL	*Texas Studies in Literature and Language*
UC	*The Upstart Crow* (Univ. of Tennessee, Martin)
UIHS	*University of Iowa Humanistic Studies*
UMS	*University of Missouri Studies*
UR	*University Review*
UTQ	*University of Toronto Quarterly*
WascanaR	*Wascana Review*
Words	*Wai Te Ata Studies in Literature*
WSL	*Wisconsin Studies in Literature*
WUS	*Washington University Studies*
YES	*Yearbook of English Studies*
YR	*Yale Review*
YSE	*Yale Studies in English*

KEY TO ABBREVIATIONS

Shakespeare's Works

Ado	*Much Ado About Nothing*
Ant.	*Antony and Cleopatra*
AWW	*All's Well That Ends Well*
AYL	*As You Like It*
Cor.	*Coriolanus*
Cym.	*Cymbeline*
Err.	*Comedy of Errors*
Ham.	*Hamlet*
1H4	*Henry IV, Part 1*
2H4	*Henry IV, Part 2*
1&2H4	*Henry IV, Parts 1&2*
H5	*Henry V*
1H6	*Henry VI, Part 1*
2H6	*Henry VI, Part 2*
3H6	*Henry VI, Parts 1&2*
H6Triad	*Henry VI Triad*
H8	*Henry VIII*
JC	*Julius Caesar*
Jn.	*King John*
LLL	*Love's Labor's Lost*
Lr.	*King Lear*
Luc.	*The Rape of Lucrece*
Mac.	*Macbeth*
MM	*Measure for Measure*
MND	*A Midsummer Night's Dream*
MV	*The Merchant of Venice*
Oth.	*Othello*
Per.	*Pericles*
PhT	*Phoenix and the Turtle*
PP	*A Passionate Pilgrim*
R2	*Richard II*
R3	*Richard III*
Rom.	*Romeo and Juliet*
Shr.	*The Taming of the Shrew*
Son.	*Sonnets*
TGV	*Two Gentlemen of Verona*
Tim.	*Timon of Athens*

Tit.	*Titus Andronicus*
TN	*Twelfth Night*
TNK	*Two Noble Kinsmen*
Tmp.	*The Tempest*
Tro.	*Troilus and Cressida*
Ven.	*Venus and Adonis*
Wiv.	*The Merry Wives of Windsor*
WT	*The Winter's Tale*

EDITORIAL ABBREVIATIONS

Co.	company
Diss.	dissertation
Ed.	editor
Incorp.	incorporated
Pr.	Press
pp.	pages
Pub.	publisher
rpt.	reprint
U.P.	University Press
U.	University

INTRODUCTION

SHAKESPEARE AND THE MEDIEVAL TRADITION:
A TWENTIETH-CENTURY REPORT

Writing in the late thirties, George Coffmann remarked that
few critics have denied the existence of native elements in
Elizabethan tragedy, but the classical influence has practically
held the center of the stage for the last thirty-five years
(70)[1]. Coffman urged the critics to reassess Shakespeare's
Medieval heritage, for he lamented the lack of critical attention in that direction. At the time of Coffman's writing,
there were less than fifty references to Shakespeare's Medieval
heritage, many of which were little more than notes. If one
peruses the standard bibliographies such as that of Ebisch and
Schücking and Gordon Ross Smith, he will turn up about a hundred
and fifty entries from 1900-1958 which are concerned with the
Medieval influence upon Shakespeare. In the following pages
I have compiled nearly 1000 articles, books, or notes from
1900-1980 that discuss the Medieval elements in Shakespeare's
plays. Of those studies, approximately 400 are concerned with
Medieval ideas in Shakespearean drama from a general point of
view while another 100 deal with particular play groups. The
bulk of the criticism focuses upon aspects of individual plays.
My approach will be to arrange these studies so as to indicate
what has been done and to suggest some areas which may prove
fruitful to investigate.

A quick glance at the subject index reveals just how much
has been written on the morality play. As a point of interest,
at the beginning of the twentieth century, the critics generally
viewed the Middle Ages and the Renaissance as being two distinct-
ly different periods. Thus literary historians such as Roy
Mackenzie, Felix Schelling, and A. W. Ward had virtually
nothing to say about Medieval elements in Shakespearean drama.
But a few writers suggested that Shakespeare was indeed tied
to his native heritage. In her work *The Evolution of Technique in Elizabethan Tragedy* (Chicago, 1914), Harriot Fansler
pointed to Shakespearean tragedies as being remarkably similar

---

[1] Numbers refer to entry numbers in this book.

to the moralities in structure and point of view (439). In
1932, L. C. Knights went so far as to say that *Troilus and
Cressida* was a morality play--in the direct line of descent
of the morality plays (886). With the publication of Willard
Farnham's *The Medieval Heritage of Elizabethan Tragedy*
(Berkeley, 1936), the connection between the morality plays
and Shakespearean tragedy was clearly expressed (441). Individual studies of the plays by Hardin Craig and Irving Ribner
pointed to the "sense of form" by which the structure of a
Shakespearean play had an imposed design (83, 404, 405). In
effect, Shakespeare borrowed the dramatic pattern of the
morality play as a way of expressing the characters' actions
within his plays. In more recent years, the critics have
written about morality ideas in virtually every Shakespearean
play.[2] Two tendencies have become all too common: numerous
studies repeat ideas which were clearly shown by previous
writers; many studies oversimplify Shakespeare and the Medieval
tradition which, in part, influenced him. Thematic studies
which discuss concepts of sin, suffering, alienation, and
awakening in Shakespearean plays and point to similar concepts
in the moralities are often too general, too simple, and too
reductive.

     To the student who is initially studying the morality
influence upon Shakespeare, it may be helpful to group the
concepts the critics have stressed, to note the controversy,
and to point to those ideas which need more questioning.
Critics have been drawn to the Vice figure perhaps more than to
any other character of Medieval drama. Bernard Spivack's
Shakespeare and the Allegory of Evil (New York, 1958) focuses
upon the study of the Vice (456). Spivack sees the Vice figure
emerging from the morality plays with the morality plays themselves undergoing numerous changes prior to the Renaissance.
Richard III, Iago, and Aaron the Moor are hybrid types of the
Vice of the morality play. Willard Farnham in *The Shakespearean
Grotesque* (Oxford, 1971) sees the Vice emerging from the devil
tradition of native English plays, and his work focuses upon
the diabolical humor often associated with the Vice (116). Falstaff, Thersites, Iago, and Caliban are members of this tradition. Geraldine Levenson's unpublished dissertation concentrates
upon the devil and clown characters in myth and art and studies
the "diabolical humor" often associated with the Vice figure
(209). The origin of the Vice has been questioned by Francis
Mares who argues that the popular festivals and the clowns of

---

[2] See entries in Section Three under particular plays. All
   morality studies are referenced even though such studies
   may also be listed elsewhere.

pre-Shakespearean drama were the original source material for
Shakespeare rather than the morality plays (224). Robert
Withington's study of the Vice suggests that he is found in the
Devil of the miracle play and the fool of the folkplay (355).
This bibliography lists some seventy other works which comment
on the Vice, and most of these argue that the Vice came to
Shakespeare by way of the morality play. It is refreshing,
therefore, to come across Robert Jones' essay "Dangerous Sport:
The Audience's Engagement with Vice in the Moral Interludes"
(180). Jones argues that the Vice played upon the audience
as well as the characters in the play. By calling attention to
the dramatic strategy which was employed, Jones breaks some new
ground, and similar studies could be applied to Shakespearean
plays.

The title of Edmund Creeth's study *Mankynde in Shakespeare*
(Athens, 1976) points to another element of the morality in-
fluence--the figure of Mankind (434). Hardin Craig called the
Humanum Genus figure the "fundamental feature of the English
moralities." Although the early moralities employed the
character Mankind, the later moralities do not. Herein lies
the central problem. If Medieval drama were developmental
and if the Mankind figure were not present in the moralities
Shakespeare was more likely to read and to see performed, how
can we account for the mankind figure in Shakespeare's plays?
Regarding the origin of the Mankind figure in Shakespearean
drama, Creeth believes that Shakespeare went to the earlier
moralities for character and thematic influence. Thus *The
Castle of Perseverance*,*Wisdom*, and *The Pride of Life* are compared to *Macbeth*, *Othello*, and *King Lear*, respectively. Ribner's
study of the history plays focuses not so much upon the origin
of Mankind but upon how Shakespeare's Mankind figure is seen in
the person of the king who vacillates between good and bad
advisors (452). In *The English Morality Play* (London, 1975),
Robert Potter sees the origins of the Mankind figure in the
Paternoster plays in the person of the seven deadly sins
(265). Morality plays to Potter are primarily dramas concerned
with the "forgiveness of sins." Craig, Farnham, and Campbell
see the héroes in the major tragedies undergoing an experience
similar to Mankind in the morality play (83, 441, and 598). A
somewhat different approach is taken by Robert Grams Hunter in
his *Shakespeare and the Comedy of Forgiveness* (New York, 1965).
Frequently, the elements of sin, contrition, and forgiveness
were transposed by Shakespeare to the situations between the
heroine and the lover. Thus Shakespeare's *Humanum Genus* figure
often offends the woman he loves, and he must undergo an
experience similar to contrition and forgiveness of the Mankind
figure in the moralities (377). As an example, the focal point
in *Cymbeline* is the testing of Posthumus and his subsequent

failure to believe in his wife's virtue. Restoration comes
with the affirmation of Imogen's innocence and the deep contrition Posthumus goes through.

Finally two other areas relating to the morality influence
are the allegory and the moralized thesis. Both of these
concepts are present in numerous morality plays, yet pointing
to these ideas in Shakespearean drama generally brings the
criticism that we are reducing Shakespeare's plays. John
Weld's *Meaning in Comedy: Studies in Elizabethan Romantic
Comedy* (Albany, 1975) addresses, in part, both allegory and
moral thesis (391). Weld argues that viewing a morality play
as opposed to reading one would give one a different impression
of allegorical characters. In the performance of a play, the
characters would behave like real people rather than abstractions. The interaction of characters with each other and with
the audience would make them less allegorical and more like
the characters found in Shakespeare's plays. Perhaps much could
be learned from the morality plays that might account for
Shakespearean characters being more than literal characters.
Allegory and moralized thesis frequently behave much in the
same way. Many critics such as M.C. Bradbrook argue that
Shakespeare's treatments of allegory and character frequently
collide, and often the result is a play which appears to be
strained (460). Thematic statement often is pursued at the
expense of both character and the classical unities of place
and action. This violation of logic and the openness in
theatrical form has been explored by both David Bevington in
From Mankind to Marlowe (Cambridge, 1962) (30) and O. B.
Hardison, Jr., in his essay "Logic Versus the Slovenly World
in Shakespearean Comedy" (375). It appears to me that further
examination of dramatic statement made through characters might
prove beneficial. *Cymbeline*, for example, has been criticized
for its lack of unity; but an examination of the characters and
the multiple places of action would indicate Shakespeare's
fondness for native theatrical form.

In yet another area of the morality influence, Alan C.
Dessen has brought some new thinking to the concept of the
legacy of the morality play. All too frequently morality
concepts are seen as monolithic and tied to the late
fifteenth-century moralities such as *Mankind* and *Everyman*.
Dessen points out that many of the moralities from 1550 to
1600 are overlooked. His own study of the "estates morality"
discusses how the mankind figure is represented by social
types--farmers, soldiers, lawyers--who have been acted upon by
a Vice figure (98). Those wishing to examine the scope of the
morality plays might find Donald Borchardt's unpublished
dissertation of interest (39). Borchardt comments upon and
lists some sixty-nine moralities. Shakespeare's experience with

the theater was so much closer to the later morality plays
than the moralities like *Everyman* or *The Castle of Perseverance*.
Perhaps there is more that could be focused upon particularly
in the areas of staging, character, and allegorical design,
   In a different area of scholarship, the critics have re-
sponded to the way in which Shakespeare's themes or characters
have been influenced by specific Medieval writers. When Ann
Thompson published *Shakespeare's Chaucer: A Study of Literary
Origins* (New York, 1978), she produced the only full-length
study of Shakespeare and Chaucer (321). Thompson shows verbal
echoes, indicates how both authors used common themes, and
discusses what Shakespeare makes of Chaucer's characters and
structures. The Medieval index to my bibliography lists over
100 other entries which have tied Shakespeare to Chaucer; some
of these are little more than notes, but many have pointed to
the kinds of ideas found in Thompson's book. Rhoda Ann Harris
also has an extensive examination of Shakespeare and Chaucer
with her unpublished dissertation from King's College (156).
Alice Miskimin's *The Renaissance Chaucer* (Yale, 1975) focuses
more on Chaucer and the Elizabethan period, but she draws
specific attention to both Chaucer's and Shakespeare's use of
allegorical ironies (238). Those wishing to pursue additional
studies of Shakespeare and Chaucer will find that the critics
have commented upon the common themes, stories, and characters
at great length; and only a few nuggets remain as E. Talbot
Donaldson has said with regret.[3] Perhaps additional studies of
of Shakespeare and Chaucer will find it more beneficial to deal
with the kinds of ideas shown by Francis Fergusson in his
study of Dante and Shakespeare. In *Trope and Allegory Themes
Common to Dante and Shakespeare* (Athens, 1977), Fergusson
breaks some new ground and points to the manner in which
Medieval allegory is employed by both writers (120). According
to Fergusson both Dante and Shakespeare were Christian writers
who shared a common vision and expressed that vision in analog-
ical terms. Few critics have written about Dante and
Shakespeare; my index lists a dozen or so studies of both
authors, and more studies should be forthcoming. Those scouting
for Medieval writers who influenced Shakespeare might well look
toward Lydgate or Caxton (few essays and no book-length studies
have been written). Most of the entries I list (about two
dozen) are brief sections from books which tie Shakespeare to
Lydgate in terms of fortune or Fall of Princes concepts.
Glynne Wickham speaks of an inherited Medieval pattern which
both Lydgate and Shakespeare employ (349), and Franklin M.
Dickey in *Not Wisely But Too Well* (San Marino, 1957) comments
that some of Shakespeare's ideas in regard to excessive love
may come from Lydgate (437). Most of the work done on Caxton
and Shakespeare has focused upon the Troy legend. Both M. C.

---

[3] As this books goes to press, Professor Donaldson published
The Swan at the Well: Shakespeare Reading Chaucer (Yale
University Pr., 1985, 192 pp.).

Bradbrook and Robert K. Presson discuss Shakespeare's borrowing
episodes of the Troy account from Caxton (867 and 901). Tucker
Brook and W. B. Drayton believe that some of Shakespeare's
ideas about decaying feudal nobility may well come from Caxton
(870 and 879). For whatever reason the critics have shied
away from both Caxton and Lydgate, and a full examination of
both authors may be appropriate.

Although it might seem that no additional studies concerning
the homiletic tradition need to be published, I believe that it
could continue to be a rich source of investigation. G. R.
Owst's *Literature and Pulpit in Medieval England* (Cambridge,
1933), Peter Milward's *Shakespeare's Religious Background*
(Bloomington, 1973), and Roy Battenhouse's *Shakespearean
Tragedy: Its Art and Its Christian Premise* (Bloomington, 1968)
would serve as points of departure (254, 237 and 426). John
Danby's assertion that the ideas in the homiletic tradition
were more significant than the abstraction in the morality
for Shakespearean drama should be a challenge (600). Similarly
Irving Ribner's "The Gods are Just" contends that the homiletic
tradition afforded Shakespeare the tools for composing *King
Lear* (632). Applications of the homiletic tradition would be
useful for other Shakespearean plays. More recently, O. B.
Hardison, Jr., in *Christian Rite and Christian Drama in the
Middle Ages* (Baltimore, 1965) has suggested that the ritual
form inherited from the liturgy and the mass is represented in
secular materials which Shakespeare employed (153). Also
Herbert Coursen's *Christian Ritual and the World of Shakespeare's Tragedies* (Bucknell, 1976) argues that the Eucharist
and the ritual associated with this sacrament is central to an
understanding of Shakespeare's plays (432). Yet we need a
more complete examination of these ideas coupled with a greater
knowledge of staging practices which support ritual techniques
in the plays. George Slover's unpublished dissertation on
liturgical stage structure offers a clearer point of view on
this topic (Indiana, 1969) (298). Further, sections of
Thomas B. Stroup's *Microcosmos: The Shape of the Elizabethan
Play* (Lexington, 1965) also comment upon the theater as a
representation of symbolic action having spiritual meaning
(314).

A number of critics have been drawn to Shakespeare's use
of feudal concepts and the chivalric code. Their attention has
been focused primarily upon *Troilus and Cressida* and *Timon of
Athens*. In his book *Comical Satyre and Shakespeare's Troilus
and Cressida* (San Marino, 1938), Oscar J. Campbell suggests
that Shakespeare used aspects of Medieval chivalric code to
comment upon the changing social conditions of the time (874).
A more focused study is E. C. Pettet's "*Timon of Athens*: The
Disruption of Feudal Morality" which points to the capitalistic

Renaissance destroying the Medieval feudal world (853).
Additional studies have been concerned with the way some
Shakespearean protagonists identify with the chivalric code,
but this code is said to be at odds with the practical world
(560, 582, 862 and 294). With the exception of M. M.
Bhattacharya's *Courtesy in Shakespeare* (Calcutta, 1940) (31),
no full-length study has been written on Shakespeare and
chivalry. Students looking for doctoral dissertation topics
will find this subject challenging and rewarding. Sections
of *King Lear* and *Cymbeline* have their ties to this aspect of
Medieval culture, but Shakespeare's subtle adaptation of
chivalry, knighthood, and romance is done to suit his own
purposes. Those wishing to explore chivalric ideas will find
useful background material in Arthur Fairchild's "Shakespeare
and the Tragic Theme" and Curtis B. Watson's *Shakespeare and
the Renaissance Concept of Honor* (Princeton, 1960) (438 and
337).

In a related area of study, the critics have been interested
in Shakespeare and the Medieval romance tradition. Carol
Gesner's *Shakespeare and the Greek Romance: A Study of Origins*
(Lexington, 1970) studies the ways in which Greek romances are
related to the Medieval romances and explores, in part, the
courtly love tradition tied to the romance (133). E. C.
Pettet's *Shakespeare and the Romance Tradition* (London, 1949)
sees Shakespeare changing the courtly love tradition so as to
bring it into a harmonious relationship with Christian love
(381). In more recent years the critics have attempted to show
how Shakespeare used romance elements--the wandering of
characters, families united and divided, ideas of faith and
patience--to establish the atmosphere and structure of the ·
play (421, 446 and 162). Those wishing to examine Shakespeare's use of romance elements have the problem of determining
whether romance-affiliated ideas (those mentioned above as
well as quest themes, courtly love ideas, and faith in the
Providential scheme of things) indeed came from the romance
tradition or from other sources both Greek and Medieval.

With the publications of *Shakespeare's Poetics* (London,
1962), Russell Fraser examined *King Lear* in terms of Medieval
and Renaissance iconography (605). Since then the research in
iconic imagery has been both interesting and productive. State
scenes, throne room scenes, trial scenes, funeral scenes,
garden scenes, and banquet scenes have also been approached
from an iconographic viewpoint by M. H. Golden in her unpublished dissertation (Columbia, 1965) (136). John Doebler's
Shakespeare's Speaking Pictures (Albuquerque, 1974) examines
woodcuts and pictures of both Medieval and Renaissance periods
and relates how they help to explicate Shakespearean passages
(103). Two excellent essays using the iconographic approach

are Mary Lascelles' "*King Lear* and Doomsday" which points to
native murals about doomsday paintings that help to explain
Lear's state of mind on the heath and Betty Doebler's
"Othello's Angels: *Ars Moriendi*" which views the bed in the
final scene in *Othello* as an iconic stage prop (618 and 730).
Nearly every play group has been studied from the iconographic
point of view.   Clifford Davidson's "Death in His Court:
Iconography in Shakespeare's Tragedies" and Martha Fleischer's
The Iconography of the English History Play (Salzburg, 1974)
indicate the range of interest in this area of research (94 and
398).   In a similar field of study, Alan C. Dessen's *Elizabethan Drama and the Viewer's Eye* (Chapel Hill, 1977) concentrates
upon the audience's awareness of visual materials and stimuli
(100).   A careful reading of Dessen's work and the iconographic
literature above will likely stimulate additional studies regarding individual scenes throughout the plays.   In addition,
David Bergeron's "The Emblematic Nature of English Civic
Pageantry" and John Doebler's "Bibliography for the Study of
Iconography and Renaissance Literature" would also prove
helpful (26 and 104).

Far too often Shakespeare's Medieval background is seen
from a literary perspective; themes, conventions, and literary
influences should be viewed with theatrical performance in
mind.   It is gratifying, therefore, that in the past twenty
years a great deal of attention has been given to the popular
theatrical tradition.   One of the most recent and notable
works is Robert Weimann's *Shakespeare and the Popular Tradition
in the Theater* (Johns Hopkins, 1978) (339).   Weimann's discussion of the mime, folkplay, mystery cycles, morality and
interludes focuses upon the popular conventions of speech and
acting.   The discussion of the two types of space used in cycle
drama (*Platea* and *locus*) clarifies the roles played by numerous Shakespearean characters in terms of each other and the
audience.   Alan C. Dessen's work on Shakespeare and the theater
has shown that certain groupings, gestures, and properties on
the stage provide the viewers with thematic statements through
the employment of visual artifice (100).   David Bergeron's
"Medieval Drama and the Tudor-Stuart Civic Pageantry," Glynne
Wickham's *Early English Stages 1300 to 1600* (London, 1963),
and Richard Southern's *The Staging of Plays Before Shakespeare*
(London, 1973) provide excellent background material for
Medieval staging principles (28, 348 and 304).   Numerous other
studies of Medieval staging influence upon Shakespeare also
show the rich native tradition Shakespeare employed in his
plays (53, 28, 102 and 188).   Although much has been written,
we need to know more about the characters in relation to stage
position, verbal expressions, and actions of the characters
with each other and the audience.

Finally, no guide to this index would be complete unless
one pointed to the numerous Medieval literary themes and conventions which abound in Shakespeare's works. Going to the
sources and becoming familiar with the concepts will provide
students with a good grasp of the Medieval and Renaissance
periods. In addition, becoming knowledgeable in this area of
research will provide opportunities for applications of these
ideas to scenes or situations in the plays which have yet to
be pointed out. In the subject index special care has been
taken to list literary themes and conventions, but the following are of special interest: (1) *ars moriendi* themes,
(2) *contemptu mundi* ideas, (3) dance of death concepts, (4)
debate elements, (5) the dream convention, (6) emblematic
ideas, (7) *exempla* studies, (8) fabliau, (9) Fall of Princes
themes, (10) *felix culpa* concepts, (11) fortune ideas, (12)
garden imagery, (13) Merlin tradition, (14) *momento mori*
themes, (15) mirror for magistrates tradition, (16) Parliament
of heaven ideas, (17) Pilgrimage of life, and (18) *ubi sunt*
themes. The courtly love tradition has been the most popular
literary theme followed closely by Medieval concepts of
fortune in Shakespearean plays. John Vyvyan called the Medieval
Rose of Love the single most important contribution of the
Medieval age to Shakespeare. Book-length studies dealing with
the courtly love influence include R. G. Hunter's *Shakespeare
and the Comedy of Forgiveness* (New York, 1965), John Vyvyan's
Shakespeare and the Rose of Love (New York, 1960), and Karl F.
Thompson's *Modesty and Cunning: Shakespeare's Use of Literary
Tradition* (Ann Arbor, 1971) (377, 390 and 322). To go into
detail and point out how all of these literary themes and conventions have been applied to Shakespeare's plays would extend
the introduction unnecessarily. However, one topic which could
be especially productive concerns the metaphor of a garden.
In recent years a number of critics have discussed the concept
of an earthly paradise in Medieval literature. A number of
applications of these ideas could be made in numerous scenes
throughout Shakespeare's plays. Such a discussion would explore
the garden as an image of paradise, the gardens of poetry and
philosophy, and the gardens of love. Terry Comito's *The Idea
of the Garden in the Renaissance* (New Brunswick, 1978) could
serve as a point of departure (74).
George Coffman, as pointed out in the beginning of this
essay, lamented that few scholars were working with Shakespeare's Medieval background, but the following pages attest
that the scholarship of the past fifty years has provided a
broad foundation of Shakespeare's debt to the Medieval world.
The rich native legacy can be seen as scholars delve into the
literary tradition, the religious and ethical concepts of that
time, and the social ideas that impacted so much upon Shakespeare's plays.

Shakespeare and
the Medieval Tradition

GENERAL WORKS

1. Adams, Henry Hitch. *English Domestic or Homiletic Tragedy 1575-1642.* New York: Noble Offset Printer, Incorp., 1917. 191 pp.

   Adams refers to Shakespeare infrequently through his work, but the first three chapters discuss the relation between Medieval and Renaissance tragedy. He includes an analysis of the *De Casibus* type of tragedy which had acquired the idea of retributive justice and shows its impact upon Elizabethan drama.

2. Albright, Victor. *The Shakespearean Stage.* New York: Columbia U. Pr., 1909. 194 pp.

   Albright examines early cycle plays, moralities, Tudor interludes, and Renaissance drama from the point of view of required stage conditions as seen in the texts of the plays. Plays are divided into the categories of those which require properties and those which do not. No direct influence is shown but the examination presents a number of physical features of the stage.

3. Allen, Don Cameron. *Mysteriously Meant: The Rediscovery of Pagan Symbolism and Allegorical Interpretation in the Renaissance.* Johns Hopkins U. Pr., 1970. 354 pp.

   In many chapters of his book, Allen explains how Medieval writers allegorized the classics. The allegorical readings generally reinforced Christian teachings, and these readings continued through the Renaissance.

4. Allison, Tempe E. "The Paternoster Play and the Origin of the Vices." *PMLA,* 39 (1924), 789-804.

   Allison shows Shakespeare's use of the Vice by clarifying the role of the Vice in Medieval drama and suggesting that the Vice in sixteenth century drama is a fusion of a group

of minor vices which were associated with Medieval comic
elements.

5. Anderson, Ruth. "Elizabethan Psychology and Shakespeare's
   Plays." *UIHS*, 3(1927), 1-183.

   Of interest are the comments upon the Medieval contribution to the concept of man's soul, body, and spirit.
   The sections on humors and "man as a microcosm" are also
   related to Medieval ideas. The essay contains scattered
   references to Medieval treatises such as *Batman upon
   Bartholomew*.

6. Artz, Frederick B. *The Mind of the Middle Ages A. D. 200-
   1500*. New York: Alfred A. Knopf, 1965. 572 pp.

   Artz presents interesting background material for the
   study of Shakespeare and the Medieval period. Artz refers
   to the doctrines of Boethius, Scholasticism, and source
   material of the Troy story and comments upon these ideas
   in relation to Shakespeare. The last chapter concerns the
   surviving Medieval economic, political and social theory
   in the Renaissance.

7. Ashton, John W. "Folklore in the Literature of Elizabethan
   England." *JAF*, 70(1957), 10-15 and 23-24.

   Nearly all of Shakespeare's plays can be related to folk
   material inherited from Medieval times. The "bed trick"
   of *MM* and *AWW* as well as the magic potions in *Rom*. and
   Cym. are found in earlier English drama. Shakespeare's
   ghosts are tied to Medieval folk tradition. There is an
   extensive bibliography on folk material and Shakespeare.

8. Atkins, J. W. H. *English Literary Criticism: The Medieval
   Phase*. Gloucester, Mass.: Peter Smith, 1961. 211 pp.

   The last chapter sketches the influence of Medieval literature in the Renaissance and includes topics such as
   patristic theory, theories of tragedy and comedy, the influence of strictly native elements upon the Renaissance
   and the Elizabethan adaptations of Medieval critical
   theory.

9. Baker, Hershel. *The Image of Man*. New York: Harper
   Torchbooks, 1947. 336 pp.

Baker studies the concept of human dignity as it is found in the Middle Ages and the Renaissance and provides a general background of the history of ideas in both eras. Chapters Eleven through Fourteen show the influence of the Middle Ages upon the Renaissance by referring to religious ideas, political concepts, the moral nature of man, and the concept of hierarchies.

10. Baker, Howard. "Ghosts and Guides: Kyd's *Spanish Tragedy* and the Medieval Tragedy." *MP,* 33 (1925), 26-72.

Although he deals mainly with the revenge theme in the *Spanish Tragedy,* Baker suggests that his thesis applies to Elizabethan revenge tragedies in general. At issue is the idea of revenge and ghosts as being exclusively Medieval in origin. Revenge characters come from Medieval metrical tragedies where they serve as adventurers on a marvelous journey. Baker refers frequently to Lydgate.

11. Baldwin, T. W. "Nature's Moulds." *SQ,* 3(1952), 237-41.

Shakespeare's conception of nature's procreative processes may be traced to Ovid or Plato, but nature's processes were commonplace in Medieval and Elizabethan times. Baldwin quotes *Batman upon Bartholomew* concerning the nature of witches in the Medieval period.

12. Bamborough, J. B. *The Little World of Man.* New York: Longmans, Green and Co., 1951. 187 pp.

Renaissance psychological theory was in many respects similar to Medieval psychology. The introduction explains the chain of being concept as derived from Medieval writers and dwells upon the theory of man as a microcosm, a concept which explains the functions of the state in relation to the body or its functions. The book refers frequently to Shakespeare.

13. Barnet, S. "Some Limitations of a Christian Approach to Shakespeare." *ELH,* 22(1955), 81-92.

Although the approach of linking Shakespeare to the Middle Ages has yielded profitable results, yet analyzing Shakespearean drama against a Medieval religious background has generally tended to oversimplify Shakespeare's plays. Far too often characters are studied as *exempla* which results in viewing Shakespeare in a reductive way.

14. Barroll, John L. "Shakespeare and Roman History." *DAI*,
    17(1957), 626 (Princeton).

    Barroll presents a general study of the Christian syn-
    thesis of Roman history as it was characterized in the
    literature of the Middle Ages. Salient works on Roman
    history written by Medieval writers are commented upon,
    with Barroll observing that they generally translated
    classical works which reinforced current Christian doc-
    trine. The Medieval concept of a moral lesson is found
    in the deaths of Brutus and Julius Caesar. Likewise
    Barroll reads *Ant.* as a work which shows erring historical
    figures whose fall would teach a moral lesson.

15. Barry, Patricia S. *The King in Tudor Drama*. (Saltzburg
    Studies in English Literature: Elizabethan and Ren-
    aissance Studies 58.) Salzburg: Inst. für Englische
    Sprache und Literatur. Univ. Salzburg, 1977. 299 pp.

    Barry surveys plays from 1485 to 1603 with kingly char-
    acters with emphasis upon techniques for depicting kings
    and theatrical imagery. Shakespeare's *H6* and *MND* are
    discussed in moral and social terms.

16. Baskerville, Charles. "Dramatic Aspects of Medieval Folk
    Festivals in England." *SP*, 17(1920), 79-87.

    Folk festivals and games in the Middle Ages are surveyed
    and viewed as surviving in the folk customs in the Ren-
    aissance.

17. ———. *The Elizabethan Jig*. Chicago: U. of Chicago Pr.,
    1929. 642 pp.

    This book presents the historical background of the jig
    from its beginning through the Jacobean age. The jig de-
    veloped from Medieval times and was called by the various
    names of games, dances, and songs. The genre was invariably
    linked with festivals and holidays. Shakespeare was in-
    fluenced by the jig in a general way in the early romantic
    comedies in the sense that the clown figures are associated
    with the tradition of the jig.

18. Bates, Katharine L. *The English Religious Drama*. New
    York: The Macmillan Co., 1902. 254 pp.

    Bates has one of the fuller earlier discussions of Med-
    ieval drama, mystery plays, miracle plays, moralities, and

interludes. There is a growth toward realism from Medieval to Renaissance drama. The development of dramatic units and the blending of comedy and tragedy is the principal Medieval contribution to Elizabethan drama.

19. Batenhouse, Roy W. "Shakespearean Tragedy as Debate." *CentR*, 8(1964), 77-98.

   This general essay touches on the Christian Medieval influence upon Shakespeare and gives a catalog of supporting and opposing views concerning Shakespeare and religion. The author determines that the terms Christian and Medieval are nearly synonymous, and he finds that Shakespeare's religious understanding is subtly woven throughout his plays.

20. Baugh, Albert C. "A Medieval Survival in Elizabethan Punctuation," pp. 1-15 in *Studies in the English Renaissance Drama*, ed. Josephine Bennett. New York: New York U. Pr., 1959.

   Baugh examines several Old English and Middle English writings in order to determine the use of the comma or period at the end of a line. He finds that it was common practice to put a comma at the end of a line, but the practice was by no means universal. He studies a number of Shakespeare's plays and sonnets and concludes that the Medieval method of punctuation was still being employed in the Renaissance by the printers.

21. Bean, John C. "Passion Versus Friendship in the Tudor Matrimonial Handbooks and Some Shakespearean Implications." *WascanaR*, 9.1(1974), 231-40.

   Bean discusses the concepts of *amour courtois* which are at odds with Christian marriage. He determines that the humanists endorsed friendship in marriage. Shakespeare emphasizes passion in marriage but falls short of endorsing the *amour* of Medieval chivalric literature.

22. Beck, Erwin, Jr. "Prodigal Son Comedy: the Continuity of a Paradigm in English Drama, 1500-1642." *DAI*, 33 (1973), 6339-A (Indiana).

   Prodigal son comedy is defined as a play in which youth rebels against a father or father figure. In Chapter Three, the *Interlude of Youth*, Beck surveys earlier morality plays in order to determine the moral, romantic, and

and satiric mode of prodigal son comedy. *AWW* is related
to the above study with Bertram and Parolles making up
"a composite roaring boy prodigal."

23. Beck, Margaret M. "The Dance of Death in Shakespeare."
     MLN, 37(1922), 372-74.

     Earlier Francis Douce noted that Shakespeare was ac-
     quainted with a painting of the Dance of Death that hung
     in the church of Stratford upon Avon. Beck notes that
     Thomas Fisher made an accurate reproduction of all paint-
     ings and frescoes that hung in the church and none are
     suggestive of the Dance of Death. Beck also discusses
     Shakespeare's use of this convention in *MM* (III, ii),
     R2 (III, ii), and *Ham.* (V, i). He finds in *Ham.* the
     following stock characters of the Dance of Death: the
     Auctor, the Lector, the Gentlewoman, the Politician, the
     Courtier, the Lawyer, the Richman, the Fool, the Heir,
     and the Lady.

24. Belton, Ellen Rothenburg. "The Figure of the Steward:
     Some Aspects of Master-Servant Relations in Elizabethan
     and Early Stuart Drama." *DAI*, 35(1975), 4415A-16A
     (Columbia).

     Servant figures developed historically from the classical
     tradition, the homiletic tradition, and the Vice and his
     confederates from the morality plays.

25. Berger, Harry. "Theater, Drama, and the Second World:
     A Prologue to Shakespeare." *CompD*, 2(1968-69), 3-20.

     Berger analyzes the psychological and symbolic aspects
     of Medieval drama as they relate to the audience and to
     the performance on the stage. Elizabethan plays are dis-
     tinguished from Medieval religious drama in terms of
     theatrical space-time and fictional space-time.

26. Bergeron, David M. "The Emblematic Nature of English
     Civic Pageantry," pp. 167-98 in *Renaissance Drama*, I
     (1968), ed. by S. Schoenbaum. Evanston: Northwestern
     U. Pr., 1968.

     The emblem and pageant share common presentation of
     figures and ideas. Both draw upon the rich native in-
     fluence and transient iconographical tradition.

27. ————. *English Civic Pageantry 1558-1642*. London: E. Arnold, 1971. 325 pp.

   As the title suggests, Bergeron discusses the nature of the pageants with regard to their "metaphorical view of the world." The *Tmp.* and *R2* are shown to have symbolic physical representation of moral, political and historical concepts which have ties to the Medieval world.

28. ————. "Medieval Drama and Tudor-Stuart Civic Pageantry." *JMRS*, 2(1971-72), 279-93.

   Civic pageantry drama owes a number of debts to Medieval drama: (1) involvement of the guild in the production of drama, (2) aspects of stage craft, (3) costume and iconographic imagery and (4) moral allegory.

29. Bethell, S. L. *Shakespeare and the Popular Dramatic Tradition*. London: Staples Pr. Ltd., 1944. 164 pp.

   Evidence for the Medieval influence upon Shakespeare is found in the multiple stage techniques use in *Rom* (I, iv) and *R3* (V, iii). Chapter Three discusses Shakespeare's use of anachronisms with particular emphasis upon these elements in the history plays. Shakespeare's treatment of character (Ch. 4) owes something to the allegorical personages in the morality plays. Thersites "recalls the old Vice," and Ulysses "conveys some suggestion of an abstract Worldly Wisdom."

30. Bevington, D. M. *From Mankind to Marlowe: Growth in Structure in the Popular Drama of Tudor England*. Cambridge: Harvard U. Pr., 1962. 310 pp.

   Most of Bevington's study relates to Marlowe; he does, however, refer to Shakespeare throughout his book. The study of Medieval traditions is applicable to Shakespeare both implicitly and explicitly. The book has individual chapters on the romance, the chronicle, the homiletic tradition, and the morality as a predecessor of Renaissance drama.

31. Bhattacharya, M. M. *Courtesy in Shakespeare*. Calcutta: Calcutta U. Pr., 1940. 225 pp.

   The first chapter lists and comments upon chivalric ideas

and courtesy in Medieval works. Chapter Two is entitled
"Renaissance Courtesy" and defines courtesy in respect to
the English chivalric code and Italian culture. Chapter
Three focuses upon the Medieval heritage of chivalry as
found in Shakespeare's plays. Chivalric ideals of manners,
honor and courage can be seen in Talbot, Hotspur, and
Henry V. The author relates aspects of *Lr.* (I, iv) to
the chivalric concept of service. Other Shakespearean
plays discussed are *Rom.*, *1H4*, and *Shr.*

32.   Black, Matthew. "Enter Citizens," pp. 16-27 in *Studies
      in the English Renaissance Drama.*   ed. Josephine Bennett.
      New York: New York U. Pr., 1959.

Black examines the use of background figures categorized
as citizens, soldiers, sailors, and watchmen, that are
numbered 1, 2, 3, 4 in Renaissance drama with particular
emphasis upon Shakespeare's plays. He traces the use of
numeraries to the English miracle cycles, but he does not
find any evidence that the morality plays or interludes
made use of this device, nor is the practice apparently
found in classical literature. It appears to be a native
English tradition which was transferred from the miracle
to the regular plays. Only five of Shakespeare's plays
are without numbered groups--*Jn.*, *MV*, *H5*, *Tro.*, and the
Tmp.

33.   Blench, G. W. *Preaching in England in the Late Fifteenth
      and Sixteenth Centuries.*   Oxford: Basil Blackwell,
      1964, 378 pp.

Blench has sections on sermon form (dispositio) and
style (elocutio) and the use of classical allusions in
the sermons from 1450-1603. The last sections treat
sermon themes and the influence of these themes on poetry
and drama. Regarding the latter, Blench demonstrates how
the following topics are common to sermons and literature:
ubi sunt theme, vanity and extravagance of women, sins of
the flesh, covetousness, and usury.

34.   Blissett, William. "Lucan's Caesar and the Elizabethan
      Villain." *SP*, 53(1956), 553-75.

Elizabethan villains can be classified into three groups:
classical, Medieval, and Renaissance. Although the thrust
of the essay is to determine the influence of Lucan's
portrayal of Caesar upon Renaissance playwrights, Blissett
also deals with the portrayal of Caesar in the Middle Ages

by Dante and Chaucer and refers to the survival of the
Medieval Caesar in Shakespeare.

35. Bloom, James Harvey. *Folklore, Old Customs and Super-
stitutions in Shakespeare's Land.* 2nd ed., rpt.
Detroit: Gale Pr., 1973. 167 pp.

Bloom discusses the evolution of folk beliefs from the
Middle Ages to the twentieth century. Topics vary and are
interestingly presented. Marriage, death, dress, birth
customs and festivals are useful for background study.

36. Boas, F. S. *Shakespeare and His Predecessors.* New York:
The Macmillan Co., 1896. 550 pp.

A brief analysis of Medieval drama and its impact upon
Renaissance plays is discussed in Chapter One. Boas notes
that *MND, Ham., JC, Mac.,* and *Tmp.* are in the tradition of
Medieval stage drama in regard to the representation of
supernatural on the stage. The Vice of the moral interludes may be the forerunner of the Shakespearean fool.

37. ———. *An Introduction to Tudor Drama.* Oxford: The
Clarendon Pr., 1933. 176 pp.

Chapter Four, "Stage-Plays at Oxford and Cambridge,"
shows the survival of festive plays dealing with the
mummeries, pageants, and Christian plays during the years
1482-1607. The plays generally emphasize comic people and
various types of buffoonery which Boas believes influenced
playwrights through Shakespeare's period.

38. ———. *Queen Elizabeth in Drama and Related Studies.*
London: George Allen and Unwin, 1950. 212 pp.

Chapter Three, "Aspects of Shakespeare's Reading," documents Shakespeare's reading of Chaucer and Gower for background material in *Tro.* Boas concludes, however, that
Shakespeare's knowledge of either classical or Medieval
works is limited.

39. Borchardt, Donald Arthur. "The Dramatic Nature of the
English Morality Play." *DAI,* 21(1961), 3353 (U. of Utah).

Although he refers to Shakespeare infrequently, the
author does emphasize the development of the morality play
as "gratifying entertainment." He studies sixty-nine
moralities in the fifteenth and sixteenth century and

and attempts to show that these plays have far more theatrical variety and creative imagination than some scholars have previously pointed out. Topics include the struggle between good and evil, ideas of comedy and tragedy, personifications, and the *humanum genus* figure.

40.   Bowers, F. T. *Elizabethan Revenge Tragedy*. Princeton: Princeton U. Pr., 1940. 288 pp.

Chapter One, "The Background of Revenge," surveys popular and political attitudes toward revenge in the Middle Ages and the Renaissance and determines that blood revenge was common in Medieval times and condoned by the law.

41.   Boyer, C. V. *The Villain as Hero in Elizabethan Tragedy*. London: Russell and Russell Incorp., 1914. 245 pp.

The influence of Medieval drama upon Shakespeare is minimal. Boyer points out that the protagonists of Seneca's tragedies are the forebearers of the Elizabethan villain. The Vice of the morality plays had little influence upon playwrights in Shakespeare's day.

42.   Bradbrook, M. C. "Shakespeare and the Use of Disguise in Elizabethan Drama." *EIC*, 2(1952), 159-68.

Shakespeare's concept of false appearance stems from the morality plays. Vices take the virtues' names: Counterfeit Countenance becomes Good Demeanance, Crafty Conveyance becomes Sure Surveyance, and Courtly Abusion becomes Lusty Pleasure. The disguise in *H5* owes something to the stories of Robin Hood and the king. The disguises of Edgar and Kent follow the tradition of the disguised protector which Shakespeare could have borrowed from the old chronicle play of *King Leir*. Shakespeare's disguises in his comedies owe a great deal to popular literature, particularly the ballads.

43.   ————. *Shakespeare and Elizabethan Poetry*. London: Chatto and Windus, 1965. 279 pp.

Chapter One surveys the Middle Ages and attempts to assess the Medieval contribution to the Elizabethan age. Topics include allegory, symbolism, the Medieval hierarchial system of thought, general theological and political ideas and the sacred use of numbers. Some discussion is given to *AWW* as a morality play.

44. Braddy, Haldeen. "Shakespeare, Abelard, and 'The Unquiet
    Grove.'" *JAF* 64(1956), 74-5.

    Braddy reports a discovery of a ballad which associates
    Shakespeare with the love story of Abelard and Heloise
    (1079-1142). The story relates that Abelard was castrated
    by relatives of Heloise for planning to get rid of her.
    After Abelard's mutilation, Heloise went to a convent.

45. Bradner, Leicester. "The Rise of Secular Drama in the
    Renaissance." *SRen* 3(1956), 7-22.

    Bradner argues that the revival of secular drama did not
    take place in the Renaissance but in the later Middle
    Ages. Moralities and Biblical plays were tremendously
    popular and a vigorous acting tradition appealing to pop-
    ular audiences had developed in the Middle Ages. Medieval
    contributions include comic elements associated with folk-
    play and well-defined type characters such as Herod, the
    braggart soldier, the comic yokel, the witty servant, and
    the shrewish wife.

46. Brewer, D. S. "The Ideal of Feminine Beauty in Medieval
    Literature, Especially *Harley Lyrics,* Chaucer, and
    Some Elizabethans." *MLR,* 50(1955), 257-69.

    Brewer traces the evolution of feminine beauty from
    classical times through the Renaissance and indicates
    that the description of a beautiful woman did not have
    great importance in literature prior to the twelfth
    century. In determining the type of beauty described
    by Geoffrey of Vinsauf, Dunbar, Chaucer, and the
    Harley Lyrics, Brewer suggests that Shakespeare reacted
    against the Medieval convention of describing women in
    Sonnets 20, 98, 106, 127, and 130.

47. Briggs, Katherine Mary. *The Fairies in English Tradition
    and Literature.* Chicago: U. of Chicago Pr., 1967,
    261 pp.

    In discussing Celtic, Scottish, and English origins of
    folklore belief, Briggs refers to Shakespeare occasionally
    in her book. The primary emphasis is upon the types of
    fairies and their distinctions and interactions with
    people. Shakespeare was well aware of native folklore
    beliefs and incorporated aspects of this tradition through-
    out his plays.

48. Brooks, Harold F. "Marlowe and Early Shakespeare," pp.
     67-94 in *Christopher Marlowe*, ed. by Brian Morris.
     London: Ernest Benn, 1968.

     Brooks' comments upon the Medieval tradition that in-
     fluenced both Marlowe and Shakespeare are of interest.
     Dramatic motifs such as Richard II's image of death and
     Mercade's handling of the news of his father's death in
     LLL are viewed as directly coming from Medieval drama.

49. Brooke, Tucker C. F. *The Tudor Drama*. London: Archon
     Books, 1964. 461 pp.

     The book details a history of Medieval and Early Ren-
     aissance drama with particular reference to mystery plays,
     moralities, and interludes. Elizabethan tragedy did not
     come from the native English period, but the author notes
     a continuing tradition from Medieval to Renaissance com-
     edy. The comic elements in *The Castle of Perseverance*
     as well as the stage directions are the early counter-
     parts of a mature Renaissance comedy and stage tradition.
     The role of Backbiter or Flypyregebet served a comic
     function much the same as buffoons in Renaissance comedy.

50. Bryant, J. A. *Hippolyta's View: Some Christian Aspects
     of Shakespeare's Plays*. Lexington: U. of Kentucky Pr.,
     1961. 239 pp.

     Bryant's thesis is that Shakespeare is a Christian
     writer whose plays reflect a Medieval typological the-
     ology. Bryant examines a dozen of Shakespearean plays
     and finds Biblical references, allusions, and Christ-
     figures. A case in point is his study of Hamlet as a
     Christ-like redeemer "who is both the scourge of evil
     and the sacrificed victim who willingly took evil upon
     himself." *Cym.* and *WT* are based upon Medieval allegor-
     ical themes.

51. Bullough, G. *Narrative and Dramatic Sources of Shake-
     speare*. 6 Vols. New York: Columbia U. Pr., 1964.

     Bullough discusses Medieval sources for the following
     Shakespearean works: *Luc.*--Chaucer's *Legend of Good
     Women; MND*--Chaucer's "The Knight's Tale"; *R2--The Chron-
     icle of Froissart; Jn.*--Bale's *Kynge Johan; 1H4*--Analogue,
     The World and the Child; Ant.--The Deeds of Caesar; Tro.--
     Lydgate's *Siege of Troy*; Henryson's *Testament of Cressid*;
     and Caxton's *The Recuyell of the Historyies of Troye*.

52. Bundy, Murray W. "Shakespeare and Elizabethan Psychology." *JEGP*, 23(1924), 516-49.

Shakespeare drew from a great body of literature which expressed ethical problems in the conventional language of faculty-psychology, a Renaissance inheritance from the Middle Ages. In addition, the morality with its personification of mental powers and moral qualities is another source for Shakespeare's inherited psychology. The Medieval concern for the trilogy can be seen in the three seats of mental processes--the liver, heart, and brain as well as the concepts of reason, memory, and imagination.

53. Burton, E. J. *The British Theatre: Its Repertory and Practice, 1100-1900.* London: Jenkins, 1960. 271 pp.

Burton's object is to see the theater from the viewpoint of staging techniques and as viable entertainment for an audience. Chapters include "ritual and folk drama," "miracle and mysteries," "moralities," "interludes," and "Renaissance theater." Parallels in regard to the Elizabethan and the Medieval stage are noted with particular stress on the physical properties of the stage and costuming.

54. Bush, Douglas. *Mythology and the Renaissance Tradition in English Poetry.* Minneapolis: The U. of Minnesota Pr., 1932. 298 pp.

Although Bush points out the importance of the classical tradition upon English literature, his first two chapters stress the importance of the Medieval heritage of Elizabethan drama. According to Bush "the native and Medieval tradition was too strong to be subdued." In addition, he states that Elizabethan poetry owed "more directly to the older English poets ... than to the classical writers." Bush also discusses Shakespeare's classical knowledge he inherited from Medieval writers.

55. Camden, Carroll. *The Elizabethan Woman.* New York: The Elsevier Pr., 1952. 333 pp.

Although Camden generally covers the Renaissance period, she frequently depicts the role of women in the Middle Ages. Topics vary from education to clothing. Of interest to Shakespeare is the discussion of marriage roles and customs as well as various types of domestic relationships.

56. Campbell, Josie P. "Farce as Function in Medieval and
     Shakespearean Drama." *UC,* 3(Fall 1980), 11-18.

     In *MND* and *1H4* farce is used as a structural device to
     enhance the dramatic action of the play. It illuminates
     key passages within the dramas and is an integral part
     of the action.

57. Campbell, Lily B. "Theories of Revenge in Renaissance
     England." *MP,* 28(1931), 281-96.

     In investigating the ethical background, nature, and
     purpose of the revenge play during the Renaissance, the
     author determines that revenge was morally evil. Working
     primarily with *Ham.,* she shows the Senecan background to
     be important but insists that the Medieval tradition is
     also of concern. The *Fall of Princes* illustrates that
     God controls man's destiny, as do the themes in the moral-
     ity plays. The ghost in Renaissance drama bears more re-
     semblance to the English native drama and the morality
     play than to Seneca.

58. Cardozo, J. L. *The Contemporary Jew in the Elizabethan
     Drama.* Amsterdam: H. J. Paris, 1925. 335 pp.

     Chapters Seven and Eight give the background to the
     Flesh-Bond story in Medieval literature with reference
     to Oriental, European and British sources. Cardozo be-
     lieves that it is uncertain whether or not the Flesh-
     Bond theme is of Oriental or Western origin. He comments
     upon the early elements of this tale in the *Cursor Mundi*
     and *Gesta Romanorum* but does not argue for any specific
     influence upon Shakespeare.

59. Carlyle, R. W. and A. J. Carlyle. *A History of Medieval
     Political Thought in the West.* 6 Vols. London:
     Blackwood and Sons, Ltd., 1930.

     The authors concentrate upon Medieval principles dealing
     with justice, religion, society, feudalism and the like.
     The study makes no attempt to relate Medieval political
     theory to Shakespeare but it would prove beneficial for
     understanding those critical essays which link Shakespeare
     to the decaying feudal order.

60. Chambers, E. K. *The English Folk-Play.* Oxford: The
     Clarendon Pr., 1933. 248 pp.

     Although this is a general work which refers to Shake-
     speare infrequently, it does trace a number of Renais-
     sance plays to Medieval origin. The Mummer's Play, the

Lament, the Sword Dance, the Plough Play, and the Morris
Dance are among those plays which Chambers notes were
popular during the Middle Ages.

61. Chandler, Frank Wadleigh. *The Literature of Roguery*.
New York: Burt Franklin, 1907. 584 pp.

Chandler defines the genre and gives the origins of
roguery in the Middle Ages and the Renaissance. He
examines early drama, jest books and popular tales and
beggar books. Shakespeare's rogues are in the Picaresque
tradition.

62. Chew Samuel. "Time and Fortune." *ELH*, 6(1939), 83-113.

The essay discusses time and Fortune as it relates to
Medieval and Elizabethan literature by referring to many
wood cuttings, pictures, engravings, and writings which
deal with time and Fortune. Chew shows Medieval conceptions of Fortune in Lydgate, Dante, *The Romance of
the Rose* and *The Mirror for Magistrates* and comments upon
Shakespeare's use of Medieval concepts of Fortune in
Ham., *Tim.*, *Lr.*, *Tmp.*, *AYL*, *Ant.*, *H5*, *JC*, and *Luc.*

63. ————. *The Pilgrimage of Life*. New York: Vail-Bailou
Pr. Incorp., 1962. 449 pp.

Chew suggests various connections between verbal and
visual imagery and between art, engravings, paintings
and literary works. Chew concentrates upon Medieval
topics such as Fortune, the Seven Deadly Sins and the
Dance of Death. Many Shakespearean passages are analyzed
in terms of Medieval and Renaissance art. His discussion
of Shakespeare's use of the housewife Fortune as seen in
Ham. and *Ant.* shows how the conventional Wheel of Fortune
theme was subtly adapted by Shakespeare.

64. Chute, Marchette. "Chaucer and Shakespeare." *CE*, 7(1950),
15-19.

Both Chaucer and Shakespeare worked for a patron; both
men were born into middle-class families; both worked at
full time jobs and wrote during their spare time; both
men lived in periods when writers were expected to act
as reformers, but neither tried to reform anyone.

65. Clark, Andrew. *Domestic Drama: A Survey of the Origins,
Antecedents, and Nature of the Domestic Play in England,
1500-1640*. (JDS 49.) Salzburg: Inst. für Englische
Sprache und Literatur, Univ. Salzburg, 1975. 455 pp.

This study emphasizes the family element in the domestic genre. References are found throughout the work to the morality tradition.

66. Clark, Donald L. "Ancient Rhetoric and English Renaissance Literature." *SQ*, 2(1951), 195-204.

Clark examines the rhetoric as used in school texts in the Renaissance and finds evidence that Cicero, Quintilian and Aristotle were frequently mentioned. In contrast, the rhetoric of the Middle Ages was a thing of beauty or a flowery pattern. *Margarita Philosophica* (1503), and the works of Geoffrey of Vensauf and Chaucer partially influenced Renaissance textbooks.

67. Clark, James M. *The Dance of Death in the Middle Ages and the Renaissance.* Glasgow: Glasgow U. Pub., 1950. 131 pp.

Clark compiles material in literary and pictorial form which treats the various aspects of the *danse macabre* theme in Medieval and Renaissance literature. He contrasts the Renaissance treatment of this theme with that of the Middle Ages. Shakespeare is mentioned briefly.

68. Clarkson, Paul S. and Clyde T. Warren. *The Law of Property in Shakespeare and the Elizabethan Drama.* Baltimore: Johns Hopkins Pr., 1942. 346 pp.

Of interest to Shakespeare is the discussion of surviving feudal concepts in Shakespeare's day. The book defines the principles of knight service, grand serjeanty, free socage, homage, and fealty. The authors determine that feudal ideas were a thing of the past in the Renaissance.

69. Clemen, Wolfgang. *English Tragedy Before Shakespeare.* London: Methuen and Co., Ltd., 1961. 301 pp.

The last three chapters discuss the rhetorical use of the lament in classical, Medieval, and Renaissance literature with particular reference to Shakespeare. Medieval writers frequently referred to Hecuba, Niobe, and Priam to express their grief, and Shakespeare's references to grief are similarly expressed. The apostrophe to Fortune is another common element.

70. Coffman, George R. "Some Trends in English Literary Scholarship with Special Reference to Mediaeval Backgrounds." *SP*, 35(1938), 500-14.

Coffman reviews Lovejoy's *The Great Chain of Being*, Farnham's *The Medieval Heritage of Elizabethan Tragedy*, Spenser's *Death and Elizabethan Tragedy*, Curry's *Shakespeare's Philosophical Patterns*, and Lewis' *The Allegory of Love*. Of particular interest to Shakespeare is Coffman's examination of Curry's work in reference to *Mac*. Like Curry, Coffman argues that *Mac*. should be interpreted in light of Medieval Christian philosophy.

71. Coghill, Nevill. "The Tragic Fact in the Roman Plays." *ShN*, 6(1956), 20.

In reporting the events of the seventh Shakespeare Conference at Stratford, Coghill notes that the Medieval concept of nobility--bringing to maturity whatever natural endowments man possesses--is at the heart of Shakespeare's Roman plays. Additional comments concern *Rom*. as belonging to Medieval fortune-type tragedy.

72. ⸻. "Shakespeare's Reading in Chaucer," pp. 86-99 in *Elizabethan and Jacobean Studies Presented to F.P. Wilson*. eds. Herbert, Davis, and Helen Gardner. Oxford: Clarendon Pr., 1959.

Coghill surveys the scholarship which advances the idea that Shakespeare used Chaucer's works and gives additional Chaucerian allusions in Shakespeare's plays. He finds Chaucerian echoes in *Mac.*, *Lr.*, *MM*, *MND*, *R2*, *Rom.*, and *Tit.* and concludes that Shakespeare "knew his Chaucer well." Chaucerian works which Shakespeare evidently read are "The Knight's Tale," "The Wife of Bath's Tale," "The Rhyme of Sir Thopas," *The Parliament of Foules*, and *The House of Fame*.

73. Colie, Rosalie. *Shakespeare's Living Art*. Princeton: Princeton U. Pr., 1974. 370 pp.

Colie attempts to view the background of verse forms, motifs, themes and literary conventions. She illustrates how Shakespeare incorporated these elements in his drama. The Medieval influence is never dealt with exclusively but is discussed in a smattering way throughout the work.

74. Comito, Terry. *The Idea of the Garden in the Renaissance*. New Brunswick, N.J.: Rutgers U. Pr., 1978. 187 pp.

Comito has chapters on (1) the garden as an image of paradise, (2) gardens of poetry and philosophy, (3) the garden of love, and (4) Medieval and Renaissance gardens: the redemption of space. Although Shakespeare is briefly

mentioned, the discussion of Medieval sources of Renaissance gardens is important and interesting. Gardens are
models "of the way the mind conceives its relation to the
world external to itself."

75. Conley, C. H. "An Instance of the Fifteen Signs of Judg-
    ment in Shakespeare." *MLN*, 36(1915), 41-44.

    Neither Holinshed's *Chronicles* nor Lucan's *Pharsalia*
    is the probable source for portents in *JC* (II, ii, 17-24)
    and *Ham*. (I, i, 115-120). Rather the Anglo-Norman version
    of the Fifteen Signs of Judgment which the author of
    Cursor Mundi translated into Middle English is the likely
    origin of Shakespeare's portents.

76. Cooper, Helen. *Pastoral: Medieval into Rensaissance.*
    Ipswich: D.S. Brewer, Totowa, N.J.: Rowman and
    Littlefield, 1977. 256 pp.

    Cooper shows that the Renaissance pastoral grew out of
    the native, vernacular heritage which used rural life to
    criticize the court. Renaissance pastoral was less alle-
    gorical and more concerned with moral and universal issues
    than the classical tradition. The discussion of this mode
    particularly focuses upon *WT*.

77. Cormican, L. A. "Medieval Idiom in Shakespeare: Shake-
    speare and the Medieval Ethic." *Scrutiny*, 17(1950),
    298-317.

    This essay illustrates the religious, moral, and psy-
    chological ideas which Shakespeare inherited from the
    Medieval world. Both Medieval and Elizabethan morality
    "supposed the primacy of eternal things." Both periods
    are intensely spiritual; both have an unresolved residue
    of paganism. Shakespeare and Medieval writers indicate
    that man can apprehend but not comprehend the design of
    the universe. Both eras relate human choice to the
    superhuman world. The Medieval ethic related human
    choice to Adam's sin or Christ's redemption. This
    concept can be seen in *Mac*. and to some extent in *Ant*.
    and *Ham*.

78. ————. "Medieval Idiom in Shakespeare: Shakespeare and
    the Liturgy." *Scrutiny*, 17(1950), 186-202.

    The range and style of Shakespeare's writings after
    1600 result from an "increased power to make dramatic
    use of a number of Medieval convictions and attitudes."
    Shakespeare moves away from the cultured language of

the classical influence toward a rugged, Anglo-Saxon,
Medieval idiom. This type of idiom can be seen in
Hebraic writings, particularly the Psalms. The *Book of
Common Prayer* greatly influenced Shakespeare,and this
work accurately represents the doctrines and ideas of
the Middle Ages. The study refers to *Ham., Mac.,* and
Oth.

79. Costello, William T. *The Scholastic Curriculum at Early
Seventeenth-Century Cambridge.* Cambridge, Mass.:
Harvard U. Pr., 1958. 228 pp.

The first chapter comments upon the survival of Medieval scholastic habit at Cambridge. The Medieval form
of *imaginatio* (imaginary disputation) is a form of
Platonic dialogue reduced to scholastic forms that made
its way into the literature of the Renaissance. The
gravedigging scene in *Ham.* and Touchstone's logic in
AYL are expert literary adaptations of scholastic disputation.

80. Courthope, W. J. *A History of English Poetry: The
Development and Decline of the Poetic Drama.* 4 Vols.
London: Macmillan and Co., 1911.

Shakespeare's poetry is in the Medieval tradition of
Teutonic woman worship, but Shakespeare modifies the
tradition by emphasizing humanistic ideas. Other studies
include the waning influence of the morality upon Shakespeare, the incorporation of fabliau elements in *Shr.,*
and traces of the metrical style of the morality in *LLL.*

81. Courtney, W. L. "New Shylock." *LA,* (November 1919),
488-90.

Courtney discusses the Jew in the Middle Ages in regard
to Shylock's character. Renaissance attitudes toward the
Jew were much the same as those of Medieval times.

82. Cox, Ernest H. "Shakespeare and Some Conventions of Old
Age." *SP,* 34(1942), 36-40.

Cox argues that Shakespeare adapted the *contemptu mundi*
theme in a number of his plays. The description of life
as a pilgrimage can be seen in *AYL, MM, R2, R3, Cor., H5,*
and *MV.* Furthermore, the description of old age as the
decaying of fruit as found in *AYL, MV,* and *R3* is similar
to lines found in Chaucer's "The Reeve's Prologue."
Finally, the description of the ages of man as found in
AYL is a well-known Medieval motif.

83. Craig, Hardin. "Morality Plays and Elizabethan Drama."
    SQ, 1(1950), 64-72.

    Craig examines the nature of the morality play and de-
    termines that its roots are specifically English in
    origin. He points out that the morality play influenced
    Tudor drama and is very closely associated with the ro-
    mantic drama of the Elizabethan period. *Dr. Faustus*,
    for example, is a morality play that has become a ro-
    mantic tragedy. The morality play pattern is found in
    Mac. as well as *Oth.*, *Lr.*, and *Ant.* The heroes of these
    plays undergo an experience similar to that of Mankind
    in the morality play.

84. ———. *English Religious Drama of the Middle Ages*.
    Oxford: The Clarendon Pr., 1955. 421 pp.

    Craig has an extensive discussion of Medieval drama,
    with the last chapter noting the transition from Medieval
    to Elizabethan drama. He writes that "the morality in
    spite of its aberrations carried on a trend of thought
    for a century and finally did something to restore the
    vision of Everyman to the world in the poems of Spenser
    and the plays of Shakespeare." *Mac.* and *Oth.* come close
    to an allegorical framework.

85. ———. *The Enchanted Glass*. Oxford: Basil Blackwell,
    1960. 293 pp.

    Medieval topics are found throughout the work but deal
    mainly with hierarchical principles, cosmological struc-
    ture, astrological concepts, faculty psychology, and
    ethical and moral principles which the Renaissance in-
    herited from the church fathers. Encyclopedias such as
    Bartholomaeus *De Proprietatibus Rerum*, and grammar school
    textbooks are frequently cited.

86. Craik, T. W. "The Tudor Interlude and Later Elizabethan
    Drama," pp. 37-57 in *Stratford Upon-Avon Studies 9*,
    ed. John Brown. London: Edward Arnold Ltd., 1966.

    Craik traces the interlude to the Middle Ages and finds
    a morality structure of temptation, sin, and repentance
    in many of the interludes. The dramatic elements of in-
    timacy and spontaneity are a part of the surviving Med-
    ieval interlude in Elizabethan drama. Shakespeare's
    familiarity with the moral interlude is evidenced in
    many plays. Kent calls Goneril "vanity" *Lr.* (II, ii, 33),
    Hamlet calls Claudius a "Vice of Kings" *Ham.* (III, iv, 98),
    and Angelo talks of writing "good Angel on the devil's

horn" *MM* (II, iv, 16).

87. Creeth, Edmund Homer. "From Moral to Tragic Recognition: a Study of Plot Structure in the Morality Tradition." Diss. U. of Cal. Berkeley, 1955.

88. Crutwell, Patrick. "Another Part of the Wood." *EIC*, 5(1955), 382-90.

   In the introductions to the New Arden Shakespeare series, the critics see Shakespeare as "more theological, more serious, more worried, and more Medieval than their forebearers saw him."

89. Cunningham, Dolora G. "The Doctrine of Repentance as a Formal Principle in Some Elizabethan Plays." *DAI*, (1954), 524-25 (Stanford).

   The conventional aspects of repentance help to shape the drama in terms of character and plot. The author sees such an influence in *Ant.*, *LLL*, *MM*, and *AWW*.

90. Cunningham, James Vincent. "Tragic Effect and Tragic Process in Some Plays of Shakespeare, and Their Background in the Literary and Ethical Theory of Antiquity of the Middle Ages." Diss. Stanford University, 1945.

91. Curtin, Madelyn Elaine Douglas. "Mistaking the Word and Simple Syllogisms: Form and Function in Shakespeare's Wordplay." *DAI*, 39(1979), 4955A (Virginia).

   Curtin studies the use of wordplay as used by the descendent of the Medieval Vice and Fool in *R3*, *TGV*, *1H4*, *Ham.*, *Oth.*, and *TN*. Wordplay includes puns, topsy-turvy-dom, jingles, and verbal repetitions.

92. Curtius, E. R. *European Literature and the Latin Middle Ages*, trans. W. R. Trask, London: Chatto and Winduo, 1953. 662 pp.

   Shakespeare loves to use the metaphor of a book when referring to people. Curtius calls this a legacy of the Middle Ages which Shakespeare raised to a "many-faceted play of ideas." Shakespeare's plays that are discussed are *Rom.*, *MND*, *Jn.*, *LLL*, *Oth.*, *R2*, *R3*, *AYL*, *Mac.*, *TN*, *Cym.*, and *Cor.*

93. Cushman, I. W. *The Devil and the Vice in English Dramatic Literature before Shakespeare*. 2nd ed. 1900; rpt. New York: The Humanistic Pr., 1970. 147 pp.

Cushman includes such topics as the origin of the Vice, the names, the functions, the dress, the language, the Vice as a comical figure, the Vice as a dramatic figure, and the Vice as a braggart. This study gives excellent background material which could be used for a study of Shakespeare and the Vice tradition, but Cushman makes no reference to Shakespeare.

94. Davidson, Clifford. "Death in His Court: Iconography in Shakespeare's Tragedies." *SI*, 1(1975), 74-86.

Shakespeare's plays relied a great deal upon Renaissance iconography. The tragedies are informed by the inevitability of death which is often portrayed by Fortune's wheel and the Dance of Death.

95. ————. "The Love Mythos in the Middle Ages and Renaissance." *BSUF*, 16(1975), 3-14.

This essay rebuffs E. Talbot Donaldson who has assailed the terminology of courtly love by calling *amour courtois* an invention of the nineteenth century. A number of Medieval works such as the *Harley Lyrics*, *The Romance of the Rose*, and *The Divine Comedy* show the commandments of love. Davidson briefly discusses courtly love in *Rom.* I, v, 96-103. Romeo and Juliet's love is raised from physical longing to spiritual love via religious imagery.

96. Dean, William K. "The Concept of the Comic in English Drama, ca 1400-1612." *DAI*, 31(1972), 914-15-A (Toronto).

Dean is concerned with the development of the comic form beginning with the Corpus Christi plays to the drama of Shakespeare. Love, reconciliation, and atonement define the limits of the comic.

97. de Montmorency, J. E. G. "Gardens of Chaucer and Shakespeare." *LA*, (June 1911), 625-29.

Chaucer and Shakespeare must have loved the month of May and gardening. The essay shows similarities in "The Knight's Tale" and the garden scene in *R2* (III, iv).

98. Dessen, Alan. "The 'Estates' Morality Play." *SP*, 62 (1965), 121-36.

The morality play tradition can be found in the estate plays of the 1580s and 90s. Social satire became a subject of such plays. Allegorical figures have changed

since Everyman, but their function is to uncover vice
within a literal kingdom. *MV* is referred to in passing.

99. ———. "Two Falls and a Trap: Shakespeare and the
Spectacles of Realism." *ELR*, 5(1975), 291-307.

The author relates how the literal and realistic
aspects of Renaissance drama were often blended with
techniques and effects of the morality plays with allegorical virtues and vices being personified.

100. ———. *Elizabethan Drama and the Viewer's Eye.* Chapel
Hill: U. of North Carolina Pr., 1977. 176 pp.

In his chapter, "Staging and Structure in the Late
Morality Play," Dessen surveys visual effects in plays
acted by early professional troupes. He argues that
more sophisticated versions of similar techniques were
used by Renaissance playwrights. These visual elements
linked various episodes to provide the viewers with a
heightened awareness of "a major theme." Thus a tradition of visual artifice informed the response of
audiences through the use of gestures, conventionalized
groupings, and properties inherited from the later
moralities. See especially Chapter Six, "The Stage
Psychomachia," (126-56) for a discussion of the Medieval
background of Psychomachia and its application to Shakespeare's plays. References are made to *The Castle of
Perseverance* and *The Interlude of Youth.* Shakespeare's
plays discussed are: *Jn., Cym., Ant., TN,* and *Tro.*

101. ———. "Homilies and Anomalies: The Legacy of the
Morality Play to the Age of Shakespeare." *ShakS,*
11(1978), 243-58.

Dessen reviews various studies which link Shakespeare's
works to the morality play in order to assess the value
of these studies. He specifically questions issues and
problems that remain unresolved and suggests research
that might prove appropriate such as the techniques and
stagecraft of the morality tradition.

102. ———. "The Logic of Elizabethan Stage Violence: Some
Alarms and Excursions for Modern Critics, Editors,
and Directors." *RenD,* 9(1978), 39-69.

Dessen reviews stage violence in the morality plays
which often portrayed violence in allegorical terms
rather than in realistic ways. He suggests allegorical

readings for violent scenes in *1H4, Lr., Cym., Oth.,*
1H6, R3, and *Cor.*

103.   Doebler, John. *Shakespeare's Speaking Pictures: Studies*
       in Iconic Imagery. Albuquerque: U. of New Mexico Pr.,
       1974. 236 pp.

       Woodcuts and pictures of both Medieval and Renaissance
       periods help to explain certain passages in Shakespeare's
       plays. Doebler comments on iconic imagery in *AYL, MV,*
       R2, and *Mac.*

104.   ————. "Bibliography for the Study of Iconography and
       Renaissance English Literature." *RORD,* 22(1979), 45–55.

       Sections III and IV are useful: "compilations and
       catalogs of Medieval and Renaissance graphics," and
       "works useful to an understanding of the relationship
       between Iconography and Medieval and Renaissance liter-
       ature."

105.   Doran, Madeleine. *Endeavors of Art: A Study of Form*
       in Elizabethan Drama. Madison: Wisconsin U. Pr.,
       1954. 482 pp.

       This book devotes numerous sections to specific Med-
       ieval influences upon Renaissance literary art and
       attempts to reconstruct aspects of literary art which
       helped shape Elizabethan playwrights, particularly Shake-
       speare. Doran discusses tragedy, comedy, rhetoric,
       Medieval narratives, the debate, ethical conflict in
       the morality play, and the influence of the mystery plays
       upon Shakespeare. Another point of interest is the
       evaluation of Medieval writers' use of of classical
       material and the influence of that material upon
       Shakespeare.

106.   Douce, Francis. *Illustration of Shakespeare, and of*
       Ancient Manners. 2nd ed. 1858; rpt. New York: Burt
       Franklin, 1968. 607 pp.

       The fairy elements in *MND* have Medieval counterparts,
       particularly in Chaucer's works. Douce has a section
       on clowns and fools and reviews the types of fools found
       in Medieval and Renaissance works. The section on *Per.*
       (394–402) shows that Shakespeare was acquainted with
       representations of the Dance of Death. The importance
       of the theme of death is given some attention in Ren-
       aissance works.

107. Dowden, Edward. "Elizabethan Psychology." *AM,* 100 (1907), 398-99.

    The Renaissance inherited Medieval psychological concepts from Bartholomew Anglious who lived in the century preceding Chaucer. *Batman upon Bartholomew* was popularly read in Shakespeare's time. The old psychology believed that a study of the mind could not be separated from the influence of the body. Other ideas stressed are the study of the four elements, the influence of astrological bodies, and the examination of theology. Dowden illuminates passages in *Lr., Tro., Mac., LLL, MV, JC, TN, Ado.,* and *Sonnets* 54 and 55.

108. Dunaway, Rebecca Kaye. "The Formative Impact of the Devil upon Selected Renaissance Dramas." *DAI,* 36(1975), 1480A-81A (Texas Tech.).

    Although not relating her work to Shakespeare, Dunaway studies the role of the Devil in the development of dramatic action and characterization in twelve non-Shakespearean plays.

109. Dunlop, Rhodes. "The Allegorical Interpretation of Renaissance Literature." *PMLA,* 82(1967), 39-43.

    This essay examines the use of allegory in Spenser, Jonson, and Shakespeare in order to determine the extent and nature of Renaissance allegory. Shakespeare's allegory does not deal so much with specific events or people as it does with certain patterns such as those associated with Fortune's Wheel and universal figurative correspondences. *1H4, R2,* and *Ham.* are related to the topics above.

110. Dunn, Catherine E. "The Medieval 'Cycle' as History Play: An Approach to the Wakefield Plays." *SR,* 7 (1960), 76-89.

    Dunn argues that there is a closer relation than is generally accepted between the Medieval mystery play and Elizabethan chronicle play. Unlike Ribner, Dunn finds that the mystery plays had a unity of purpose and method which can be seen only when dealing with the totality of these plays. The relationship between the two dramas is "philosophical rather than structural." There is a background of epic proportions in the mystery cycle and Elizabethan chronicle; both have a didactic element; both deal essentially with unchangeable facts.

111. Dyer, T. F. Thiselton. *Folk-Lore of Shakespeare.*
      New York: Dover Pub., 1966. 526 pp.

      In Chapter Eleven (296-331) Dyer refers to Shakespeare's
      knowledge of the mystery and morality plays. *TN, Ham.,*
      1H4, R3, Lr., and *AYL* contain passages which indicate
      Shakespeare's acquaintance with Medieval plays.

112. Edwards, Ralph William. "Shakespearean Laughter: A
      Study of Shakespeare's Bases of Laughter and Their
      Implications." *DAI,* 22(1961), 1554-55 (Boston U.).

      Edwards shows variations of the Medieval aspects of
      laughter in a number of Shakespeare's tragedies, comedies,
      and histories by comparing Shakespeare's plays to moral-
      ities and early religious plays.

113. Erskine, John *The Elizabethan Lyric.* New York:
      Columbia U. Pr., 1916. 344 pp.

      In stressing the growth of the lyric in English lit-
      erature, Erskine has a short section explaining the types
      of lyrics found in Shakespeare's plays. He discusses the
      pastourelle in *AYL* and the *aubade* in *Cym.*

114. Fairchild, Arthur H. R. "Shakespeare and the Arts of
      Design." *UMS,* 12(1937), 1-198.

      Part Four comments upon Shakespeare's use of architec-
      ural ruins, feudalism, and chivalric ideals. Shakespeare
      was a "medievalist at heart and regretted the new materi-
      alism; he was convinced that the ideals of honor, courte-
      sy, and munificence were of higher worth than those of
      practical efficiency, expediency, and diplomatic maneuver
      in government." *Ham.* is viewed in light of Medieval
      concepts of feudalism and its opposite Machiavellian
      opportunism.

115. Farmer, R. "Essay on the Learning of Shakespeare,"
      pp. 162-215 in *Eighteenth Century Essays on Shakespeare.*
      ed. by D. Nichol Smith. 2nd ed. 1903; rpt. New York:
      Russell and Russell, 1962. 358 pp.

      This classic essay should be read for a view of how
      the seventeenth and eighteenth centuries perceived
      Shakespeare's knowledge of Medieval and classical writers.
      Farmer concludes that Shakespeare's knowledge of the
      ancients was rather limited.

116. Farnham, Willard. *The Shakespearean Grotesque.* Oxford:
      The Clarendon Pr., 1971. 175 pp.

The vice and devil tradition of native English plays is essential for an understanding of Shakespearean drama. Farnham discusses the transformation of the Vice as he appears in drama from the Medieval to the Renaissance period by referring to the following characters from Shakespeare's plays: Falstaff, Hamlet, Thersites, Iago, and Caliban.

117. Felver, Charles Stanley. "Shakespeare and Robert Armin his Fool--A Working Partnership." *DAI*, 16(1956), 2446 (U. of Michigan).

The second and third chapters are of interest since Biblical and Medieval notations about fools and folly are compared to sixteenth century continental and English concepts. Felver determines how much fool-lore was commonplace in Elizabethan source material and how much Shakespeare derived from Robert Armin and Medieval sources.

118. Ferguson, Wallace K. *Renaissance Studies*. Ontario: The U. of Western Ontario, 1963. 170 pp.

Chapter Two, "The Reinterpretation of the Renaissance," offers a valuable discussion of Medieval and Renaissance history of ideas. Ferguson refers to art, history, education, and literature and finds a tendency to see the Middle Ages in the Renaissance. In the past, scholars have "ignored the whole body of Medieval feudal and ecclesiastical literature and leaped straight to the age of Petrarch."

119. Fergusson, Francis. "Trope and Allegory: Some Themes Common to Dante and Shakespeare." *DS*, 86(1968), 113-26.

Dante and Shakespeare use the "same traditional vision of human life to give order and meaning to their poetry." Both have similar principles of art, derived from "the venerable habit of four-fold allegory." The author finds similar usage of the Medieval concepts of letter, trope, allegory, and analoge in Dante's Canto XVI of the *Purgatorio* and *MM*.

120. ————. *Trope and Allegory Themes Common to Dante and Shakespeare*. Athens: U. of Ga. Pr., 1977. 164 pp.

Dante and Shakespeare shared a classical and Christian heritage which brought about a type of writing that focused upon moral and religious levels of meaning.

Analogous themes and situations are shown such as that
involving Paolo and Francesca and Romeo and Juliet as
well as Ugolino and Macbeth.

121. Finn, Dorothy Mercedes. "Love and Marriage in Renais-
      sance Literature." *DAI*, 15(1955), 2188-89 (Columbia).

      This study traces classical and Medieval ideas of love
      and marriage through numerous Renaissance writers. The
      Medieval ideas concern friendship and the courtly love
      theme. Finn has a section on the Christianization of
      courtly love as an offshoot of the sensual Medieval
      love theme.

122. Fishel, Oskar. "Art and the Theatre--II." *BM*, 15(1935),
      4-15; 54-67.

      Fishel studies various aspects of Medieval stages by
      examining carved clocks which date back to 1405. He
      believes Medieval stage designs are embodied in the
      Globe, as well as many other stages of the Renaissance.
      The study concentrates upon structural aspects such as
      side-chambers and right and left wings.

123. Flanigan, Clifford C. "The Liturgical Drama and its
      Tradition: A Review of Scholarship, 1965-1975."
      RORD, 18(1975), 81-102.

      The author reviews important studies noting the con-
      tributions to the scholarship of liturgical drama. Of
      importance to Shakespearean scholarship is the adaptation
      of liturgical principles to Renaissance drama.

124. Fleming, John V. "Medieval Manuscripts in the Taylor
      Library." *PULC*, 38(1977), 107-19.

      Some of the material in the manuscripts in the Robert
      H. Taylor Collection at Princeton provided Shakespeare
      with texts for his plays. Fleming specifically mentions
      the *Chronicles of Brut* as well as Boccaccio's *De Casibus
      Virorum Illustrium*.

125. Freeman, Rosemary. *English Emblem Books*. London:
      Chatto and Windus, 1948. 156 pp.

      Freeman lists and discusses the background of emblems
      in Medieval and Renaissance literature. The heraldic
      emblems in *Per.* may be attributed to Medieval emblems
      concerning chivalry. Freeman believes, however, that
      emblematic literature did not influence Shakespeare
      that significantly.

126. Friedman, Simon. "Some Shakespearing Characterizations
of Women and Their Traditions." *DAI*, 34(1974), 312A
(Yale).

The discussion that is pertinent is Shakespeare's presentation of women as influenced by women in romance
and in domestic drama. Friedman further examines heroines
and women in the tragedies.

127. Frye, Roland Mushat. *Shakespeare and Christian Doctrine*.
Princeton: Princeton U. Pr., 1963. 314 pp.

Frye argues against any allegorical interpretation of
Shakespeare's plays and sees little influence of Medieval
drama on Shakespeare. The book comments upon the religious ideas of Shakespeare from the point of view of
Renaissance theology. The Medieval religious influence
is basically ignored.

128. Gallagher, Ligera Cecile. "Shakespeare and the Aristotelian Ethical Tradition." *DAI*, 16(1956), 1898
(Stanford).

The Aristotelian ethical tradition as received by Shakespeare through the Medieval Thomist adaptation is probably the most widely known ethical system in Shakespeare's
day. *R2*, *MV*, *Oth.*, and *Lr.* are examined in light of this
philosophy, particularly emphasizing the following concepts: (1) virtuous choice ending in happiness, (2)
virtuous choice ending in frustration, and (3) the Christian pattern of redemption which consists of enduring the
natural effects of sin as part of the means to expiate
guilt and to achieve happiness.

129. Galloway, David. "Records of Early English Drama in the
Provinces and What They May Tell Us About the Elizabethan Theatre," pp. 82-110 in *Elizabethan Theatre
VII*, ed. by G. R. Hibbard. Hamden, Conn.: Archon Books
in Collaboration with the U. of Waterloo, 1980.

Of concern is the discussion of the *Records of The
Early English Drama* project. The author surveys printed
texts of provincial records and details the strong native
drama tradition.

130. Gardiner, H. C. *Mysteries' End ... The Last Days of the
Medieval Religious Stage*. New Haven: Yale U. Pr.,
1946. 140 pp.

In detailing the continuation of the Medieval religious
stage through 1603, Gardiner argues that religious drama

was extremely popular during the 1580s, yet it was soon
to pass out of existence due to political pressures.
This work supplements others which contend that mystery
and morality plays were easily accessible to Shakespeare.

131. Gatch, Katherine. "Shakespeare's Allusion to the Older
      Drama." *PQ*, 7(1928), 27-44.

      Gatch shows the way that Shakespeare's treatment of
      the Herod figure, the devil, and the Nine Worthies was
      influenced by earlier drama. Other discussions include
      death as an antic and face puppetry.

132. Gayley, Charles Mills, ed. *Representative English Come-*
      dies. 4 Vols. New York: The Macmillan Co., 1912.

      The introduction concerns the surviving Medieval comic
      elements in the mystery plays, moral interludes and in
      the character of the Vice. Moral plays offered a reso-
      lution to the problems within a play by emphasizing the
      providential scheme of things.

133. Gesner, Carol. *Shakespeare and the Greek Romance: A*
      Study of Origins. Lexington: The U. of Kentucky Pr.,
      1970. 216 pp.

      In Chapter Two (14-46) Gesner discusses the Medieval
      background--chaste and adulterous love, courtly love
      tradition--and sees the Greek romances forming the bases
      of Medieval romances. Greek romances influenced
      Boccaccio as well as the chivalric cycles. Chapter
      Three (47-51) studies the extant Greek romances in the
      Medieval and Renaissance periods.

134. Gira, Catherine R. "Shakespeare's Venus Figures and
      Renaissance Tradition." *SI*, 4(1978), 95-114.

      Gira explores the enigmatic and complex Venus figures
      in Shakespeare's plays. Although there was a rich native
      tradition predominantly based upon the classics, Shake-
      speare's portrayal of Venus is similar to the Italian
      tradition, the works of Titian and Botticelli.

135. Glazier, Phyllis Gorfain. "Folkloristic Devices and
      Formal Structure in Shakespearean Drama." *DAI*, 34
      (1973), 3341-42-A (Berkeley).

      Glazier concentrates upon the riddle, proverbs, games,
      and dramatic devices and shows how they aid in the under-
      standing of *MV*, *AWW*, *Lr.*, *Mac.*, and *Per*.

136. Golden, Martha Hester. "The Iconography of the English History Play." *DAI*, 26(1965), 1631 (Columbia).

Golden studies emblems concerning the state scene, throne room scene, trials, funerals, and deathbed scenes. Other aspects evaluate the "garden scene," King as commoner, seduction, banquet, and finally battle and murder scenes. Armor, weapons, daggers, music, beds, and corpses are also considered.

137. ———. "Stage Imagery," pp. 810-20 in *Reader's Encyclopedia of Shakespeare*. ed. by Oscar J. Campbell and Edward G. Quinn. New York: Crowell, 1966.

Golden stresses the importance of visual topoi (speaking pictures) in Shakespeare's scenes. Stage emblems are apparent in clothing, embroidery, colors, jewels, badges, painted cloths and windows. Each contributes to the meaning of the play.

138. Goldschmidt, E. P. *The Printed Book of the Renaissance*. Amsterdam: Gerard Th. van Heusden, 1966. 93 pp.

Section Two takes up two points of interest: the survival of Medieval books which are illustrated by woodcuts and the scope of classical themes in Medieval literature which the Renaissance inherited. Goldschmidt also determines that the illustrated book in which the text is accompanied by paintings depicting a scene described in the text is a Medieval conception which the Renaissance printers rejected. Renaissance printers stressed the picture book, "the book of plates accompanied by explanatory letter-press."

139. Goodman, Randolph G. "That Strumpet the Stage: Poems About Playgoers, Players, and Playwrights." *DAI*, 13(1953), 450 (Columbia).

Goodman surveys the audience, actors, and playwrights from the Middle Ages through the Renaissance and determines the audience's attitude toward dramatic performances by the playwrights and poets. The secularization of the audience caused the Medieval cycles to cease and brought the beginning of the company of actors under a patron.

140. Gorfain, Phyllis. "Remarks Toward a Folkloristic Approach to Literature: Riddles in Shakespearean Drama." *SFQ*, 41(1977), 143-57.

Gorgain illustrates the use of folklore devices (riddle, oath, curse, proverb) in *Mac.*, *Lr.*, *AWW*, *Cym.*, and *MV*. These devices should not be seen as separate or apart from theme and character, for they complement by providing further insight into the play.

141. Green, Henry. *Shakespeare and the Emblem Writers*. London: Trubner and Co., 1870. 571 pp.

This book attempts to be an exhaustive compilation of all emblem literature to which Shakespeare had access. Green discusses Medieval emblems such as the Dance of Death, and shows the theme in a number of Shakespeare's plays. Other sections of this book focus upon historical emblems, heraldic emblems, mythological emblems, emblems illustrating fables, emblems associated with proverbs, those associated with nature and animals, and those connected with poetic ideas, morality, and aesthetics.

142. Greene, David M. "Medieval Background of the Elizabethan Emblem Book." Diss., 1958 (Berkeley).

143. Greenfield, Thelma N. *The Induction in Elizabethan Drama*. Eugene, Oregon: U. of Oregon Pr., 1969. 173 pp.

In Chapter Two the dumb show is discussed in Medieval moralities and liturgical drama. References to Medieval personification characters abound throughout the work.

144. Greer, C. A. "Shakespeare a Researcher." *N&Q*, 200 (1955), 479-80.

Greer considers Shakespeare's reading to be limited to the works of his contemporaries. Those studies which attempt to relate Shakespeare to recondite Medieval and classical works are discredited.

145. Hales, J. W. "Shakespeare's Reading of Chaucer." *QR*, 134(1873), 225-85.

Shakespeare was well acquainted with Chaucer's "The Knight's Tale" and *Troilus and Criseyde*. Hales finds Chaucerian echoes and allusions in *MND*, *Tro.*, *Rom.*, *TNK*, and *Ven.*

146. ————. *Essays and Notes on Shakespeare*. London: George Bell and Sons, 1892. 300 pp.

In Chapter Three, "Chaucer and Shakespeare," Hales discusses similarities between the two writers. Both tell

the story of Lucretia, both decline to use the romance
of chivalry, both quickly outgrew the use of allegory,
both recount the story of Julius Caesar, portray the
tragic end of Pyramus and Thisbe, and comment at length
upon Cleopatra. Hales also comments upon the porter
scene in *Mac.* and sees a number of affinities between
the porter and Belial in the Coventry mysteries.

147. Hallen, William. "What Needs My Shakespeare?" *SQ*,
2(1952), 3-16.

Of interest is Haller's comments regarding the sermon
in Medieval and Renaissance times. The sermon in dramatic form would produce a morality play in the Middle
Ages, while the sixteenth century sermon would yield
an Elizabethan tragedy.

148. Halliwell-Phillips, James O. *Outlines of the Life of
Shakespeare.* London: Longmans, Green, and Co.,
1907. 416 pp.

It is highly probable that Shakespeare saw a number
of mystery plays in his youth. Although there is no
evidence to support the idea that mystery plays were
performed at Stratford, yet there are accounts of mysteries performed at Bristol. Shakespeare's notions of
Herod and of Black Souls appear to be derived from
Medieval drama.

149. Hanford, James H. "The Origin and Development of the
Allegorical Debate in Medieval Literature." Diss.,
Harvard University, 1909.

Topics of Hanford's dissertation include "The debate
of Heart and Eye," "Classical eclogue and Medieval debate," "The Medieval debate between wine and water,"
and "The debate element in Elizabethan drama."

150. ————. "The Debate Element in Elizabethan Drama,"
pp. 445-56 in *Anniversary Papers by Colleagues and
Pupils of George Lyman Kittridge,* ed. by F.N.
Robinson. Boston: Ginn and Company Pub., 1917.

Hanford suggests that the debate element in Renaissance
literature is a survival of the morality play and the
antiquated style of scholastic disputation. Debate
topics illustrated are body and soul, life and death,
youth and age, pride and lowliness, love and riches,
and fortune and nature. The induction scenes in

Renaissance drama are based upon the debate.   Hanford
studies the debate element in *LLL*.

151.   Hankins, John Erskine.   "Pains of the Afterworld in
       Milton and Shakespeare." *PMLA*, 11(1956), 482-95.

       Hankins discusses Shakespeare's indebtedness to Med-
       ieval visions which describe Hell such as the visions
       of Drythelm, Alberic, Tendale, and the Monk of Evesham.
       Shakespeare's plays mentioned are *Lr.*, *Ham.*, *WT*, *Tim.*,
       and *Oth*.

152.   ————.   *Backgrounds of Shakespeare's Thought*.   Hamden,
       Conn.:   Archon Books, 1978.   196 pp.

       This book traces the broad intellectual heritage that
       Shakespeare used and derived from various sources.   Many
       passages are quoted with an emphasis upon philosophy,
       science, and Medieval Latin.

153.   Hardison, O. B.   *Christian Rite and Christian Drama in
       the Middle Ages*.   Baltimore: Johns Hopkins U. Pr.,
       1965.   328 pp.

       For a discussion of the relation of Medieval drama to
       the Renaissance see pp. 1-23.   Hardison sees the two
       time spans as evolutionary.   Also, for particular com-
       ments upon Shakespeare's debt to Medieval drama see pp.
       287-292.   This study ties Shakespeare to his Medieval
       background in numerous ways, but particular emphasis
       is upon the liturgical tradition.

154.   Harnack, Harvey A.   "The Typological Devine: A Study
       in the Figural Expression of Renaissance Kingship."
       DAI, 37(1977), 5851-A (Okla. State).

       Harnack defines typology in its major modes, and
       traces its historical development with special reference
       to monarchial typology.   In *Cym.* one finds an expression
       of "monarchial typology delicate in compliment and
       qualified by gentle admonition.

155.   Harrier, Richard.   "Another Note on 'Why the Sweets
       Melted.'" *SQ*, 18(1967), 67.

       The association of melting sweets with fawning dogs is
       found in Medieval pageants where displays of flattery
       point to sweets and bisquits thrown on passing lords.
       Image clusters which depict dogs and melting sweets can
       be found in *R2*, *Ham.*, and *Tim*.

156. Harris, Rhoda Ann. "Chaucer in the Elizabethan and
     Jacobean Drama with Particular Reference to Shake-
     speare." Diss., King's College (London), 1972.

157. Harrison, Thomas P. "Shakespeare's Birds." *TSL*, 3
     (1958), 53-62.

     In discussing three types of source material from
     which Shakespeare may have derived ornithological in-
     formation, Harrison refers to scientific works, rural
     works, and Medieval encyclopedias like the one by
     Bartholomaeus Anglicus.

158. Hart, Alfred. *Shakespeare and the Homilies*. Melbourne:
     Melbourne U. Pr., 1934. 261 pp.

     Hart touches briefly upon the influence of Medieval
     homilies upon *1H4* (II, i, 13-139). References to treason
     and rebellion or the prompting of the devil appear to
     come from Medieval homiletic literature.

159. Hawkins, Harriett. *Poetic Freedom and Poetic Truth:
     Chaucer, Shakespeare, Marlowe, and Milton*. London:
     Oxford Pr., 1976. 135 pp.

     Of interest is Hawkins' introduction--"Poetic Injus-
     tice: Some Winners and Losers in Medieval and Renais-
     sance Literature." References are made to *Rom.*, *JC*, *Cym.*,
     MV, *Ham.*, and *Oth*. Points of comparison are made to
     Chaucer's "The Clerk's Tale," "The Knight's Tale," and
     "The Miller's Tale."

160. Hawkins, Richard H. "Some Effects of Technique Developed
     in the Native English Drama on the Structure of Shake-
     speare's Plays." *DAI*, 31(1971), 4121-A (Washington
     State).

     1, *2*, *3*, *H6*, *LLL*, *Rom.*, and *WT* reflect a morality play
     otructuro. Thooo playo arc influcnccd by the native
     English tradition, especially the techniques of alter-
     nation, suppression, and compression.

161. Haydn, Hiram. *The Counter Renaissance*. New York:
     Scribner, 1950. 705 pp.

     Haydn places the Medieval English period from 1341 to
     1626. Thus his discussion of Shakespeare's time shows
     the blending of Medieval and Renaissance ideas. Polit-
     ical thought, literature, and philosophy are some sub-
     jects elaborated upon. Chapter Ten deals exclusively
     with Shakespeare and "the counter Renaissance."

162.   Hengerer, Joyce H. "The Theme of the Slandered Woman
        in Shakespeare." *DAI, 29*(1968), 1078-A (Wisconsin).

        This work studies the influence of the Medieval tra-
        dition of the slandered woman in homilies, allegories,
        and romances and sees the continuation of this tradi-
        tion in *Ado., Cym.* and *WT.* The study defines slander
        in the Medieval sense of Envy, the most pernicious of
        all the Seven Deadly Sins.

163.   Herndle, George C. *The High Design: English Renaissance
        Tragedy and the Natural Law.* Lexington: U. of
        Kentucky Pr., 1970. 337 pp.

        Medieval attitudes toward natural law are surveyed,
        and Herndle argues for their continuation in the Renais-
        sance. He applies the concepts of the Medieval world
        picture to his discussion of tragedy.

164.   Herrington, H. W. "Witchcraft and Magic in the Eliz-
        abethan Drama." *JAF, 32*(1919), 447-85.

        Plays dealing with witchcraft and magic in Elizabethan
        drama were popular and generally pleased the audiences.
        Herrington sees this as a continuation of magic and en-
        chanters as seen in the Middle Ages. Accounts of magi-
        cians and enchanters such as Merlin, Trithein, Cornelius,
        Agrippa, and Paracelsus are traced.

165.   Hertzbach, Janet Stvropoulos. "From Congregation to
        Polity: The English Moral Drama to Shakespeare."
        DAI, 39(1979), 4274-A (Indiana).

        Medieval plays such as *The Pride of Life, The Castle
        of Perseverance,* the Digby *Mary Magdalene,* and *Youth*
        are examined in order to show the concept of citizenship
        and political responsibility. References are made to
        R2, and *1* and *2H4.*

166.   Hieatt, A. Kent. "Medieval Symbolism and the Dramatic
        Imagery of the English Renaissance." *DAI,* 1955, 817
        (Columbia).

        This study ties Renaissance dramatic imagery to short
        and long tropes of Medieval literature. English allegory
        and dramatic imagery have common symbols and iconography.
        "Literary symbolism ... is to be found in certain Med-
        ieval allegories." Hieatt sees English allegory and
        Renaissance dramatic imagery as "common manifestations
        of one enduring" literary heritage.

167. Hogan, Jerome William. "The Rod and the Candle: Conscience in the English Morality Plays, Shakespeare's *Macbeth* and Tourneur's *The Atheist's Tragedy*." *DAI*, 35(1975), 4524-A (Cuny).

Chapter Four examines the character of conscience in a number of English morality plays such as *Mundus et Infans* and *Impatient Poverty*. Some discussion of these concepts is applied to *Mac.* and *H8*.

168. Holaday, Allan. "Shakespeare, Richard Edward, and the Virtues Reconciled." *JEGP*, 66(1967), 200-07.

The essay corrects a remark by Chew that the Parliament of Heaven theme is not found in Tudor-Stuart drama beyond the limits of the morality plays. Holaday find the Parliament of Heaven theme in *MV*. Instead of arguing a direct Medieval morality influence, he notes that Richard Edward's *Damon and Pithias* is based upon the Parliament of Heaven concept, and the allegory in Edward's play is closer to the type of allegory found in Shakespeare than the cruder type found in the moralities.

169. Holbrook, David. *The Quest for Love*. Tuscaloosa: U. of Alabama, 1965. 376 pp.

Holbrook studies the topic of love in the works of Chaucer, Shakespeare, and D.H. Lawrence. The introduction gives an overview of love and its many themes as seen in the authors mentioned. The section on Chaucer as well as the one on Shakespeare deals with similar aspects of love as viewed by both authors. For example, Holbrook notes that both authors see the wholesomeness of sexuality as a basis for the well-being of the individual.

170. Hole, Christina. *English Home Life, 1500-1800*. London: Batsford, 1947. 184 pp.

Part One (1-90) contrasts the Renaissance and Middle Ages in regard to the following topics: home, sickness, marriages, death, sports, games, children, education, and religion.

171. Holznecht, Karl Julius. *The Background of Shakespeare's Plays*. New York: American Book Co., 1950. 481 pp.

Many chapters in this work refer to the Medieval influence upon Shakespeare. In "The Drama before Shake-

speare" the author discusses the importance of the miracle and morality plays for Shakespearean drama in relationship to stages and themes. More comments upon
Medieval staging techniques are found in "The Influence
of the Theatrical Conditions upon Shakespeare." The
work contains scattered references to Medieval sources
in the chapter "The Sources of Shakespeare's Plays."
Finally, he evaluates the Medieval contributions to
tragedy in "Shakespearean Tragedy."

172. Hoskins, Frank L. "Master-Servant Relations in Tudor
      and Early Stuart Literature with Special Reference
      to the Drama of Shakespeare and His Contemporaries."
      DAI, 15(1955), 1387-88 (Columbia).

      Chapter Three considers Shakespeare's dramatic treat-
      ment of master-servant relationships in light of the
      changing feudal, social world and the new Renaissance
      mercantilism. There are numerous references to the
      tragedies, comedies, and the histories.

173. Hosley, Richard. "Three Kinds of Outdoor Theatre Before
      Shakespeare." *ThS*, 12(1971), 1-33.

      Hosley distinguishes three types of theater prior to
      Shakespeare: the place and scaffolds theater, the
      pageant-wagon theater, and the booth-stage theater.

174. Huber, Edward. "Three Shakespearean Myths: Mutability,
      Plenitude, and Reputation," pp. 95-119 in *English
      Institute Essays*. New York: Columbia U. Pr., 1948.

      Shakespeare's concept of mutability is associated with
      the decay of beauty and the transience of bodily things
      and is related to the *de contemptu mundi* tradition, while
      his ideas of plenitude indicate an awareness of the riches
      of the world, the joy of love, and the briefness of
      beauty which are derived from Chaucer and *The Romance of
      the Rose*. Ideas of reputation are associated with im-
      mortality and involve the notion that a man's virtue
      would survive him.

175. Huzinga, Johan. *The Waning of the Middle Ages*. London:
      Edward Arnold and Co., 1923. 328 pp.

      Individual chapters on chivalry, conventions of love,
      and religious imagery are of interest. The last chapter
      (297-309) assesses the Medieval contribution to the Ren-
      aissance with Huzinga noting that feudalism, ideas of
      chivalry, courtesy, and scholasticism refused to give

way to Renaissance humanism.

176. James, D. G. *The Dream of Learning.* Oxford: The
    Clarendon Pr., 1951. 126 pp.

    See pages 1-32 for a discussion of Shakespeare and
    Bacon and the new learning. James asserts that the
    tradition of allegory in drama was very much alive.
    Yet he insists that Shakespeare did not write in the
    Christian tradition.

177. Janecek, Thomas John. "The Literary History of the
    Parliament of Heaven Allegory from Origination in
    Christianity to Culmination in the Renaissance Drama
    of England." *DAI*, 36(1976), 6371-71A (Ill. Urbana-
    Champaign).

    The author traces the history of the "Parliament of
    Heaven" allegory and assesses its impact upon selected
    Medieval and Renaissance drama. He refers to the plays
    in the *Ludus Coventriae* cycle and discusses the allegory
    in Shakespeare's *MM* and *MV*.

178. Jarrett, Bede. *Social Theories of the Middle Ages:
    1200-1500.* Boston: Little, Brown and Co., 1926.
    280 pp.

    Of interest is the section on usury (150-180) which
    spells out the Medieval attitude toward money-lending.
    Jarrett comments that the theme of usury in *MV* is fully
    in the Medieval tradition.

179. Jones, Emrys. *The Origins of Shakespeare.* Oxford: The
    Clarendon Pr., 1977. 290 pp.

    Jones shows that the significance of the mystery
    cycles upon Shakespearean drama is far greater than
    hitherto acknowledged. Particular emphasis is placed
    upon *Tit.*, *Jn.*, *1H6*, *2H6*, and *3H6*. He also has a dis-
    cussion of the morality *Mudus et Infans*.

180. Jones, Robert C. "Dangerous Sport: The Audience's
    Engagement with Vice in the Moral Interludes."
    RenD, 6(1973), 45-64.

    The Vices are more attractive than the virtues. Play-
    wrights tried to control the Vice so that his moralizing
    force was not ruined. The Vice plays upon the audience
    as well as characters in the play. Although the study is
    not directed specifically to Shakespeare, it has impor-

tant applications for Shakespearean Vices.

181. Jorgensen, Paul A. *Redeeming Shakespeare's Words.*
      Berkeley: U. of Calif. Pr., 1962. 131 pp.

      Jorgensen's method of word analysis reveals insights
      into the meaning of Shakespeare's plays. Thus "honesty"
      is examined in *Oth.* by going to the use of the word in
      morality plays as well as plays contemporary to
      Shakespeare.

182. Jusserand, J. J. *A Literary History of the English
      People.* 1909, 3rd ed. New York: G. P. Putnam
      and Sons, 1926. 633 pp.

      In "The Predecessors of Shakespeare" (3-148), morality
      characters and abstractions are discussed. The play-
      wrights in Shakespeare's day began to give names to
      abstract characters of the moralities. Jusserand
      argues that morality characters became apart of Renais-
      sance drama.

183. Kantorowicz, Ernst. *The Kings Two Bodies.* Princeton:
      Princeton U. Pr., 1957. 567 pp.

      Medieval political theology is centered in the king
      who shows both spiritual and natural attributes. Chap-
      ter Two discusses Medieval and Renaissance political
      theory in Shakespeare's *R2.* The rite of degradation,
      and the political nature of the play are emphasized.

184. Keeton, George W. *Shakespeare's Legal and Political
      Background.* London: Sir Isaac Pitman and Sons,
      Ltd., 1967. 417 pp.

      In giving Shakespeare's political background (225-47),
      Keeton emphasizes the turbulant politics of the period
      which ranged from the Medieval view of absolutism, to
      the view of society as a type of divine institution.
      In addition, there was the view of Philip Melancthon
      who saw authority residing in the law of nature.

185. Keilstrup, Lorraine M. "The Myth of Cain in the Early
      English Drama." *DAI,* 35(1974), 2942-43-A (Nebraska).

      The author surveys the Cain character in Hebrew writings
      and Medieval works such as *Beowulf, Piers Plowman, The
      Chester Creation, The Hegge Cain and Abel* and *The York
      Sacrificium Cayne and Abell* to establish the rebel
      character. There is a discussion of *Lr., Tit., R3,* and

MV in regard to the above ideas.

186. Kellet, Ernest Edward. *Suggestions: Literary Essays.*
1923; rpt. Freeport, New York: Books for Libraries
Pr., 1969. 212 pp.

Chapter Two, "Some Medievalisms in Shakespeare," illustrates Medieval themes in Shakespeare's plays and gives
parallel themes in the writings of the Middle Ages. *MV*
(III, v) illustrates the Medieval idea of compensation,
that misfortunes in this life will bring favor in the
next. Kellet refers to "The Wife of Bath's Tale" and
"The Merchant's Tale" in presenting the Medieval background. *AYL* (I, ii) uses Medieval ideas of nature and
fortune. The fits of nature are frequently canceled
out by the vagaries of fortune. He finds a similar
handling of this theme in "The Parliament of Foules,"
"The Merchant's Tale," and *Kingis Quair.* Another use
of Medieval ideas in Shakespeare's works is the analogy
to the body politic with the physical body. *Cor.* (I, i)
cites the fable of the belly and the members of the
body while *Ham.* (I, ii) refers to the body politic in
terms of the physical body.

187. Kermode, Frank. *On Shakespeare's Learning.* New Haven:
Yale U. Pr., 1965. 22 pp.

This work summarizes the scholarship which deals with
Shakespeare's knowledge of the classics and of Medieval
literature. Kermode finds Shakespeare's contemporaries
stressing the Medieval and native English tradition.
Some discussion is given to the presence of Thomist
ideas in Shakespeare's plays.

188. Kernodle, George. *From Art to Theatre: Form and Convention in the Renaissance.* Chicago: Chicago U. Pr.,
1944. 255 pp.

Efforts to explain the Renaissance theater as a development of Medieval religious stages have generally
failed. Kernodle explains that we must look to the
tradition of Medieval and early Renaissance art. He
examines paintings, sculpture, stained glass, tapestries,
and *Tableaux vivants* in order to see the development of
stage wings, proscenium arches, inner stages, curtains,
side doors, upper galleries, heavens and canopies.
For those who are working with the liturgical tradition
and Shakespeare this important study should be read
carefully.

189. Kesler, Charlotte Ruth. "The Importance of the Comic
      Tradition of English Drama in the Interpretation of
      Marlowe's *Doctor Faustus*." *DAI*, 15(1955), 1387-88
      (Missouri).

      As the title indicates, the study deals mainly with
      Marlowe but has important implications for a similar
      study of Shakespeare. Kesler observes: "The Elizabe-
      than tragedy represented the flowering of the native
      tradition. Shakespeare and his contemporaries retained
      the concept of multiple unity, the habit of symbolic
      interpretation, and the comedy of evil." Kesler studies
      the mockery of evil in art and religion which later
      found literary expression in the English mystery cycles
      where evil was presented in terms of comic counterpoint.

190. Kiefer, Harry Christian. "Elizabethan Attitudes toward
      Music in Shakespeare's Plays." *DAI*, 22(1961), 177-78
      (Columbia).

      "Many Elizabethan attitudes toward music were rhetor-
      ical commonplaces; some were acquired from classical,
      patristic, and Medieval sources, especially Boethius'
      De Institutione Musica." Many Shakespearean plays are
      referred to while determining attitudes toward music.

191. Kinghorn, A. M. *Medieval Drama*. London: Evans
      Brothers Ltd., 1968. 152 pp.

      Chapter One considers that Shakespare depended upon
      old, established ideas and conventions of Medieval
      drama. The book cites examples from *MND*, *Ham.*, and
      TN in which Shakespeare refers to various aspects of
      Medieval drama. An example is Shakespeare's acquaint-
      ance with the character of Herod. In contrast to Med-
      ieval drama, Shakespeare's plays ask questions and give
      no answers, whereas Medieval drama raised the questions
      and attempted to give answers. Other contrasts dis-
      cussed include character development, realism, and
      stylistic qualities.

192. Kirkpatrick, R. "On the Treatment of Tragic Themes
      in Dante and Shakespeare." *MLR*, 77(1977), 575-84.

      There is a distinct "theatricality" in Shakespeare's
      writing which is lacking in Dante's. The author attrib-
      utes this sense of the dramatic to our reaction to the
      physical pressure on the stage. Passages cited to
      support these assertions come from *Oth.* and *The Divine
      Comedy*.

193. Kittredge, G. L. "Notes on Elizabethan Plays." *JEGP*, 2(1898), 7-13.

Kittredge suggests that Chaucer's *Troilus and Criseyde* was the source for many Elizabethan plays.

194. Klein, David. *Milestones to Shakespeare: A Study of the Dramatic Forms and Pageantry that were the Prelude to Shakespeare*. New York: Twayne, 1970. 126 pp.

Klein has a chronological discussion of early English drama. Early English plays influenced Renaissance drama in terms of realism, the juxtaposition of violence and ridicule, and the disregard of the unities of time, place, and action.

195. Knights, L. C. *Poetry, Politics, and the English Tradition*. London: Chatto and Windus, 1954. 32 pp.

The social conditions of sixteenth-century England had much in common with the political and social thought of the Middle Ages. The human and moral basis of politics and the recognition of an authority higher than the political is a Medieval contribution to Shakespeare. Knights refers to *Piers Plowman*, vernacular sermons, and social moralities.

196. ————. "In Historical Scholarship." *SR*, 68(1955), 233-40.

Knights cautions against reductive criticism which seems so prevalent today. Shakespeare's treatment of Medieval conventions is important but his transformation and assimilation of that tradition are more so.

197. ————. *Shakespeare's Politics: With Some Reflections on the Nature of Tradition*. London: The British Academy, 1957. 18 pp.

In surveying Medieval political theory by going to the works of Dante, Aquinas, Boethius, and John of Salisbury, Knights determines that "Medieval political theory is ethical through and through." He discusses *Mac.*, *Cor.*, *Lr.*, *Tro.*, and *Jc* and finds certain characteristics of Shakespeare's political concepts are Medieval in nature. For example, the King reigns for the good of the state rather than his personal pleasure. Also love and justice are combined for the good of the body politic.

198. ————. *Further Explorations*. Stanford: Stanford U. Pr., 1965. 204 pp.

Chapters One and Three are of particular interest and
stress power, authority, honor, order, and freedom as
seen in Shakespeare's plays. Knights believes that
Shakespeare subordinates politics and emphasizes ethics
and religion, an influence of the Medieval tradition.
Cor. is studied in detail from the point of view of
Medieval political theory.

199. Kolin, Philip C. "The Elizabethan Stage Doctor as a
      Dramatic Convention." *DAI*, 34(1973), 3406-A
      (Northwestern).

Of interest is Kolin's survey of the ancestors of the
physician in the folk play, cycle and morality plays.
The doctor convention is discussed in *Wiv.*, *Cym.*, and
Mac.

200. ————. "A Report on the 1977 MLA Special Session in
      Renaissance Drama." *RORD*, 21(1978), 1-9.

Kolin reports on a seminar on Renaissance drama which
concerned the legacy of the morality play in Shakespeare's
age. Several types of morality plays existed, but the
tendency has been to view moralities as a monolithic
body. Such a view with its moralized thesis tends on
being too reductive.

201. Koskenniemi, Inna. "On the Use of 'Figurative Negation'
      in English Renaissance Drama." *NM*, 67(1966), 385-401.

The essay examines the use of verbal negation through
nouns and words indicating smallness such as "it is
not worth a groat." The use of verbal negation is
common in Medieval literature and still survives in many
Elizabethan plays. Shakespeare is referred to in
passing.

202. Kozilkowski, Stanley J. "Homo Fortunatus: A Study of
      the Humanized Image of Fortune in Tudor Dramatic
      Literature." *DAI*, 32(1972), 2059-A (Mass.).

This study traces the influence of the portrayal of
Fortune from the Psychomachia in secular moralities to
Elizabethan plays. The author sees a court of Fortune
tradition which attempts to express man's struggle
by the interplay of Fortune's attributes of folly and
vice. *MV*, *Oth.*, and *Ant.* are commented upon.

203. Krempel, Daniel Spartakus. "The Theatre in Relation to
      Art and to the Social Order from the Middle Ages to the
      Present." *DAI*, 14(1954), 421 (U. of Illinois).

The chapter on the Medieval theater and art discusses
symbols which depict the story of man's salvation through
the church. Renaissance art reflects upon man's freedom
and expresses a far more materialistic world than does
art in Medieval times. The Renaissance theater, however,
was "basically Medieval which is seen in the use of
Medieval dramatic form."

204. Kristeller, Paul Oskar. *Renaissance Philosophy and the
Medieval Tradition.* Latrobe, Pa.: The Archabbey Pr.,
1965. 120 pp.

The Middle Ages and the Renaissance have many points
in common. The Renaissance humanists were the successors
of the Medieval grammarians. The humanists have a greater
knowledge of classical lore than the Medievalists. The
humanists inherited Medieval scholasticism and Thomism
as well as an unbroken tradition of political theory,
medicine, and astrology. The book contains scattered
references to Shakespeare.

205. Lacey, Stephen Wallace. "Structures for Awareness in
Dante and Shakespeare." *DAI,* 33(1934), 4421-A
(SUNY, Buffalo).

Dante's works "mirror the process and intention of
psychoantlytic therapy, but Shakespeare's works do
not. The author focuses primarily upon the *Sonnets* and
Tit. in coming to his conclusion.

206. Lamson, Roy. Jr. "English Broadside Ballad Tunes, 1550-
1770." Diss.,

207. Lanier, Sidney. *Shakespeare and His Forerunners.*
New York: Doubleday, Page and Co., 1902. 324 pp.

Chapter Two compares the supernatural element in *Ham.*
with the supernatural ideas in the Medieval poem "Address
of the Soul to the Dead Body." The supernatural in *Ham.*
is treated skeptically but there is the firmest persua-
sion of reality about the ghost and supernatural ideas
in the Medieval poem. Chapter Three compares the savagery of nature in *Beowulf* with the peaceful aspects
of nature in *MND.* Chapter Four compares birds in
Middle English literature with Shakespeare's "The
Phoenix and the Turtle." Of particular interest is
Lanier's discussion of Mandeville's, Dunbar's and
Chaucer's poems in relation to Shakespeare. Another
chapter comments upon the role of women in the Middle
Ages and in the Renaissance. This book is one of the
first full-length studies relating Shakespeare to his past.

208. Laslett, Peter. *Family Life and Illicit Love in Earlier Generations*. Cambridge: Cambridge U. Pr., 1977. 270 pp.

Of concern is the discussion on marriage and love in Laslett's chapter "The Age at Sexual Maturity in Europe since the Middle Ages." He has a brief discussion of love and marriage in Shakespeare's works.

209. Levenson, Geraldine Bonnie. "'That Reverend Vice': A Study of the Comic-Demonic Figure in English Drama and Fiction." *DAI*, 38(1977), 283-84-A (Brit. Col.).

The recurrent association of the devil and clown both in myth and art is studied in terms of "diabolical humor." The study begins with an examination of the Vice in the moralities and interludes and shows parallels with morally ambiguous figures such as Falstaff.

210. Levin, Richard. *The Multiple Plot in English Renaissance Drama*. Chicago: U. of Chicago Pr., 1971. 277 pp.

The emphasis in this work is analytical rather than historical, but Levin does discuss the origin of the multiple plot by relating the technique to Medieval drama. He finds the clown subplot developing from the morality play and sees a similar handling of the clown's role in *1* and *2H4* and *H5*. Levin comments throughout his work on the possible influence of the morality play, but he is rather cautious concerning Shakespeare's debts to the moralities.

211. ————. "Some Second Thoughts as Central Themes." *MLR*, 67(1972), 1-10.

Modern Elizabethan criticism is preoccupied with inclusive central themes that dictate dramatic action. Such criticism is often stagnant and reduces the plays to a type of morality drama.

212. Lewis, Clive S. *The Allegory of Love: A Study in Medieval Tradition*. Oxford: The Clarendon Pr., 1936. 378 pp.

This is an important work presenting background material on the Medieval courtly love tradition in Chaucer, Gower, and Spenser. Lewis refers briefly to Shakespeare and notes a satirical treatment of this tradition in *MND*.

213. ———. *English Literature in the Sixteenth Century,*
Excluding Drama. Oxford: The Clarendon Pr., 1954.
696 pp.

Chapters One and Two deal with the interaction of
philosophical and literary concepts between the Middle
Ages and the Renaissance. The Christian humanists re-
tained the worst of all habits of Medieval allegorical
interpretation while failing to respond to the central
meaning of a work.

214. Lewis, Ewart. "Organic Tendencies in Medieval Political
Thought." *APSR,* 32(1938), 849-76.

In this philosophical study, Lewis attacks Otto Von
Gierke's theory of the relationship between the group
and the state. Gierke asserts the primacy of the state,
while Lewis argues that the ethical and spiritual ful-
fillment of the individual is the proper Medieval view.
Although the essay ranges far from literature, it may
be helpful for those wishing to understand Shakespeare's
history plays in regard to Medieval political theory.

215. Littledale, H. "Folklore and Superstitions: Ghosts
and Fairies, Witchcraft and Devil," pp. 516-45 in
Shakespeare's England. ed. C.T. Onions. Oxford:
The Clarendon Pr., 1916.

Of interest is the explanation of Shakespeare's concepts of animals as a survival of the Medieval tradition.
The essay credits Medieval preachers for the idea of the
pelican as a type of Christ. The author also points out
Shakespeare's knowledge of the pelican in *Ham.* (IV, v)
and *Lr.* (III, iv). In *Ado.* (II, i) Shakespeare refers
to the Medieval idea of women not marrying and leading
apes to Hell.

216. Loske, Olav. "The Story and the Play." *Orbis,* 11(1956),
237-244.

Loske compares Shakespeare's technique of playwritting
to that of Medieval and classical playwrights. In many
ways, Shakespeare faced the same type of problems as did
his Medieval forebearers. Both dramatized stories which
were known to the audience. The Medieval audience knew
the ultimate outcome of the morality or miracle play
and the characters' actions were also known from the
beginning of the play. They knew that the Vice would
fare badly, and thus what was important was "how the

characters would meet their fates." *Lr.* and *Ham.* are
analyzed in regard to the dramatic restrictions noted
above.

217. Lord, John Bigelow. "Certain Dramatic Devices in the
Comedies of Shakespeare and in Some of the Works of
his Contemporaries and Predecessors." *DAI*, 12(1951),
66 (U. of Illinois).

The author discusses dramatic principles, conventions,
and devices in miracle and morality plays and shows re-
semblances and contrasts with similar topics in Shakespeare's plays. The topics include reform, the vow,
love, reward, the bribe, love tokens, betrayal, the
substitute, the hidden character, and the use of disguise. Shakespeare's plays are frequently cited.

218. Lovejoy, Arthur O. *The Great Chain of Being.* Cambridge:
Harvard U. Pr., 1936. 381 pp.

In Chapters Three and Four (67-143) Lovejoy discusses
the survival of the Medieval chain of being and also
emphasizes the concepts of plentitude and the conflict
of cosmography in the Renaissance. The study provides
background material for political ideas in Shakespeare's
history plays.

219. Lucy, Margaret. *Shakespeare and the Supernatural.*
Liverpool: Jaggard and Co., 1906. 38 pp.

The language and imagery associated with the supernatural aspects found in *Mac.*, *MND*, and *Tmp.* are similar
to the supernatural ideas found in Medieval drama. The
audience would be familiar with Shakespeare's treatment
of supernatural material, for they would recall the
native English plays.

220. Lukacs, Georg. "Theatre and Environment." *TLS*,
23 April (1964), 347.

Shakespeare's scenic art succeeded in "preserving the
popular outward forms of the Middle Ages while using
these forms as the artistic medium for the new Renaissance tragedies of conflict between individuality and
social feeling."

221. Mackenzie, Roy W. *The English Moralities from the Point
of View of Morality.* Boston: Ginn and Co. Pub.,
1914. 278 pp.

Of interest is Chapter Ten (257-270) which comments
upon the use of the homily in the moralities and the
prevalence of the homiletic and morality tradition in
Renaissance literature. The author suggests that there
is no connection between the history play of Elizabethan
times and earlier English chronicles. Tillyard, Ribner,
and others refute Mackenzie's statement.

222. MacKinnon, Effie. "Notes on the Dramatic Structure of
the York Cycle." *SP*, 28(1931), 433-39.

In dealing with the dramatic structure of the York
cycle, Mackinnon suggests a number of unconscious relationships between the English chronicle play and the
earlier craft cycles. Shakespeare could not greatly
alter the historical account of his characters, and the
York dramatist could not alter his audience's notions
of God and Lucifer. Shakespeare's presentation of the
historical events was close to the actual facts. Likewise, the composers of the York plays were limited to
the events narrated in Biblical and apocryphal sources.
Both dramatic types are didactic: the chronicle play
appeals to patriotism, while the York cycle deals with
religious themes.

223. Marder, Louis. "Romance Plays and Other Subjects." *SN*,
5(1955), 41.

Shakespeare's knowledge of classical ideas came to him
indirectly from Medieval and Renaissance sources. Marder
opposes those who find that Shakespeare avidly read
classical works.

224. Mares, Francis Hugh. "The Origin of the Figure Called
the 'Vice' in Tudor Drama." *HLQ*, 22(1958), 11-29.

Mares argues that the Vice comes into drama by way of
popular festivals rather than the morality play. The
Vice should not be associated with moral allegory but
with the clown of pre-Shakespearean drama. The essay
refers to Shakespeare infrequently.

225. Matthews, Honor. *Character and Symbol in Shakespeare's
Plays*. New York: Schockin Books, 1962. 211 pp.

The entire book is devoted to a study which relates
Shakespeare to Medieval ideas. Chapter One discusses
Medieval homiletic literature in regard to Lucifer and
his fall and then relates the three parts of *H6* and *R3*

to the homiletic tradition. In the chapter "The Parliament of Heaven," Matthews notes that the legal imagery
used by Shakespeare in regard to the debate between
Justice and Mercy is "one of the clearest examples of
the influence of Medieval patterns on his imagination."
Other comments concern lines in *Oth.* and *Rom.* as parallel-
ing the Medieval Parliament of Heaven concept. Some
discussion is given to the presence of the debate tradition in *Err.*, *MV*, *MND*, *Rom.*, *H5*, *Tro.*, and *TGV*. Chapter Four, "Justice, Mercy and False-Seeming," focuses
upon the character "false-seeming" as found in morality
plays and shows a similar usage in *Ado.*, *Ham.*, *Cor.*, *JC*,
Oth., *MV*, and *MM*. In "Medieval Thought in the Romances,"
Matthews shows Shakespeare's adaptation of Medieval
concepts of sin and redemption. The emphasis in this
chapter is upon the three-fold pattern of sin, judgment,
and redemption with references to works in the Middle
Ages.

226. McClennen, Joshua. "On the Meaning and Function of
      Allegory in the English Renaissance," pp. 1-38 in
      Contributions in Modern Philology. Number 6, 1947.

      Allegory is defined by examining works which use and
      explain the term. The author refers to dictionaries
      and scriptures.

227. McDonnell, Robert Francis. "The 'Aspiring Minds': A
      Study of Shakespearean Characters Who Aspire to
      Political Sovereignty Against the Background of Liter-
      ary and Dramatic Tradition" *DAI*, 19(1958), 1365-66
      (Minnesota).

      This study analyzes the characters who aspire to sov-
      ereignty in Senecan drama, the *De Casibus* tradition,
      Lydgate's *Fall of Princes*, and *The Mirror for Magistrates*.
      A separate chapter shows that Richard III, Bolingbrook,
      Julius Caesar, Edmund, and Macbeth are a part of the
      tradition of the aspiring hero who places himself against
      God or Fortune. The moral villainy of the hero is sym-
      bolized by something unnatural about him. Richard III
      is hunchback; Edmund is illegitimate; Macbeth has a
      dwarfish appearance after donning Duncan's robes.

228. McDowell, Dimmes A. "Courtly Love in the Early English
      Renaissance: 1485-1557." Diss., 1953 (Cornell U.).

229. McDowell, J. H. "Conventions of Medieval Art in Shake-
      spearean Staging." *JEGP*, 67(1948), 215-219.

Medieval and Elizabethan staging use similar principles, and a study of Medieval staging practices will suggest solutions to difficult problems in Shakespearean staging. Subjects discussed are successive scenes, the fore-stage, interior scenes, set pieces, and special effects. Many frescoes, tapestries, ivories, woodcuts, illuminations and details in cathedral architecture were examined before McDowell came to his conclusions. Some discussion is given to multiple-setting scenic representations which were derived from Medieval "houses."

230. ————. "Medieval Influences in Shakespearean Staging." *PM,* 26(1949), 52-53.

The Medieval stage had a series of small units called "houses" which were placed in a row at the rear of the stage. The curtained inner stage of the Elizabethan theater and the fore-stage of the Globe correspond to the Medieval "houses."

231. McKeon, R. B. "Rhetoric in the Middle Ages." *Speculum,* 17(1942), 1-32.

The essay documents the types of rhetoric, rhetorical writers, and the various distinctions by which rhetoric had been known in the Middle Ages. The school of Nizolius and Majorogius held that all philosophy and all subjects were assimilated to rhetoric. Another school of Agricola and Ramus emphasized rhetoric as a dialectic process of discovering the art of reason. There is a brief discussion of the impact that Medieval rhetoric had upon the Renaissance.

232. McRoberts, J. Paul. "Shakespeare and the Medieval Tradition: An Annotated Bibliography." *DAI,* 33 (1972), 5686-7A (Kent State).

McRoberts annotates all the known critical works in English from 1900-1970 which are concerned with the Medieval influence upon Shakespeare.

233. Meader, William Granville. *Courtship in Shakespeare.* New York: Columbia U. Pr., 1954. 266 pp.

Shakespeare drew upon the courtly love tradition of preceding centuries for his romantic plots. Meader refers to Andreas Capellanus' *The Art of Courtly Love* and notes that Shakespeare rejected those aspects of the love tradition which run counter to Christianity. The book discusses the stages of courtship in Shakespeare

such as inception, development, bethrothal, ordeal, and
union.

234.   Mehl, Dieter. "Emblematic Theatre." *Anglia*, 95(1977),
       130-38.

       Mehl calls for a moderation of emblematic and icono-
       graphic aspects of Elizabethan staging. The test for
       employing these studies should be whether or not Shake-
       speare's audience would be familiar with them.

235.   Mendelsohn, Leonard R. "The Legend of Troy in English
       Renaissance Drama." *DAI*, 27(1966), 1033A (Wisconsin).

       The dramatic problems in Shakespeare's *Tro*. share the
       numerous faults of the other Troy stories found from
       late Medieval times through the Renaissance. The study
       deals with themes, characterization, and metaphoric
       structure in the various Troy stories and plays.

236.   Mills, Laurens J. *One Soul in Bodies Twain*. Blooming-
       ton: The Principia Pr. Incorp., 1937. 378 pp.

       Mills compiles a list of classical and Medieval works
       which discuss the friendship motif. Medieval writers
       and works include Walter Map, *The Gesta Romanorum*, Guy
       of Warwick, Caxton, *Athelston*, *Amis and Amiloun*, *Eger
       and Grime*, Gower, Chaucer, Usk, and Lydgate. Aspects
       and variants of the friendship theme are seen in *Sonnets
       40, 41, 42, 133, 144* and in *MV*, *Oth.*, *Ham.*, *TGV*, and *Tim*.
       False friends disappear when fortune changes is shown
       in *Tim*.

237.   Milward, Peter. *Shakespeare's Religious Background*.
       Bloomington: Indiana U. Pr., 1973. 312 pp.

       Milward has various references to Shakespeare's debt
       to the Medieval homiletic tradition throughout his
       work. There is also a section on the Biblical influence
       upon Shakespeare.

238.   Miskimin, Alice S. *The Renaissance Chaucer*. New Haven:
       Yale U. Pr., 1975. 315 pp.

       Although the aim of this work is to show how the Eliz-
       abethans viewed Chaucer, we note a number of peripheral
       suggestions. Chaucer's material, his dramatic personae,
       his tolerance of human limitation and his allegorical
       ironies are nearer to Shakespeare than to Spenser.
       The book compares Chaucer's *Troilus and Criseyde* with

Shakespeare's *Tro.* in regard to character portrayal and the Troy legend.

239. Mohl, Ruth. *The Three Estates in Medieval and Renaissance Literature.* New York: Columbia U. Pr., 1933 425 pp.

The estates of the world is a literary form arising out of the concept of feudalism with particular references to classes, order, and degree. Mohl's study deals mainly with this genre in Medieval literature, but she makes frequent remarks to the survival of the convention in Shakespeare. *Tro.* (I, iii) emphasizes the necessity of classes in a stable society. During the Renaissance, however, the genre was in decline for literature no longer reflected the feudal world.

240. Moore, John B. *The Comic and the Realistic in English Drama.* Chicago: The U. of Chicago Pr., 1925. 231 pp.

Moore has sections on "The Realistic and Comic to John Haywood," "Comic Situations and Plots," and "Comic Belief and Tragic Belief."

241. Moorman, F. W. "The PreShakespearean Ghost." *MLR,* 1(1905-06), 89-95.

Jonson, Chapman, Tourneur, Marlowe and Shakespeare stripped the ghost of its rant and fustian and invested it with new dignity. Pre-Shakespearean ghosts were derived from classical sources. Moorman contends that the popularity of the morality play with its fondness for moral abstractions as *dramatic personae* made the conception of the historical ghost difficult.

242. Moorman, F. W. "The Pre-Shakespearean Ghosts and Shakespeare's Ghost." *MLR,* 1(1906), 192-201.

Shakespeare's ghosts have their roots in Senecan drama and not the morality play. The fondness "for moral abstractions as *dramatic personae* made the entrance of the historical ghost somewhat difficult.

243. Moulton, Richard G. *The Moral System of Shakespeare.* London: Macmillan and Co., 1903. 373 pp.

For the most part, Moulton stresses Shakespeare's classical heritage, but he makes various comments in Chapter Nine on the Medieval heritage of Elizabethan drama. Both Medieval and Renaissance drama use romance

stories and narrative sources. The audience tended to
restrict the type of drama which could be portrayed.

244. Munrow, David. *Instruments of the Middle Ages and
      Renaissance.* London: Oxford U. Pr., 1976. 95 pp.

      This book compiles and comments upon musical instru-
      ments which were used in the Medieval and Renaissance
      periods.

245. Nagler, A. M. "Sixteenth-Century Continental Stages."
      SQ, 5(1954), 359-70.

      Of interest is the discussion of the survival of the
      Medieval stage in the Renaissance. Topics include the
      use of the multiple stage and the adaptation of narrative
      material for staging.

246. Nearing, Homer, Jr. "Local Caesar Traditions in
      Britain." *Speculum,* 24(1949), 218-27.

      Nearing examines the conflicting evidence from the
      chronicles regarding the many Caesar traditions. Caesar
      supposedly built the Tower of the Isle of Man, the
      Tower of London, a stone house in Scotland, the Castle
      of Dover, Canterbury, and Rochester. William of Malm-
      esbury ascribes the hot springs of Bath as one of Caesar's
      buildings.

247. ————. "The Legend of Julius Caesar's British Con-
      quest." *PMLA,* 64(1949), 889-929.

      Nearing traces the Caesar legend from classical and
      Medieval sources. The attitude that the native English
      chroniclers have toward Caesar is diverse. Wace's *Brut*
      sees Caesar as a great man while Geoffrey of Monmuth
      praises the bold-hearted Britons. Lydgate's *Serpent*
      stresses the treachery of civil discord. Shakespeare's
      use of the legend is seen in *R2, R3,* and *Cym.*

248. Niva, Wildon N. "Significant Character Names in English
      Drama to 1603." *DAI,* 20(1959), 2296 (U. of Pennsyl-
      vania).

      The first significant names in English drama date from
      the middle of the fourteenth century, appearing in mys-
      tery and morality plays. Niva discusses crude attempts
      of name-calling such as derision and invective and
      determines that significant names are likely to be comic

or satiric. One chapter discusses Shakespeare's character names in light of the above discussion.

249. Notestein, Wallace. *A History of Witchcraft in England from 1518 to 1718*. New York: Russell and Russell, 1965. 442 pp.

Chapters One through Five trace the development of witchcraft from the Middle Ages to the Renaissance. Witchcraft was generally a minor matter in Medieval times but under Elizabeth and James, civil punishments were often imposed and interest in witchcraft grew as legislation was proposed against it.

250. Nutt, Alfred. *The Fairy Mythology of Shakespeare*. 2nd ed., 1900; rpt. New York: Haskell House Pub., 1968. 40 pp.

In tracing the background of Shakespeare's fairy lore, Nutt explores the influence of the romance, particularly that which focuses upon the Arthurian cycle. Celtic mythology explains man's relation to nature and to the universe in a symbolic manner. References to Shakespeare appear throughout the book.

251. Nuttall, Anthony D. *Two Concepts of Allegory: A Study of Shakespeare's The Tempest and the Logic of Allegorical Expression*. New York: Barnes and Noble, 1967. 175 pp.

The work examines two types of allegory in Medieval and Renaissance literature: that which was proposed by C.S. Lewis and termed non-metaphysical and that which is less rigid and termed metaphysical. The former makes a rigid division between allegory and sacrementalism, while the latter sees a community of purpose between them. Dante is studied in particular in relation to allegory. The chapter on *Tmp.* disagrees with those who interpret the play in specific allegorical terms. The play is read in relation to associations or possible types and figures and thus broadens the view of allegory and moves away from specific Medieval influences.

252. O'Donnell, Joseph Leo. "Ethical Principles of the Christian Middle Ages in Shakespeare." MA Thesis, Western Ontario, 1941. 206 pp.

This study applies the concepts of Thomist and Aristotle to a number of Shakespeare's plays.

58   *General Works*

253. Owen, Lucy DeGeer. "The Representation of Forgiveness
      in Shakespeare and Medieval Drama." *DAI*, 36(1976),
      4516-17A (Virginia).

      Concepts of repentance and forgiveness found in Med-
      ieval drama such as *The Second Shepherds' Play* and *The
      Woman Taken in Adultery* are present in Shakespeare's
      MM and *Tmp*. Owen discusses the "jolting perception
      of one's bondage to sin and the acceptance of a love
      that transcends sin."

254. Owst, G. R. *Literature and Pulpit in Medieval England.*
      London: Cambridge U. Pr., 1933. 616 pp.

      Of interest are Owst's remarks concerning the *Gesta
      Romanorum*, a collection of homiletic tales. Owst sees
      the survival of homiletic material in *Lr.*, the bond and
      three caskets in *MV*, the closing scene in *Shr.*, and
      parts of *Per.* He finds Puck and Ariel "descendants of
      merry Medieval devils who are to be found in grim hom-
      iletic devil humour." The themes in *Ham.*, *Mac.*, *Cor.*,
      and *Ant.* serve as variations on *exemplum* concepts.

255. Page, Susan Carolyn Ulichney. "The Emergence of the
      Humanist Tragic Hero: A Study in the Dramatization
      of the Psychomachia in the Morality Plays and in
      Selected Plays of Shakespeare." *DAI*, 41(1980),
      2617-18A (Purdue).

      Page discusses the evolution of the tragic hero from
      the morality plays through Renaissance drama with special
      emphasis upon *R3*, *MM*, and *Ham*. The movement is from
      Thomist theology to Christian humanism. Early plays
      studied are: *Nature*, *Four Elements*, *Mundus et Infans*,
      and *Youth*.

256. Parker, M. D. H. *The Slave of Life.* London: Chatto
      and Windus, 1955. 264 pp.

      Chapter One treats religious and philosophical concepts
      which reflect a Medieval state of mind. Ulysses' speech
      in *Tro.* (I, iii) is a survival of the Medieval concept
      of hierarchies. Scattered references are found in the
      book in regard to Shakespeare's Medieval religious ideas.
      Parker attributes a number of these ideas to St. Thomas
      and St. Augustine.

257. Parks, H. B. "Nature's Diverse Laws: The Double Vision
      of the Elizabethans." *SR*, 63(1950), 402-418.

This essay shows the conflict which develops when Renaissance writers attempted to reconcile the Medieval world system with naturalistic attitudes arising in the Renaissance. Parks analyzes moral and social order in Spenser and Shakespeare and discovers that both attempted to reconcile a traditional moral system with ethical ideas which are frequently opposite of the Medieval system. Topics discussed are sexuality, the concept of evil, and the change of the villain in drama.

258. Parr, Johnstone. *Tamburlaine's Malady and Other Essays on Astrology in Elizabethan Drama.* Tuscaloosa, Ala.: U. of Alabama Pr., 1953. 158 pp.

As the title suggests, Parr emphasizes astrology as found in Renaissance literature and of interest are four sections of the book--"Sources of the Renaissance Englishman's Knowledge of Astrology" (112-150), "Shakespeare's Artistic Use of Astrology" (57-69), "The 'Late Eclipses' in *King Lear*" (70-79), and "Edmund's Birth under Ursa Major" (80-84). In the first of these, Parr points out that Renaissance concepts of astrology derived from Medieval astrological treatises and pamphlets as well as classical and Arabic writings. According to Parr, Guido Bonatus' *Liber Astronomicus* "was perhaps the most thorough and elaborate treatise on astrology that the Renaissance inherited from the medieval period." Another popular medieval work was Bartholomaeus Anglicus' *De proprietatibus Rerum*.

259. Parrill, William Bruce. "The Elizabethan Background of Hell, the Devil, the Magician, and the Witch, and Their Use in Elizabethan Fiction." *DAI*, 25(1965), 5937 (Tennessee).

Elizabethan dramatists drew from classical legends, the Bible, the literature of the Middle Ages, and the material of their own times while writing about the supernatural. Parrill discusses Shakespeare's use of background material in *Mac.*

260. Patch, Howard P. *The Goddess Fortuna in Medieval Literature.* Cambridge: Harvard U. Pr., 1927. 215 pp.

References to Shakespeare occur infrequently, but the subject is important (as Patch indicates) to Shakespeare and the Renaissance. Patch has individual chapters on the philosophy of Fortune, themes in Medieval literature, motifs, and themes associated with Fortune.

261. Patchell, Mary F. *The Palmerin Romances in Elizabethan*
      Prose Fiction. New York: Columbia U. Pr., 1946.
      157 pp.

      The work defines the peculiar characteristics of the
      late Medieval and Renaissance Spanish romance of chiv-
      alry and assesses its influence upon English fiction.
      Patchell finds that it is uncertain whether Shakespeare
      was familiar with the Spanish romance. Chapter Four
      associates Shakespeare's ridicule of *fine amour* in *Tro.*
      with the similar treatment of love by Spanish writers.
      Since Shakespeare is writing in the Christian tradition,
      he cannot help showing the utter futility and defeat
      of worldly love.

262. Patterson, Frank Allen. "Shakespeare and the Medieval
      Lyric," pp. 431-52 in *Shakespeare Studies.* ed. by
      Brander Matthews. New York: Russell and Russell
      Incorp., 1962.

      The essay uncovers a number of Medieval lyric forms
      in Shakespeare's works such as the *aube* in *Rom.* Other
      types discussed are the *chanson d'aventure, pastourelle,*
      reverdie and the debate. The essay gives the Medieval
      background for the various poetic types and shows sim-
      ilar usage in a number of Shakespeare's plays and poems.

263. Phillias, James E. *The State in Shakespeare's Greek*
      and Roman Plays. New York: Columbia U. Pr., 1940.
      230 pp.

      Chapter Four, "The Significance of Analogical Argu-
      ment," shows how the Renaissance inherited the Medieval
      practice of using numerous analogies in explaining the
      state and society. The rhetorical device of the analogy
      embodied both Medieval religious and philosophical prin-
      ciples even in the Renaissance. Chapter Seven, "Social
      Corruption," presents the Medieval background in terms of
      source material for Shakespeare's *Tro.* Medieval writers
      debased the Greeks, since it was thought that the English
      were descendants of the Trojans.

264. Pollard, Alfred W. *English Miracle Plays, Moralities,*
      and Interludes. Oxford: The Clarendon Pr., 1923.
      250 pp.

      The introduction gives a rather lucid view of Medieval
      drama with Pollard drawing distinctions among the various
      types of Medieval plays. He shows the survival of native
      drama in Shakespeare's day and comments upon the Porter's

speech in *Mac.* as the most notable survival of the miracle play in Shakespeare's day.

265.   Potter, Robert. *The English Morality Play.* London:
       Routledge and Kegan Paul, 1975.   286 pp.

Potter has a discussion of Medieval plays with an
emphasis upon the structure of innocence, fall, and
redemption.   Chapter Three concerns the "morality of
state" and shows the influence of Skelton and Medwall.
The next section focuses upon the political morality.
References to Shakespeare abound, but particular discussions concern *1H4* as a political morality as well
as *Lr.* and *Ham.* as morality plays.   Chapter Eight
traces the understanding that seventeenth, eighteenth,
and nineteenth centuries had of the native English
influence upon Shakespeare.

266.   Powell, C. L. *English Domestic Relations 1485-1653.*
       New York; Columbia U. Pr., 1917.   274 pp.

Powell studies matrimony, family life, and literary
types as found in the literature, law, and history of
the period.   The writer sees Kate in *Shr.* as a comic
character who originally had roots in the morality play.
The patient wife, a figure known to many Medieval writers,
is found in Hermioine in *WT* and Catherine in *H8.*

267.   Powell, Jocelyn. "Marlowe's Spectacle." *TDR,* 8(1964),
       195-210.

Powell's essay deals exclusively with Marlowe's plays,
but the discussion on the emblematic tradition and the
spectacle of the morality tradition is extremely clear.
Those wishing a greater understanding of visual images
in Elizabethan drama will find this essay useful.

268.   Putnam, Adelaide Donalda. "Folklore and Balladry in
       Shakespeare." MA Thesis, McGill U., 1933.

269.   Ramsay, Robert Lee, ed. *Magnyfycence* by John Skelton.
       London: Oxford U. Pr., 1908.   100 pp.

Ramsay's introduction is indispensable, mainly by way
of implication, for linking Shakespeare to the morality
play.   Ramsay surveys the moralities with an emphasis
upon analyzing influences and techniques.   The section
dealing with characterization (lxxxix-cvi) studies the
concept of the hybrid character, a mixture of personified

abstraction and social type. He comments upon the development of the Vice and fool in morality plays and
classifies the types of fools as natural and artificial.
Shakespeare's fools are in the same tradition as those
in Medieval plays. King Lear's fool belongs to the
natural category, while Touchstone and Feste are
artificial.

270. Reese, M. J. *Shakespeare: His World and His Work.*
     London: Edward Arnold and Co., 1953. 589 pp.

Chapter Two, "Miracle Plays and Moralities," focuses
upon the importance of Medieval drama for Shakespeare.
Reese observes that when Shakespeare is at his best,
the morality habit of mind is hidden. At other times
the morality pattern is quite evident. The Duke's role
of Providence stands out as a barren convention beside
the vitality of Isabella and Angelo. *1H4* is an orthodox
morality with Falstaff representing Riot and Iniquity.
Other observations concern the dialogue of Richard III
and Iago as being close to the Vice's jocularity.

271. Reynolds, George F. "Some Principles of Elizabethan
     Staging." *MP*, 3(1905), 69-97.

Renaissance stage practices borrowed from Medieval
conventions a number of habits which seem strange to
the modern theatergoer. Some of these practices are
incongruous properties on the stage, shifting of the
scene before the actors clear the stage, and the stage
representing two widely separated places at the same
time. Reynolds refers to Shakespeare infrequently.

272. Reynolds, J. A. "Variations on a Theme in the Western
     Tradition," pp. 83-92 in *Sweet Smoke of Rhetoric,*
     ed. by N.G. Lawrence. Coral Gables: U. of Miami
     Pr., 1964.

Reynolds argues against those who view the Renaissance
as distinct from the Middle Ages. He calls Shakespeare
a late Medievalist and lists a number of Medieval ideas
in Shakespeare's works. Some of the ideas include the
existence of the soul after death, the possibility of
Divine or Satanic intervention into man's affairs, the
concept of order and decorum in the state, and the
Medieval hierarchical scheme.

273. Ribner, Irving. *William Shakespeare.* Toronto:
     Blaisdale Pub. Co., 1969. 280 pp.

Ribner gives thumbnail sketches of the Medieval influence upon Shakespeare on the following topics: (1)
"Medieval Universe," (2) "Concepts of Physical Nature,"
(3) "Man and Microcosm," (4) "The Great Chain of Being,"
(5) "Church and State," (6) "Morality and Law," and (7)
"Political Theory."

274. Rice, James G. "Shakespeare's Curse: Relation to
Elizabethan Curse Tradition and to Drama." Diss.
U. of North Carolina, 1949.

275. Richmond, Velma E. Bourgeoise. "The Development of the
Rhetorical Death Lament from the Late Middle Ages to
Marlowe." *DAI*, 20(1966), 2807 (U. of North Carolina).

The rhetorical death lament is a genre which had its
beginnings with Geoffrey de Vinsauf's lament for Richard
I, and it can also be seen in Medieval romances. Several
chapters trace the death lament in Medieval narratives
and Elizabethan drama. The author notes that there is
a "marked continuity of ideas and expression" with the
death lament, and Shakespeare's early use of the lament
shows his dependence upon Medieval concepts and motifs.

276. Ristine, F. H. *English Tragicomedy, Its Origin and
History*. New York: The Columbia U. Pr., 1910. 247 pp.

The section on the Medieval heritage (11-18) notes
that both Renaissance and Medieval tragi-comedy accent
the didactic nature of the play, mingle comedy with
tragedy, and point to serious action crowned with a
happy ending.

277. Robinson, David M. "The Wheel of Fortune." *CP*, 41
(1946), 207-16.

The essay establishes that the Wheel of Fortune was
originally found in Greek literature and passed to
Latin literature and was finally seen in English
Medieval literature.

278. Root, R. K. *Classical Mythology in Shakespeare*. 2nd
ed. 1903; rpt. New York: Gordian Pr. Incorp., 1965.
134 pp.

In the introduction Root defines the terms Medieval
and Renaissance and relates aspects of these definitions
to Shakespeare. "Medievalism has its gaze on the spiritual, while that of the Renaissance on the sensuous."

Root develops the thesis that Shakespeare was essentially Medieval even though he drew largely upon classical sources for structural aspects of his plays. As
Shakespeare's dramatic art grew, he came to rely more
upon Medieval spiritual concepts and less upon classical
ideas. In a separate section, Root is careful to show
Shakespeare's debt to those Medieval writers who translated classical works. For example, he probably was
influenced by Caxton's *Recuyell* for the character of
Aneas. Root also points out Shakespeare's dependence
upon Chaucer for the stories of Dido and Pyramus and
Thisbe.

279.   Rosier, James Louis. "The Chain of Sin and Privation
       in Elizabethan Literature." *DAI*, 18(1958), 583
       (Stanford).

       Chapter One defines and traces the concept of "the
       chain of sin" to ideas espoused by Augustine and
       Aquinas which are closely associated with evil as
       found within Medieval theology. Rosier discusses
       Shakespeare's use of the "chain of sin" motif in
       R3, *Tit.*, and *Mac.*

280.   Rossiter, A. P. ed. *Woodstock, A Moral History*.
       London: Chatto and Windus, 1946. 255 pp.

       Rossiter traces Shakespeare's history plays to the
       Tudor political plays and finally to the Medieval
       morality play. The purpose of the history play is
       primarily didactic or propgandistic and is concerned
       with politics on various levels. It inquires into
       the nature of man and the nature of the governor.
       The morality habit of mind persisted from the chron-
       iclers to the history playwrights. The Elizabethan
       dramatist operated in the framework of the morality
       tradition.

281.   ————. *English Drama from Early Times to the Eliz-
       abethans*. London: The Mayflower Pr., 1950. 169 pp.

       This book contains chapters on the morality play,
       interludes, mystery plays, gothic drama, staging, pre-
       Shakespearean drama, and Elizabethan drama. The author
       studies the influence of Medieval drama on Shakespeare
       and compares and contrasts the following ideas: staging,
       realism, character portrayal, vocabulary, allegory,
       morality play, ancient fertility rituals, morality play
       devices which include dialogue and staging, and the

contention of spring and winter, and the Vice. In Rossiter's words "the Morality habit of mind is a Medieval heritage of the first importance to the understanding of Elizabethan drama."

282. Roston, Murray. "Shakespeare and the Biblical Drama." *IEY*, 9(1964), 36-43.

Shakespeare inherited the Medieval insistence on an orderly and retributive world from Tudor Biblical drama rather than the morality play. This moral awareness (originally seen in the moralities) served to offset the stoic sense of callous and arbitrary fate which the Senecan drama gave to the Elizabethan stage.

283. Russell, H. K. "Elizabethan Dramatic Poetry in the Light of Natural Philosophy." *PQ*, 12(1933), 187-95.

Medieval and Renaissance doctrines of natural and moral philosophy had a profound effect upon Elizabethan playwrights. Russell quotes from *Secreta Secretorum*, attributed to Aristotle, to establish the relationship between the passions and parts of the body. The essay characterizes Falstaff, Brutus, and King John in terms of natural philosophy and concludes that the Elizabethan language of passion is less figurative and more factual than modern readers generally realize. Statements regarding the burning or freezing of the body are to be taken as vivid statements of fact rather than poetical imagination.

284. ————. "Tudor and Stuart Dramatizations of the Doctrines of Natural and Moral Philosophy." *SP*, 31 (1933), 1-27.

This study traces the seduction and repentance of man in Medieval and Renaissance drama and determines that the plot structure is similar in both dramas. The humanist educators adapted Medieval religious drama to teach their students the surrender of loyalty to reason, while the Medieval playwrights dealt with the salvation of man's soul. Some twenty Medieval and Renaissance plays are referred to in light of the above concepts.

285. Salter, F. M. *Medieval Drama in Chester*. Toronto: U. of Toronto Pr., 1955. 138 pp.

The last chapter gives a general discussion of the contribution made by the *Chester Plays* to Renaissance drama.

Salter deals in part with the value of contrast in Medieval drama and its continuation in Renaissance drama. There is some discussion of the surviving aspects of the Medieval stage as found in the Globe. Other topics briefly mentioned are stock characters and the tradition of music and song.

286.   Sarton, George. *The Appreciation of Ancient and Medieval Learning During the Renaissance (1450-1600)*. Philadelphia: U. of Pennsylvania Pr., 1957. 233 pp.

This work surveys many areas which are not literary, but it does deal with surviving Medieval principles in the Renaissance. Topics include medicine, natural history, mathematics and astronomy. The first chapter sums up the Medieval contribution to the Renaissance and refers to Elizabethan writers who quote Medieval texts.

287.   Schell, Edgar T.   "The Pilgrimage of Life: The Imitation of an Action in Renaissance Drama." *DAI*, 27(1966), 1039-40-A (Berkeley).

The second part of this dissertation argues that Shakespeare's second historical tetraology "imitates by means of analogous characters, and themes the patterns of action found in the morality drama and the allegorical pilgrimage poems." *Mac.* and *Lr.* are "the tragic form of the pilgrimage of life developed in the mid-century moralities and hybrids."

288.   Schelling, Felix E.   *The Elizabethan Chronicle Play*. 2nd ed. 1902, rpt. New York: Haskell House, 1964. 310 pp.

The history play's concern is for nationalistic feeling and is closely tied to the St. George play, folklore, balladry and the Robin Hood Plays. Only tenuous connections exist between the Elizabethan history play and Medieval mysteries and moralities.

289.   Schiffhorst, Gerald, ed.   *The Triumph of Patience: Medieval and Renaissance Studies*. Orlando: U. Pr. of Florida, 1978. 146 pp.

This book has a collection of essays on patience as it relates to Medieval and Renaissance thought. A number of works are referenced from 1480-1680 which includes an inventory of devotional literature, emblem

books, and moral treatises. Shakespeare's depiction
of patience is briefly presented on pages fourteen
and fifteen.

290. Schirmer, Walter Franz. "The Importance of the
Fifteenth Century for the Study of the English
Renaissance with Special Reference to Lydgate," pp.
104-110 in *English Studies Today*, ed. by G. I.
Duthie. London: Oxford U. Pr., 1951.

Lydgate is far more than a "drivelling monk," for he
is a key link between Chaucer and Shakespeare. The
author believes that Shakespeare's history plays are
based upon the rise and fall concept of Fortune's
Wheel (inherited from Lydgate) and the extension of
this Medieval idea is a valuable link in the chain
which binds Medieval and Renaissance thought.

291. Schofield, William Henry. *Chivalry in English Literature;*
2nd ed. 1912; rpt. New York: Kennikat Pr., 1964.
263 pp.

Shakespeare was influenced by the Medieval concepts
of chivalry and knightly conduct which can be seen in
Jn, R2, R3, 1H4, H5, and *1,2,3,H6.* Schofield briefly
comments on "feudal anachronisms" in the above plays.
Other sections of this work point out Shakespeare's
debt to Chaucer for source material of *Tro.* and *Luc.*
There is some discussion concerning Shakespeare's debt
to Gower for portions of *Per.*

292. Scott-Giles, C. W. *Shakespeare's Heraldry.* New York:
E.P. Dutton and Co. Incorp., 1950. 202 pp.

The thrust of the book points out that the armorial
devices on shields, garments, and flags "play a con-
spicuous and colourful part in the Mediaeval scene."
Medieval emblems which Shakespeare's historical characters wear include the *fleur-de-lys,* cinque foil,
excallop shell, leather bottle, wheatsheaf, boar's head,
Cornish chough, and the martlet. The first chapter
discusses heraldry in Medieval and Tudor times and
relates various aspects of heraldry to Shakespeare.
The author has a discussion on *Jn., R2, 1* and *2H4, H5,*
1H6, R3, and *H8.* The heraldry in *Jn.* is the simplest,
consisting of bold signs on weapons of war, while in
R2 these devices are more numerous and varied appearing
on flags, seals, helms, servants, and costumes. This
important work is one of the few studies on heraldry.

293. Sen, R. K. "Shakespeare and Scholasticism with Partic-
      ular Reference to Romantic Love." *BDECU*, 5(1967),
      113-35.

      Medieval scholasticism influenced the romantic atti-
      tude of love in three different directions: neo-Plato-
      nism with the cult of Sophia, the growing cult of the
      Virgin, and the concepts of Medieval chivalry.

294. Siegel, Paul N. *Shakespearean Tragedy and the
      Elizabethan Compromise.* New York: New York U. Pr.,
      1957. 243 pp.

      Chapter Three defines Christian Humanism as being
      essentially Medieval particularly in its concern for
      hierarchy. At the apex of the hierarchy is the new
      monarch who has altered the aristocratic ideal, yet
      he stresses the good of the social scheme.

295. ————. "Shakespeare and the Neo-Chivalric Cult of
      Honor." *CR*, 8(1964), 39-70.

      The feudal chivalric tradition of honor conflicts
      with the Christian humanists idea of honor in *1H4*, *Tro.*,
      AWW, *Cor.*, and *Tim.*

296. ————. ed. *His Infinite Variety.* New York: J.B.
      Lippincott Co., 1964. 412 pp.

      This book contains a variety of essays on Shakespearean
      drama depicting many points of view. Included is an
      article by E.M.W. Tillyard explaining Shakespeare's
      history plays in relation to the conventions derived
      from the morality tradition. S.L. Bethell analyzes
      Shakespeare's poetic drama by relating it to Medieval
      theological patterns. G. Wilson Knight discusses
      mythic aspects in Shakespearean drama and signifies the
      importance of Medieval Christian terminology in
      Shakespeare's plays.

297. Sinsheimer, Hermann. *Shylock: The History of a
      Character of the Myth of the Jew.* London: Victor
      Gollancz Lt., 1947. 147 pp.

      Shakespeare's characterization of Shylock is wholly
      in the Medieval tradition associated with Jews. The
      anti-Christian element and the usury theme clearly
      stem from the body of Medieval literature dealing with
      Jews. The author does not argue that Shakespeare used
      one particular work for his portrayal of Shylock but

deals generally with the tradition. Scattered throughout the work are various references to Shakespeare and
Medieval conventions, and the last chapter (114-40)
focuses upon Shylock's Medieval elements.

298. Slover, George W. "The Elizabethan Playhouse and the
     Tradition of Liturgical Stage Structure." *DAI*,
     30(1969), 435A (Indiana).

     The Elizabethan stage appears in the age of trans-
     ition from Medieval to modern and is intelligble only
     in the context of its Medieval heritage. Slover fur-
     ther states that the Elizabethans are the last to
     conceive their stage on an analogy to the sanctuary;
     the last, therefore, to understand dramatic action as
     analogous to liturgical action.

299. Smith, Hallett. "Bare Ruined Choirs: Shakespearean
     Variations on the Theme of Old Age." *HLQ*, 39(1976),
     233-49.

     Smith discusses the concepts of old age in a number
     of Shakespeare's plays--*MM*, *AYL*, *Rom.*, and *Lr.* Some
     of the commentary focuses upon the *momento mori* theme
     of Medieval Christianity.

300. Smith, Warren D. "The Elizabethan Rejection of Judical
     Astrology." *SQ*, 9(1958), 159-76.

     The church (from the beginning of Augustine) forbade
     the use of astrology because it conflicted with free
     will. Furthermore, Medieval and early Renaissance
     political theory disapproved of astrological readings.
     Shakespeare used astrology to heighten his dramatic
     purposes.

301. Smyth, M. M. "Dante and Shakespeare." *NC*, 64(1908),
     603-21.

     Dante's and Shakespeare's moral philosophy is com-
     pared by examining the concepts of sin as evidenced
     in their works. Smyth notes that both writers are
     extremely careful to show the effects and ravages of
     sin. Other comparisons include political views, re-
     ligious convictions, and character analysis.

302. Snyder, Susan. "The Left Hand of God: Despair in
     Medieval and Renaissance Tradition," pp. 18-59 in
     Studies in Renaissance, Vol. 12. New York: The Ren-
     aissance Society of America, 1965.

Snyder carefully details the despair theme in Medieval works and shows its application to Spenser's the Redcrosse knight. The study is applicable to Shakespeare by association in that valuable background detail is provided.

303.   Soellner, Rolf H. "Anima and Affectus: Theories of the Emotions in Sixteenth Century Grammar Schools and Their Relations to the Works of Shakespeare." *DAI*, 14(1954), 351 (U. of Illinois).

Of interest is the first chapter which shows the Renaissance inheritance of Medieval psychological ideas. Soellner then reconstructs the theories of emotions which were taught in Elizabethan schools.

304.   Southern, Richard. *The Staging of Plays before Shakespeare*. London: Faber, 1973. 603 pp.

Southern's concern is limited to those plays written between 1460 and 1589. The work helps to visualize theatrical setting and staging technique. Some lengthy discussion is given to the Tudor hall screen and dramatic action in an open structure, the great hall.

305.   Spargo, John Webster. *Juridical Folklore in England Illustrated by the Ducking-Stool*. Durham: Duke U. Pr., 1944. 163 pp.

Spargo illustrates the various ways shrewish and wayward women were punished in the Medieval and Renaissance periods. The most common punishment was the tying of a woman to a chair and dipping her in water until she repented.

306.   Spencer, Theodore. *Death and Elizabethan Tragedy*. Cambridge: Harvard U. Pr., 1936. 288 pp.

In Chapter One, "The Medieval Background," Spencer discusses some of the works of the Middle Ages which deal with the theme of death and indicates that the Elizabethan period inherited Dance of Death concepts as well as the *de contemptu mundi* ideas of Pope Innocent III. Chapter Three discusses the language of death in Elizabethan drama in general and in *Ham.* and *Rom.* in particular. Spencer writes "the late medieval emphasis on the skeleton had created a personified image, which almost automatically attracted to itself the wealth of adjective and metaphor which the sixteenth century exuberantly discovered." Spencer refers to death as a sergeant, death's darts, death as an arrester, and death as a jailer.

307. ───. *Shakespeare and the Nature of Man.* New York: The Macmillan Co., 1942. 225 pp.

The last chapter "The Dramatic Convention" describes Shakespeare's dramatic techniques in relation to Medieval drama. The cycle plays emphasized the narrative method which influenced the chronicle play. In addition, the narratives of great men brought low through the caprice of Fortune is a familiar pattern in Shakespeare's plays. Spencer comments on Shakespeare's adaptation of allegory and the influence of the morality play in *1* and *2H4*, *H5*, *H6*, and *R3*. The author concludes that Shakespeare blended the Biblical and the morality play into serious chronicle plays.

308. ───. "The Elizabethan Malcontent," pp. 523-35 in *Adams Memorial Studies.* ed. by James G. McManaway. Washington: The Folger Shakespeare Library Pr., 1948.

The first part of this essay studies the malcontent from a historical point of view by referring to Medieval melancholy and the *de contemptu mundi* influence of Innocent III. Stoicism, Medieval Christianity, and Renaissance humanism also contributed ideas which are necessary for a background study of the malcontent.

309. Spivak, Charlotte. *The Comedy of Evil on Shakespeare's Stage.* Rutherford, N. J.: Fairleigh Dickinson U. Pr., 1978. 184 pp.

Chapter Six (138-173) studies Shakespeare's use of the homiletic stage tradition--the Dance of Death, the *memento mori,* and other "gargoyle elements" of Medieval drama. These concepts are seen in the tragedies, comedies, history plays, and romances. In addition, comic representations of evil are traced through the art and literature of the Medieval period.

310. Springer, Marlene, ed. *What Manner of Woman: Essays on English and American Life and Literature.* New York: New York U. Pr., 1977. 357 pp.

Ann S. Haskell depicts the portrayal of women by Chaucer in his age (1-14), while Catherine Dunn reflects upon the changing image of woman in Renaissance society (15-38).

311.   Staines, David. "To Out-Herod Herod: The Development
       of a Dramatic Character." *CompD*, 10(1976), 29-53.

       Staines discusses the development of the Herod figure
       in apocryphal and Biblical works as well as liturgical
       drama. The diversity of the presentations of Herod in
       the mystery cycles "gives him a host of contrasting
       descendants in the Elizabethan theater." Shakespeare's
       Ham. is referred to briefly.

312.   Stevenson, David L. *The Love-Game Comedy.* New York:
       Columbia U. Pr., 1946. 259 pp.

       Many sections of this book are devoted to the Renais-
       sance inheritance of Medieval views of love and sex.
       The first chapter, "Shakespeare's Love-Game Comedies,"
       stresses Shakespeare's indebtedness to the literature
       of the Middle Ages for "three mutually incompatible
       attitudes" of love. The first of these is the courtly
       love concept which emphasized the ritual of desire;
       the second idea is the Pauline tradition which stressed
       that all desire was evil as were women who provoked it;
       the third attitude toward love was the acceptance of
       sensual experience. Stevenson believes that Shakespeare
       was highly influenced by Lyly who had attempted to
       reconcile these attitudes toward love. Chapters Three
       through Six deal with the amorous controversy in Med-
       ieval literature with particular emphasis upon Chaucer's
       attempt to resolve the three incompatible attitudes
       toward love noted above. Chapter Ten discusses the
       courtly love tradition in Shakespeare's *Sonnets*. The
       author points out that Shakespeare inherited the lan-
       guage of love with its symbols of the eye and heart,
       but the "courtly and Petrarchan symbols of love were
       transmuted." Chapters Eleven and Twelve analyze the
       comedy of courtship in *LLL*, *AYL*, *Ado.*, and *Tro.* Shake-
       speare's plays attempted "to formulate a consistent
       philosophy of love from Medieval inconsistencies."

313.   Stone, Charles Venable. "Dramas of Christian Time:
       Temporal Assumptions and Dramatic Form in the Medieval
       Mystery Cycle, the Morality Play, and Shakespeare's
       Second Tetralogy." *DAI*, 33(1973), 3603-A (Minnesota).

       Stone discusses Medieval dramatic tradition from the
       viewpoint of time both historically and subjectively.
       Subjective time is viewed as a talent which man may
       utilize or waste. These Medieval concepts of time are
       applied to *R2*, *1H4*, *2H4*, and *H5*.

314. Stroup, Thomas B. *Microcosmos: The Shape of the Elizabethan Play*. Lexington: The U. of Kentucky Pr., 1965. 235 pp.

   Stroup's work demonstrates a number of Medieval ideas in Shakespeare's plays. In Chapter One, "The World as a Stage," he comments upon the Renaissance theater as a symbol of the world or a symbolic representation of the cosmos, an inheritance of Medieval drama. He also demonstrates at length that the action within Shakespeare's plays represents universal and cosmological conflict, an aspect of staging which, he believes, is another influence of Medieval drama. In "The Pageant of the World," Stroup contends that the pageantry, processions, and ceremonies of Medieval drama were continued in Renaissance drama, particularly Shakespeare's plays. In "The Places of Action," the writer notes that Shakespeare chose the various scenes of action within his plays with particular attention to "their appropriateness of power to suggest action of worldwide and cosmic import." In so doing, the author emphasizes that the scenes have a private, public, and spiritual context. Other sections of his book point out Shakespeare's adaptation of the *psychomachia*.

315. Swain, Barbara. *Fools and Folly during the Middle Ages and the Renaissance*. New York: Columbia U. Pr., 1932. 234 pp.

   Swain surveys the function and type of fools found in Medieval drama and discusses the qualities usually associated with the fool. There is an unbroken tradition of fools and folly from the Middle Ages through the Renaissance.

316. Symonds, John Addington. *Shakespeare's Predecessors in the English Drama*. New York: Cooper Square Pub., 1967. 536 pp.

   This book has individual chapters on the morality play, miracle play, chronicle drama, English comedy, and tragedy. The study touches on Shakespeare when the author comments that the Vice of Medieval drama can be seen in *Jn*. Symonds calls the morality play a transition between miracle plays and the drama which emphasized characters.

317. Taylor, George C. "The Relation of the English Corpus Christi Play to the Middle English Religious Lyric." *MP*, 5(1907), 1-37.

This essay reviews the general body of lyric poetry
in the Middle Ages and shows its influence upon Medieval drama. In discussing the *ubi sunt* lyric, however,
Taylor indicates that its influence can be detected in
the Renaissance, particularly in the works of Skelton
and Shakespeare.

318.   _____. "Some Patristic Conventions Common to Shake-
       speare and Milton." *SP*, 28(1931), 652-55.

Taylor inquires if any Medieval and Renaissance
theologian had definitely influenced Shakespeare and
disagrees with those critics who use patristic conventions in interpreting Shakespeare. Taylor is
convinced that Shakespeare's knowledge of patristic
literature and his allusions to Biblical ideas were
not beyond the average playgoer of his day.

319.   _____. "The Medieval Element in Shakespeare." *SAB*,
       12(1937), 208-16.

A number of studies are reviewed which stress the
Medieval influence upon Shakespeare. Taylor refers
to Farnham, Root, Bradley, and Cushman and finds their
studies extremely favorable.

320.   Taylor, William Edwards. "The Villainness in Elizabe-
       than Drama." *DAI*, 17(1957), 1756 (Vanderbilt).

Taylor attributes the Renaissance concept of feminine
villainy to three sources: Medieval ecclesiastical
literature, Senecan drama, and Italian literature.

321.   Thompson, Ann. *Shakespeare's Chaucer: A Study in
       Literary Origins*. New York: Barnes and Noble, 1978.
       239 pp.

This important work is the only full length study on
Shakespeare's debt to Chaucer. A persuasive case is
made that Shakespeare's *Tro.* is greatly indebted to
Chaucer's long poem. Shakespeare's *TNK* owes much to
Chaucer's "The Knight's Tale." Thompson shows the
subtle use that Shakespeare made of Chaucer's themes,
characters, and structure. The appendix lists Shakespeare's reference to Chaucer with virtually every
Shakespearean play being influenced by Chaucer.

322.   Thompson, Karl F. *Modesty and Cunning, Shakespeare's
       Use of Literary Tradition*. Ann Arbor: U. of Michigan
       Pr., 1971. 176 pp.

Thompson assumes that Shakespeare's audience would be
familiar with Medieval literary conventions. For the
most part he comments upon the courtly romance tradition,
various views of tragedy, revenge tragedy, didactic
nature of morality plays, and the doctrine of Medieval
correspondences.

323. Thorndike, Lynn. "The Survival of Medieval Intellectual
Interests into Early Modern Times." *Speculum*, 2
(1927), 146-59.

Although this study does not specifically refer to
Shakespeare, the essay is a useful compendium on the
surviving Medieval influence upon the Renaissance.
Thorndike discusses knighthood, the guild system,
chemistry, math, medicine, politics, education, physics,
scholasticism, rhetoric, alchemy, and astrology. The
following Medieval writers are discussed: Martianus
Capella, Duns Scotus, Costa ben Luca, Nicholas Oresme,
Albertus Magnus, Guy de Chauliac, and Richard Suiseth.

324. ————. "Medieval Magic and Science in the Seventeenth
Century." *Speculum*, 28(1953), 692-704.

Even though this study does not make any particular
reference to Shakespeare, its presentation of diverse
Medieval concepts is informative. The essay refers
to gems, herbs, animals, astrology, humors, prescriptions,
remedies, and powders. The essay has a section on
alchemy and relates its importance to literature. By
tracing the impact of Medieval science and magic from
1600 to 1700, Thorndike determines that Medieval ideas
were largely rejected by seventeenth-century writers.

325. Thorp, M. F. *The Triumph of Realism in Elizabethan
Drama*. Princeton: Princeton U. Pr., 1928. 142 pp.

Of interest is the first chapter which examines the
type of plays published in London between 1557 and 1590.
Of those listed in the Stationer's Register, thirty-four
out of seventy-nine were moralities or had morality
features. This study establishes the lingering appeal
of the moralities "long after the classical impulse
had transformed other native literary forms."

326. ————. "Shakespeare and the Fine Arts." *PMLA*,
46(1931), 672-98.

The essay concerns Shakespeare's knowledge of stained

glass, frescoes, paintings,and tapestries with particular emphasis upon fifteenth century paintings depicting
the siege of Troy.

327. Tillyard, E. M. W. *The Elizabethan World Picture*.
      London: Chatto and Windus, 1943. 108 pp.

      Chapter One discusses the survival of Medieval con-
      cepts in the Renaissance with particular reference to
      Shakespeare. The subjects include astrology, contempt
      of the world theme, Medieval and Renaissance ideas of
      Platonism and chivalry, and the concept of hierarchies.
      Other chapters refer to the chain of being, Medieval
      concepts of sin, and the lingering influence of native
      religious ideas.

328. ————. *The English Renaissance: Fact or Fiction?*
      Baltimore: Johns Hopkins Pr., 1952. 114 pp.

      The purpose of this work is to distinguish the Ren-
      aissance from the Middle Ages in relationship to art,
      science, religion, and philosophy. Tillyard refers
      frequently to Medieval writings while contrasting and
      sometimes comparing attitudes in both ages. Individual
      chapters on the lyric, criticism, and the epic are
      presented.

329. Toole, William B. *Shakespeare's Problem Plays*.
      London: Mouton and Co., 1966. 242 pp.

      Chapter One reviews criticism concerning Shakespeare's
      problem plays and discusses in particular Coghill's
      theory of the Medieval heritage of Shakespearean com-
      edy. Toole also links Dante's allegory of Christian
      typography and the structure of English mystery and
      morality plays to Shakespearean drama. There are
      individual chapters on *Ham.*, *AWW*, *MM*, and *Tro.* The
      pattern of thought which provides unity in these plays
      is tied to the Medieval concept of temptation, sin,
      remorse, repentance, penance, and pardon. Thus the
      morality framework plays a dominant part in the
      structure of Shakespeare's plays.

330. Trachtenberg, Joshua. *The Devil and the Jew: The
      Medieval Conception of the Jew and Its Relation to
      Modern Anti-Semitism*. New Haven: Yale U. Pr., 1944.
      279 pp.

      The author analyzes Shylock as a Jew thoroughly in

the Medieval tradition. Shakespeare associates the
Jew with the Devil, shows that Shylock is willing to
butcher a Christian, and emphasizes Shylock's extreme
usury. All of these characteristics are part of the
Medieval conception of the Jew.

331. Tuve, Rosemund. *Allegorical Imagery*. Princeton:
Princeton U. Pr., 1966. 461 pp.

Tuve examines how Medieval allegory has been passed
on to the Renaissance with particular reference to
Spenser. Chapters One and Two detail the survival
of Medieval emblems in the early Renaissance. Chapter
Two also discusses the allegory of vices and virtue.
Other aspects of the book concern "imposed allegory"
and "romances."

332. Ure, Peter. "On Some Differences Between Senecan and
Elizabethan Tragedy." *DUJ*, 10(1948), 17-23.

Like Farnham and Baker, Ure discounts the Senecan influence on Elizabethan drama and finds the Medieval
background to be important. Ure emphasizes the concept
of hierarchy and Medieval world order.

333. Vyvyan, John. *The Shakespearean Ethic*. London:
Chatto and Windus, 1959. 205 pp.

Chapters Four and Fourteen relate Shakespeare to the
allegorical tradition of the Middle Ages. According
to Vyvyan, "Ophelia is the girl we know as well as
representing a quality in Hamlet's soul." Allegory
in *WT* is also discussed, and Vyvyan finds similarities
between Shakespeare's psychological ideas and those
expressed in *The Romance of the Rose*. The author
concludes that the allegorical influence upon Shakespeare was significant.

334. Ward, A. W. *History of English Dramatic Literature to
the Death of Queen Anne*. London: Macmillan and
Co., 1899. 518 pp.

In his discussion of Medieval drama, Ward writes of
general tendencies of Medieval drama which worked their
way into Shakespearean drama. He finds few specific
concepts in Shakespearean drama which are directly
linked to the Medieval world. The discussion of religious ideas ties the drama of the Middle Ages to
the Elizabethan Age.

335. Wasson, John. "The Morality Play: Ancestor of
      Elizabethan Drama." *CompD*, 13(1979), 210-21.

      Wasson reexamines the contention that morality plays
      were models for the major types of Renaissance drama.
      He finds few links between Medieval and Renaissance
      drama in regard to the chronological, thematic, or
      structural grounds. The Medieval influence upon Ren-
      aissance drama comes from "the saints' lives on history
      plays," mummers' plays, folk tales, miracle plays, and
      especially the Thomas a Becket plays.

336. Watkins, W. B. C. *Shakespeare and Spenser*. Princeton:
      Princeton U. Pr., 1950. 339 pp.

      This book focuses upon how allegory was used during
      the Renaissance and the Middle Ages. There was always
      the chance of allegory becoming too concrete and hence
      less moral and more comic. Medieval allegory could
      portray psychological realism as is seen in the *Roman
      de la Rose* and was immensely fluid and fertile. Shake-
      speare and Spenser share with the Medieval scholar the
      exploiting of manifold meaning that both allegory and
      symbol share.

337. Watson, Curtis Brown. *Shakespeare and the Renaissance
      Concept of Honor*. Princeton: Princeton U. Pr., 1960.
      452 pp.

      The Renaissance concept of honor is radically differ-
      ent from that found in the age of Dante. Shakespeare's
      concept of honor is shaped by pagan humanist philosophy,
      while the Medieval concept of honor is closely associ-
      ated with Christianity. Watson discusses at length
      the dualism of pagan and Christian values in the Middle
      Ages and refers to the following writers and ideas:
      Augustine, Boethius, Francis, Aquinas, Dante, and the
      Medieval chivalric code. According to Watson differ-
      ences between Renaissance and Medieval ideas of honor
      can be clearly seen in the following concepts: (1) the
      virtuous Renaissance individual seeks public approbation
      to confirm his belief in his own moral worth; the same
      idea is heretical to Medieval moral philosophers; (2)
      posthumus reputation gives the Renaissance individual
      a sense of permanence, while posthumous reputation for
      those in the Medieval world was considered evanescent
      and fickle. This important work provides excellent
      background material for Shakespeare and the Middle Ages.

338. Welsford, Enid. *The Fool: His Social and Literary History*. New York: Farrar and Rinehart, 1935. 374 pp.

The author finds a number of common characteristics in the parasite, the buffoon, the Medieval court fool, the Lord of Misrule, and the court fool of Renaissance drama. The section on the surviving Medieval elements (243-70) is noteworthy. The fool is the keynote of the play, and Shakespeare employs the Medieval ambiguity of the terms fool and foolish throughout the major portion of *Lr*. In a sense the good are foolish to love and to crave affection. King Lear is brought to the position of a fool in order to be wise. Welsford also finds a morality framework throughout *Lr*. with a balanced cast of characters representing good and evil.

339. Weimann, Robert. *Shakespeare and the Popular Tradition in the Theater*. ed. by Robert Scwartz. Baltimore: Johns Hopkins U. Pr., 1978. 325 pp.

This important work shows Shakespeare's debt to the popular native tradition in drama. The first chapter concerns the drama of miming. The character of the fool evolves from the mime. Another chapter shows the relationship between folk play and Elizabethan drama. Weimann's chapter on the mystery cycles discusses how the use of space on the *platea* (open area) and the *locus* (specific scenic unit) of Medieval plays was incorporated on the Elizabethan stage. The morality heritage, dramatic speech, and punning are also discussed. Chapter Six is entitled "Shakespeare's Theater: Tradition and Experiment."

340. Weisinger, Herbert. "The Renaissance Theory of the Reaction Against the Middle Ages as a Cause of the Renaissance." *Speculum*, 20(1945), 461-67.

The author points out that Renaissance religious writers deplored the literature of the Middle Ages and found an interest in the classical writings. Renaissance artists also reacted against the gothic style and saw a community of interest in the classic mode. Very few Medieval writers were thought highly of with the exception of Bede and Alcuin, who were credited for a slight revival of learning.

341. ————. *Tragedy and the Paradox of the Fortunate Fall*. East Lansing: Michigan State Col. Pr., 1953. 300 pp.

The Medieval and Renaissance concepts of *felix Culpa*
are examined in relationship to myth and ritual of
other cultures (190-227). Myth and ritual were generally incorporated into Medieval Christian thought and
are ubiquituous to western thought.

342. Weisinger, Herbert. "The Study of Shakespearean
     Tragedy since Bradley." *SQ*, 6(1955), 387-96.

Although Bradley's lectures did much to advance Shakespearean criticism, the criticism since his time should
also be considered important. Weisinger classifies
Shakespearean criticism into six schools, one of which
is the surviving Medieval element in Elizabethan drama.
The author credits Campbell, Farnham, Tillyard, and
Thorndike for advancing the study of native English
and Medieval ideas in Shakespeare and notes that the
results of such studies have tended to discount the
concept of the Renaissance as a distinct era. To an
extent such studies repudiate the revival of classical
culture in the Renaissance while affirming the importance
of the Medieval influence. The author agrees with
Campbell that Shakespeare is a superior writer of
Medieval *exempla*. Another Medieval convention reviewed
is the Fall of Princes theme, though critics who see
Shakespeare's use of this concept fail to agree upon
its importance in relation to all of his plays.

343. West, Robert Hunter. *The Invisible World*. Athens,
     Georgia: U. of Georgia Pr., 1939. 200 pp.

The first few chapters briefly sketch the history of
demonology throughout the ages and refer frequently to
the works of Thomas Aquinas. Another section relates
to patristic and Medieval demonology and Renaissance
concepts on the same topic.

344. Whitaker, Virgil K. *Shakespeare's Use of Learning*.
     San Marino: The Huntington Library, 1953. 346 pp.

In emphasizing the classical influence upon Shakespeare, Whitaker also notes the importance of Medieval
ideas. He discusses Shakespeare's debt to Chaucer,
Gower, the prevalence of the theme of fortune in Shakespeare's plays, and the surviving ideas of the Medieval
courts of love. The section on *JC* illustrates the
presence of morality play concepts in a play which is
basically classical.

345. White, T. H. *The Bestiary*. New York: G. P. Putnam
and Sons, 1954. 270 pp.

   This work is mainly a translation of a Latin bestiary
   of the twelfth century, but the numerous notes often
   refer to Shakespeare. Shakespeare's knowledge of birds
   and beasts appears to come from the literature of his
   day with the exception of those birds and animals found
   in "The Phoenix and the Turtle." In this work Shakespeare was acquainted with the birds of the *Physiologus*,
   such as the Phoenix, the Chaladrius, and the Medieval
   peculiarities of swans, doves, and crows.

346. Whitmore, Charles E. "The Elizabethan Age in England,"
pp. 203-88 in *The Supernatural in Tragedy*, ed. by
Charles Whitmore. New York: Phaeton Pr., 1915.

   The revenge-ghost is an Elizabethan invention formed
   by fusing Medieval and Senecan concepts of the ghost.
   The ghosts in *R3*, *JC*, and *Ham*. are "wholly in the
   Medieval tradition."

347. Wickham, Glynne. "Shakespeare's 'Small Latine and Less
Greeke,'" pp. 209-30 in *Talking of Shakespeare*. ed.
John Garrett. London: Hudder and Stroughton, 1954.

   Wickham sees the above quotation as representing two
   philosophical ideas in the Renaissance. Jonson depicts
   classical and Hellenic culture, while Shakespeare is
   immersed in Medieval concepts. Shakespeare's audience
   is fundamentally Medieval. The pattern that Shakespeare
   used in his histories, tragedies, and comedies is
   basically Medieval, one he inherited from Lydgate and
   Chaucer.

348. ————. *Early English Stages 1300 to 1600*. 2 Vols.
London: Rutledge and Kegan Paul, 1963.

   Volume One is a collection of source material relating to stage practices in the Middle Ages. Wickham
   examines mosaics, frescoes, stained glass, and statu-
   aries in order to determine the description and precise
   function of the Medieval stage. He believes that the
   drama was not a self-contained art form, since everyday
   pursuits and past-times contributed more to stage practices than many people have realized. For example, the
   conventions of heraldry contributed a great deal to
   color symbolism in stage costumes. Wickham argues that
   "Shakespeare's theatre represented a climax of centuries

of medieval experiments rather than a new beginning
of Renaissance inspiration." Wickham argues that the
"mansion staging of *decor simultane* of the Middle Ages
was imported intact into the first permanent theatres
of Elizabethan London." The Elizabethan playwrights
received structural form and consecutive scenes from
the miracle cycles, while they received thematic concepts of salvation, and damnation from the moralities.
The pageantry of Medieval plays was incorporated into
the regular drama rather than passing out of existence.

349.   ————. *Shakespeare's Dramatic Heritage.* New York:
        Barnes and Noble, 1964. 265 pp.

    Wickham's discussion of Medieval tragedy relates to
fortune and the Christian concepts of the fall of man
which speak of personal as well as social misery and
disaster. "Shakespeare took over this pattern in its
entirety and applied it to English history, starting
with the deposition and murder of Richard II and spread-
ing outwards to the involvement of the whole nation in
the misery and carnage of the War of Roses." Wickham
emphasizes that Shakespeare's audience was steeped in
Medieval religious ideas, and Shakespeare's plays
should be interpreted by keeping this in mind.

350.   Williamson, George. "Elizabethan Drama and Its
        Classical Rival." *CUC*, 31(1929), 251-56.

    Shakespeare's abandonment of the unities may be
partially due to his neglect of the classical chorus
as well as his disregard of Biblical plays that are
found in the Medieval dramatic tradition.

351.   Wilson, F. P. "Shakespeare's Reading." *ShS*, 3
        (1950), 14-21.

    The author questions those critics who claim that
Shakespeare's reading included many Latin, Greek, and
Medieval works. He doubts that Shakespeare read
Boccaccio and was indebted to him for the wager plot
in *Cym.* This essay raises the question as to how extensively Shakespeare read Chaucer. Those Medieval
elements which seem to appear in Shakespeare's writings
may be seen in many Renaissance works.

352.   ————. *The English Drama 1485-1585.* New York:
        Oxford U. Pr., 1969. 244 pp.

The book refers to Shakespeare in passing while tracing the development of English drama. The craft cycles disappeared about the end of the sixteenth century because of the condemnation of these plays by ecclesiastical authorities. Wilson discusses comedy, tragedy, and Tudor attitudes toward morality plays.

353. Wilson, J. Dover. "Shakespeare's 'Small Latin' How Much?" *ShS*, 10(1957), 12-26.

Wilson examines whether or not Shakespeare knew classical legend from reading classical writers or from Medieval writers who incorporated classical ideas in their stories. Although the argument cannot be proven decisively, Wilson contends that Shakespeare relied upon Chaucer for many of the classical concepts. *Troilus and Criseyde* and *The Legend of Good Women* were used frequently by Shakespeare.

354. Withington, Robert. *English Pageantry: An Historical Outline*. 2 Vols. Cambridge: Harvard U. Pr. 1918.

Withington details the survival of folk elements, early masques, and pageants associated with "royal entry" from the thirteenth century onward. He also describes the pageantry associated with the Lord Mayor's show.

355. ————. "The Development of the Vice," pp. 155-67 in *Of Barrett Wendell*. ed. William R. Castle. Cambridge: Harvard U. Pr., 1926.

The essay associates the Vice with comic elements in early Medieval drama with a particular emphasis of the Vice's being aligned with the Devil of the miracle play and the Fool of the folk play. Launcelot, Gobbo, Iago, and Falstaff can trace their ancestry to the Vice of the moralities.

356. ————. *Excursions in English Drama*. New York: D. Appleton-Century Co., 1937. 263 pp.

Withington is cautious about over-emphasizing Shakespeare's Medieval heritage, and his chapter "On the Continuity of Dramatic Development" (174-206) suggests that more study needs to be done on Shakespeare's use of homiletic literature. The author accepts a number of Owst's ideas with reservation and notes that Owst

finds "influences where none exist." The section on
the Vice (42–89) repeats much which was previously
noted above.

357.   ———. "The Continuity of Dramatic Development."
        SAB, 10(1960), 73–81.

        There is a connection between Medieval homilies and
        Shakespeare's *Ham.*, *Mac.*, and *Ant.* On one level these
        tragedies deal with the purging of sin by depicting
        waste, shame, and folly. Another point of interest
        is Shakespeare's techniques of appealing to the audi-
        ence's imagination in presenting a setting, a dramatic
        device which comes from Medieval plays, particularly
        passages in the *Chester Deluge*.

358.   Wright, Herbert. "How Shakespeare Came to Know the
        Decameron." *MLR*, 1(1955), 45–48.

        Wright speculates that Shakespeare may have used the
        French translation of Antoine le Macon of Boccaccio's
        Decameron which was circulated widely in England during
        Shakespeare's time. He quotes a number of passages
        from Shakespeare's plays and attempts to prove that
        Shakespeare was capable of reading French.

359.   Wright, Louis B. "Social Aspects of Some Belated
        Moralities." *Anglia*, 54(1930), 107–48.

        The morality play with its emphasis upon Medieval
        religious principles was transformed during the late
        1500s to a play involving political and social condi-
        tions of the day. Gradually the moralities came to
        deal with money, commercialism, and various classes
        of people.

360.   ———. *Shakespeare's Theater and the Dramatic
        Tradition.* Washington: The Folger Shakespeare
        Library, 1958. 36 pp.

        This book is basically an introductory study since
        it gives a running account of native Medieval staging
        and describes a number of Elizabethan theaters. Wright
        relates Shakespeare's comedies to earlier English
        models.

361.   Wynne, Arnold. *The Growth of English Drama.* 2nd ed.
        1914; rpt. Freeport, New York: Books for Libraries
        Pr., 1968. 269 pp.

The first three chapters focus upon common ideas in
Medieval and Renaissance drama. Wynne finds the Renaissance love of the supernatural as a continuation
of the supernatural found in the miracle and morality
plays. He believes the Vice in Medieval drama can be
found in a number of Shakespeare's plays and briefly
comments upon his presence in *TN*.

362. Yoker, Audrey. *Animal Analogy in Shakespeare's
Character Portrayal.* New York: King Crown Pr.,
1947. 150 pp.

Chapter One discusses Shakespeare's use of the tradi-
tion of animal analogy with particular reference to the
Aesopian tales as they were handed down through the ages.
Other sections speculate that Shakespeare may have re-
lied upon the *Physiologus* and *Bestiaries* and may have
been indebted to Medieval writers such as Caxton,
Vincent of Beauvais, and anonymous writers who reworked
Aristotle's *Historia Animalium*.

II
MEDIEVAL INFLUENCE UPON PARTICULAR PLAY GROUPS

The Comedies

363. Arthos, John. "The Forming of the Early Comedies."
SRO, 3(1967), 1-8.

There is an opportunity for fruitful investigation
concerning the surviving Medieval influence of music
and choreography in Shakespeare's plays. Music and
choreography must be understood if one is to fully
appreciate Shakespearean dramatic form.

364. Barger, C. L. *Shakespearean Festive Comedy*.
Princeton: Princeton U. Pr., 1959. 261 pp.

In Chapter One, "The Saturnalian Pattern," Barber
indicates that the concepts of festivity, holiday, and
social customs in Shakespeare's plays come in part from
the morality tradition, mummings, morris dances, and
native English social observances. In Chapter Eight
Barber argues that Falstaff is a descendant of the Vice
and clown of the morality play. The actions and relationships between Falstaff and Hal were shaped by
the "morality play encounters between Vices and Virtues."

365. Bradbrook, M. C. *The Growth and Structure of Elizabethan Comedy*. London: Chatto and Windus, 1962. 206 pp.

Of particular relevance are Chapters One through Four
which discuss Chaucer's influence upon Shakespeare, the
Medieval and Elizabethan audience, the continuity of
the oral tradition in Shakespeare's day, and public
stages in Medieval and Renaissance times. The Medieval
narrative tradition was the basis of Shakespearean
comedy, but Shakespeare modified the earlier comedy
by having his characters interact with one another.
Another section comments upon Shakespeare's use of the
disguise and relates this dramatic technique to Italian
comedy and the Vice of the morality play.

366.   ———.   "Folklore Festivals,"   pp. 237-39 in *Reader's
       Encyclopedia of Shakespeare*.   ed. by Edward J. Quinn,
       New York: Crowell, 1968.

       Bradbrook comments upon folk festivals and the sur-
       vival of folk legend in comedies and romances for the
       most part.   Few folk elements are employed in the
       histories and tragedies.

367.   Charlton, H. B.   *Shakespearean Comedy*.   New York:
       Barnes and Noble, Incorp., 1938.   303 pp.

       This book assesses Shakespeare's indebtedness to
       classical and Medieval ideas for the comedies.   *MND,
       AYL,* and *TGV* are in the Medieval romance tradition
       since courtesy, chivalry, feudalism, and the religion
       of love are found throughout the plays.   Charlton
       associates Shakespeare's lovers with the state of the
       lover in *The Romance of the Rose*.

368.   ———.   "The Dark Comedies."   *BJRL,* 21(1938), 78-128.

       Charlton calls *Tro., MM,* and *AWW* Shakespeare's dark
       comedies.   Shakespeare trained himself to write romantic
       comedies by experimenting with "dark" comedy.   In *Tro.*
       he played "classical idealized heroism" against Medieval
       romanticism and points out the deficiencies of each.
       Romantic love is ridiculed as is the concept of honor
       and the noble warrior.

369.   Coghill, Nevill.   "The Basis of Shakespearean Comedy:
       A Study in Medieval Affinities."   *E&S,* 3(1950), 1-28.

       The two basic types of comedy in the Renaissance are
       the romantic and the satiric, and most Renaissance play-
       wrights use satire in an attempt to ridicule man and
       his follies.   Shakespeare, however, "reached for his
       Chaucer" when he wrote comedy.   The Medieval concept
       of comedy concerns a story which begins in sorrow and
       ends in felicity.   Coghill defines the term by re-
       ferring to the works of Dante, Chaucer, Vincent de
       Beauvais, and Matthieu de Vendome.   Aspects of the
       Medieval pattern are seen in *Err.* and *Shr.*   Other topics
       discussed are the *amour courtois* concept, the Medieval
       convention of the hen-pecked husband, and the *exemplum*
       influence.   The last section of his essay concerns the
       morality play influence upon *MV,* and *Tmp.*   Coghill notes
       similarities between Shakespeare's treatment of allegory
       and the use of allegory in *Piers Plowman* and *The Castle
       of Perseverance*.

*   Dean, William K. "The Concept of the Comic in English Drama, ca 1400-1612." See 96.

370.   Feldman, Sylvia D. *The Morality Patterned Comedy of the Renaissance.* The Netherlands: Mouton and Co. Pub., 1970. 165 pp.

     This is an important work showing the continuation of Medieval ideas in Renaissance drama. Morality drama has a didactic intention, character groupings, and action and structure of the morality play. Feldman defines the morality pattern by discussing *The Castle of Perseverance, Wisdom, Mankind,* and *Everyman.* The book examines *AWW* in detail as a morality patterned drama.

371.   Frye, Northrup. "The Argument of Comedy." *EIE,* (1948), 58-73.

     Frye classifies the new comedy as Aristotelian, old comedy as Platonic, Dante's comedy as Thomist, and Shakespeare's comedy as elusive but tied to Medieval influences. Many of Shakespeare's characters are adaptations of the Medieval Vice. In addition, Shakespeare's comedies, like the ones of Peele, Lyly, and Greene, use themes from romance and folklore while avoiding the comedy of manners. Frye sees Shakespearean comedies deriving from the drama of folk ritual, the St. George play, the mummer's play, and the Feast of the Ass and the Boy Bishop. He calls this type of drama the comedy of the green world, and its themes are the triumph of life over the wasteland and the death and revival of the year impersonated by figures. *LLL* shows the Medieval influence of the debate of winter and spring, while *Wiv.* contains the elaborate ritual of the defeat of winter known to folklorists as "carrying out Death" with Falstaff being the victim.

372.   ————. "Characterization in Shakespearean Comedy." *SQ,* 3(1953), 271-277.

     The thrust of Frye's essay concerns the classical influence upon Shakespearean comedy, but in categorizing the various functions and points of comic structure, Frye discusses how the Vice in Shakespeare's plays derives from the morality play.

373.   Galway, Margaret. "Flyting in Shakespeare's Comedies." *SAB,* 10(1935), 183-191.

Medieval flyting was basically used for comic purposes
as is seen in the Towneley play which represents Noah's
wife declining to enter the ark. Galway indicates the
extent and nature of Shakespeare's use of this convention by pointing to some forty episodes or scenes
in the comedies, especially *MM*, *Wiv.*, and *Shr.* Shakespeare uses flyting for the purpose of comic satire.

374. Habicht, Werner. "The Wit Interludes and the Form of
      Pre-Shakespearean Romance Comedy," pp. 73-88 in
      Renaissance Drama 8(1965), ed S. Schoenbaum.
      Evanston: Northwestern U. Pr., 1965.

      Habicht sees the morality element surviving in Wit
      interludes by way of allegory and thematic pattern.
      Such plays achieved a "unity of moral theme and roman-
      tic spectacle."

375. Hardison, O. B., Jr. "Logic Versus the Slovenly World
      in Shakespearean Comedy." *SQ*, 31(1980), 311-22.

      Hardison analyzes aspects of Medieval drama which the
      Renaissance world inherited. The key points are that
      "the drama is comic in structure, open in form, and as
      various and irrational as society itself." He discuss-
      es aspects of the above concepts in *Shr.*, *Err.*, and *MND*.

376. Hassel, R. Chris, Jr. *Faith and Folly in Shakespeare's
      Romantic Comedies.* Athens, Ga.: U. of Georgia Pr.,
      1980. 255 pp.

      Hassell studies the Christian background of the com-
      edies by exploring Pauline, liturgical and Erasmian
      concepts that Shakespeare employed. Rather full treat-
      ment is given to *LLL*, *MND*, *Ado.*, *TN*, and *MV*.

377. Hunter, Robert Grams. *Shakespeare and the Comedy of
      Forgiveness.* New York: Columbia U. Pr., 1965.
      272 pp.

      Hunter explores a suggestion by J.M. Manly that Med-
      ieval drama had strongly influenced Renaissance play-
      wrights. Shakespeare, like his Medieval predecessors,
      wrote dramas which were a dialectic of mercy and for-
      giveness. Both selected stories in which sin, contri-
      tion, and forgiveness were already present. Shake-
      speare's *humanum genus* figure generally offends the
      woman who loves him and is later forgiven by her. Like
      Medieval authors, Shakespeare sees charity and love as

regenerative forces in restoring sinful humanity. The book has an extensive discussion of *Cym.*, *WT*, *Ado.*, and *AWW* in regard to the above ideas.

378. Lascelles, Mary. "Shakespeare's Pastoral Comedy," pp. 70-86 in *More Talking of Shakespeare*. ed. John Garrett. New York: Books for Libraries Pr., 1959.

Shakespeare's pastoral is a blending of the Daphnis and Chloe stream, Montemayor's Diana, oracular prophecy of Greek gods, Robin Hood legends, and tales of Medieval chivalry.

* Lord, John Bigelow. "Certain Dramatic Devices in the Comedies of Shakespeare and in Some of the Works of his Contemporaries and Predecessors." See 217.

379. Muir, Kenneth. *Shakespeare's Source Comedies and Tragedies*. London: Methuen and Co. Ltd., 1979. 267 pp.

Eminently readable, Muir details the sources and Shakespeare's adaptation of them to fit his own drama. See individual plays for a reading of the Medieval influence.

380. Parrott, Thomas M. *Shakespearean Comedy*. New York: Oxford U. Pr., 1949. 417 pp.

The opening chapter surveys the type of comedy found in Medieval drama and makes pertinent comments upon the survival of such comedy in Shakespeare's plays. The Porter's scene in *Mac.* and the grave digging scene in *Ham.* owe something to the tradition established in the miracle plays where comedy was introduced to entertain the audience. Parrott also comments that Shakespeare's clowns resemble the Vice of the morality play and the clown of the interludes.

381. Pettet, E. C. *Shakespeare and the Romance Tradition*. London: Staples Pr., 1949. 208 pp.

Chapter One gives an overall discussion of the concept of romance as it relates to Shakespearean drama, with Pettet commenting upon classical, Medieval, and continental influences upon Shakespeare. There is a discussion of the surviving influence of the miracle and morality play in the Renaissance. Pettet observes a change in the courtly love tradition since Chaucer,

with Shakespeare bringing sexual love into a more harmonious relation with religion. The author argues that
Shakespeare reacted against the Medieval conception of
courtesy and chivalry in *MND*, and Pettet terms this
reaction as "the cult of rejection." He also discusses
TGV, *Err.*, *LLL*, *Ado.*, *Rom.*, *AYL*, and *TN* from the point
of view of "the cult of rejection." In his chapter,
"The 'Dark' Comedies," Pettet has a lengthy comparison
of Chaucer's *Troilus and Criseyde* with Shakespeare's
Tro. and finds that Shakespeare expresses a sense of
shallowness and sham with the doctrines of romantic
love and the code of chivalric honor.

382. Presson, Robert K. "Some Traditional Instances of
      Setting in Shakespeare's Plays." *MLR*, 61(1966), 12-22.

      Presson studies the garden setting metaphor in *The
      Romance of the Rose* and shows parallels in *Rom.*, *Cym.*,
      Ado., and *R2*. The essay also compares Shakespeare's
      forest in *Tit.* and *LLL* to Chaucer's forest settings.

383. Rodway, Allan Edwin. *English Comedy: Its Role and
      Nature from Chaucer to the Present Day*. Berkeley:
      U. of California Pr., 1975. 288 pp.

      The discussion of comedy in the Medieval and Renais-
      sance periods (57-113) includes the following topics:
      clerical and chivalric pretensions, knighthood, women,
      courtly love, dream romances, and the fabliaux. Chaucer
      and Dunbar are discussed in the Medieval period, while
      Shakespeare and Jonson are primarily addressed in the
      Elizabethan period.

384. Russell, William M. "Courtly Love in Shakespeare's
      Romantic Comedies." *DAI*, 29(1968), 4502-A
      (Catholic U. of America).

      Russell examines the concept of courtliness not from
      the point of view of Medieval doctrinal points but from
      the characteristic development of carnal and spiritual
      values in a love relationship. He finds that comic
      uses of the courtly love themes adds romantic texture
      in *TN*, *AYL*, *MND*, and *Ado.*, while the same theme contrasts
      with romance elements in *Shr.*, *MV*, and *Wiv.*

385. Salinger, Leo. *Shakespeare and the Tradition of Comedy*.
      London: Cambridge U. Pr., 1974. 356 pp.

      Of particular interest is "Early Elizabethan Romances"

(31-39), "Medieval Stage Heroines" (39-59), and "Survival of Medieval Staging" (67-75). Salinger finds that Shakespeare was influenced by Medieval stage heroines for Hermoine in the *WT*, and in a general sense Medieval stage romances shaped "Shakespeare's formation as a playwright."

*   Stevenson, David L. *The Love-Game Comedy*. See 312.

386.   Talbert, E. W. *Elizabethan Drama and Shakespeare's Early Plays*. Chapel Hill: U. of North Carolina Pr., 1963. 400 pp.

Chapter Two, "Aspects of the Comic," deals with the surviving Medieval comic influence upon Shakespeare. The subjects include the "Lord of Misrule," the Medieval *demande d'amour*, ballads, flyting, mystery and morality plays, and the dance and song of Medieval drama.

387.   Thompson, K. M. "Shakespeare's Romantic Comedies." *PMLA*, 67(1952), 1079-93.

An appreciation of Shakespeare's comedies depends upon understanding the tradition which Shakespeare inherited. The essay focuses upon the English courtly love tradition which stemmed from "Chaucer, elaborated by the Fifteenth-Century Chaucerians and changed by their Sixteenth-Century successors." The movement is from the romance of adultery to the humorous mockery of this convention, and finally to the romance of marriage. The humor in *LLL* depends upon the irony and paradox involved in the love-game conventions. The parody of love conventions is discussed in *TGV* as well as the ironical use of feudal metaphors as a source of comedy in *TN*.

388.   Thorne, William Barry. "The Influence of Folk Drama upon Shakespearean Comedy." *DAI*, 25(1965), 6603 (Wisconsin).

The study dwells upon Shakespeare's use of native folk drama by concentrating upon the following topics: the Mummer's play, the Maying theme, the flight to the woods theme, the Lord of Misrule, and the rebirth of the New Year. Further, the work analyzes characters, incidents, settings, themes, and structural principles in relation to the above in eight Shakespearean plays.

389. Tillyard, E. M. W. *The Nature of Comedy and Shakespeare.*
       English Association Presidential Address, London:
       Oxford U. Pr., 1958. 15 pp.

       The author agrees with Coghill's idea that Shake-
       spearean comedy is linked with the Medieval comic spirit.
       Tillyard adds that Shakespeare's method is also derived
       from the classical tradition and goes in the direction
       of the didactic and satiric. In addition, Tillyard
       finds that Shakespeare exploits ideas associated with
       farce, the picaresque, and fantasy.

390. Vyvyan, John. *Shakespeare and the Rose of Love: A*
       Study of the Early Plays in Relation to the Medieval
       Philosophy of Love. New York: Barnes and Noble,
       1960. 193 pp.

       LLL, TGV, Rom., MM, and *WT* use the five-act structure
       derived from Terence. The Medieval Rose of Love appears
       in the fifth act of those plays where it acts as a force
       of goodness to overcome the forces of evil. Vyvyan has
       a chapter on *The Romance of the Rose* and associates many
       of Shakespeare's ideas of love with this work. The
       allegory of love and the mysticism associated with this
       allegory was by far the most vital contribution of the
       Middle Ages to Shakespeare.

391. Weld, John. *Meaning in Comedy: Studies in Elizabethan*
       Romantic Comedy. Albany: State U. of New York Pr.,
       1975. 255 pp.

       Much of this work studies the religious tradition of
       Shakespeare's audiences. Weld discusses the morality
       drama in regard to the "radical independence of dra-
       matic vehicle and tenor." The use of morality concepts
       is specific rather than abstract. Part One presents
       the dramatic tradition while Part Two concerns the
       following plays: *Err., Shr., MND,* and *MV.*

392. Wickham, Glynne. "Medieval Comic Traditions and the
       Beginnings of English Comedy," pp. 40-62 in *Comic*
       Drama. ed. by W.D. Howarth. New York: St. Martin's
       Pr., 1978.

       Wickham discusses the origins of comedy in the Med-
       ieval secular and liturgical tradition. Chaucer,
       Lydgate, Heywood, and Medwall are briefly referred
       to. Applications of the liturgical readings of plays
       are shown in *LLL* and *MND.*

The Histories

* Bergeron, David M. "The Emblematic Nature of English
  Civic Pageantry." See 26.

393. Bethell, S. L. "The Comic Element in Shakespeare's
     Histories." *Anglia*, 71(1953), 82-101.

     Bethell analyzes three types of comedy in Shake-
     speare's early history plays: the comedy of the common
     people; the Elizabethan humour of the comic villain
     which is derived from the comic devils of the miracle
     plays and the Vice of the moralities (sees this in
     R3 and the Bastard in *Jn.*); thirdly, the use of wit
     in dialogue to express comically a serious theme.

394. Bornstein, Diane. *Mirrors of Courtesy*. Hamden, Conn.:
     Archon Books, 1975. 158 pp.

     The author deals in part with the chivalric tradition,
     especially as it touches upon the Hal-Hotspur battle.

395. Cane, Walter. "The Morality Themes and Patterns in
     Shakespeare's Second Historical Tetralogy." *DAI*,
     27(1967), 3422-A (Vanderbilt).

     Shakespeare uses the basic pattern of the religious,
     moral plays but adapts the pattern to that of a polit-
     ical morality. *R2* through *H5* are concerned with sec-
     ular salvation--the destiny of England and its restora-
     tion to wealth and health. Shakespeare uses a cyclic
     pattern which resembles the morality play and is
     similar to the various stages of the redemptive process.

396. Carr, Virginia M. "One More into the Henriad: A
     'Two-Eyed' View." *JEGP*, 77(1978), 530-46.

     Carr interprets the kingship roles in Shakespeare's
     history plays as a struggle between the Christian
     humanist tradition and the Machiavellian. The tension
     is not resolved, since "the king must embrace both sets
     of values."

397. Chapman, Robert. "The Wheel of Fortune in Shakespeare's
     Historical Plays." *RES*, 1(1950), 1-7.

     Shakespeare's histories are "closely linked with the
     Fortune theme of Medieval literature." Chapman dis-
     cusses the idea that kings are the sport of Fortune,

and the kingly state corresponds to the four positions
on the Wheel of Fortune—rising, ruling, falling, and
casting off. Shakespeare also employs the Medieval
principle of Fortune's buckets. The Medieval conception of Fortune is shown in the writings of Dante,
Lydgate, Gower, Chaucer, and Boccaccio, and particular
applications of the Fortune theme are shown in *R2, 1*
and *2H4, H5, H6 Triad,* and *H8.* Chapman concludes that
"Shakespeare made a brilliant use of the implications
of the Medieval conception of Fortune."

398. Fleischer, Martha Hester. *The Iconography of the*
       English History Play. (Elizabethan and Renaissance
       Studies 10) Salzburg: Inst. für Englische Sprache
       und Literatur, Univ. Salzburg, 1974. 363 pp.

Fleischer establishes and points out the conventional
meanings associated with iconographic images. The
study is divided into state scene images, garden images,
and battle images. Shakespeare's history plays are
referred to frequently. The bibliography is extensive
as is the index.

399. Kernan, Alvin. "The Henriad: Shakespeare's Major
       History Plays." *YR,* 59(1969), 3–32.

The tetralogy of *R2* to *H5* involves the movement from
ceremony and ritual to history and drama and parallels
the movement from the Medieval to the Renaissance world.

400. Krugel, Sister Mary Flaula. "An Ideological Analysis
       of Honor in William Shakespeare's *Richard II, I* and
       II Henry IV, and *Henry V.*" *DAI,* 24(1963), 4177–78
       (St. Louis U.).

Kruegel relates honor in the plays mentioned above
to the theories of honor set down by Plato, Aristotle,
and Cicero as well as the Christian concepts espoused
by Paul, Augustine, and Aquinas. She determines that
the pagan concepts of honor are viewed with skepticism.
Shakespeare treats pagan pursuits of glory by ridicul-
ing them from a Christian point of view.

401. Matte, Nancy Lightfoot. "The *Ars-Morendi* in Selected
       Shakespearean History Plays." *DAI,* 38(1978),
       6145-A (Arizona State).

Matte discusses death and Elizabethan attitudes about
dying in *R2, R3, 1H4, 2H4,* and *H5.* She surveys funeral

monuments, devotional works, paintings, printed illustrations, and objects of personal ornamentation to
obtain insight into Elizabethan death attitudes.

402. Morrison, George Peter. "Shakespeare's Lancastrian
Tetralogy in the Light of the Medieval Mystery Cycles:
A Theory for Unity." *DAI*, 38(1978), 5499-A (S.U.N.Y.,
Stony Brook).

Although the study shows no allegorical relationship
between Shakespeare's characters and those of the
mystery cycles, yet it does show similarities in the
overall plan, the enormous scope of the two dramas,
and the historical approach. The author believes that
"the liturgy of the Christian church provided an organ-
izing principle" in Shakespeare's treatment of secular
history. *R2*, *1H4*, *2H4*, and *H5* are discussed in light
of the above ideas.

403. Ribner, Irving. "The Tudor History Plays: An Essay in
Definition." *PMLA*, 69(1954), 591-609.

The English history play adopted "the morality play
structure as a vehicle for executing the true historical
function." Ribner cites plays, such as Bale's *Kynge
Johan* which reflects the evolution of the morality play
into the political, morality play. Later the history
play became more complex as the morality pattern incorporated Senecan devices.

404. ————. "Morality Roots of the Tudor History Play."
TSE, 4(1954), 21-43.

"The history play is a highly didactic vehicle which
is deeply rooted in English stage tradition extending
back to Medieval times." One of the first new movements
in the morality play was the shift from religious questions to political questions. The growth of this aspect
is traced in Skelton's *Magnyfycence*, *Albion Knight*, and
Bale's *Kynge Johan*. The morality play pattern reflects
"initial felicity, temptation by evil, yielding, suffering, repentance and final salvation." The pattern is
shown in *1* and *2H4* when Shakespeare makes Prince Hal
choose between the Vice, Falstaff, and the life of
honor represented by the Chief Justice. Hal goes
through the typical experiences of Mankind in the
morality play. Similar ideas are shown in *R2* and *Jn*.
This essay provides important background material which
relates Shakespeare to the morality tradition.

405. ————. *The English History Play in the Age of Shake-*
      speare. New York: Barnes and Noble, 1965. 194 pp.

      Throughout this work Ribner argues that Medieval drama
      helped to shape Shakespeare's historical plays. He be-
      lieves that the miracle play influenced Shakespeare's
      dramatic methods. Also, Ribner presents a full study
      of the morality play and traces its impact on various
      plays up to Shakespeare's day. Ribner sees the king
      in Shakespearean drama as an adaptation of the *humanum*
      genus figure in the morality play. Other sections of
      this book discuss folk ritual and the possible influence
      of the Robin Hood plays upon Shakespeare. Some study
      is given to the Wheel of Fortune theme and the didactic
      quality of the history plays.

406. Saccio, Peter. *Shakespeare's English Kings: History,*
      Chronicle, and Drama. New York: Oxford U. Pr., 1977.
      268 pp.

      Saccio studies English history plays and shows their
      development from chronicle sources. Shakespeare's
      history plays are mentioned frequently.

407. Sheriff, William E. "Shakespeare's Use of the Native
      Comic Tradition in his Early English History Plays."
      WSL, 2(1965), 11–17.

      The native comic convention is seen in *Jn.*, *H6 Triad*,
      and *R3* in regard to character and action. One is assured
      that order will come from disorder.

408. Stokes, James David. "Roots of the English History
      Play." *DAI*, 40(1979), 2051–52A (Washington State).

      Stokes examines the native tradition which influenced
      the English history play. The features include a two-
      movement, four-part structure; hero-centered narrative
      framework, inseparability of the main character from
      the historical process, and the appearance of realism
      and metaphysical within a single work. A discussion
      of *R2* and *Cym.* is emphasized.

409. Stribrny, Zdenek. "The Idea and Image of Time in
      Shakespeare's Second Historical Tetralogy." *SJW*,
      111(1975), 51–66.

      The author discusses the plays in terms of the Renais-
      sance suppression of old baronial privileges with feudal
      honors being destroyed to make way for a new social
      order.

410. Tillyard, E. M. W. *Shakespeare's History Plays.*
New York: The Macmillan Co., 1946. 336 pp.

The morality play prompted the formality of Shakespeare's first tetralogy and supplied a single per-
vasive theme, one which overrides but in no way inter-
feres with the theme he derived from Hall. In none of
the plays is there a hero; the reason for this is that
there is an unnamed protagonist dominating all four.
It is England, or in morality terms Respublica. Like
the themes which lend structural unity in the morality
plays, Shakespeare sows in one play the seeds which
will germinate in the next. Other Medieval influences
discussed are formalism and stylization of speech and
Medieval hierarchial tendencies.

411. Turner, Robert Y. "Shakespeare and the Public Con-
frontation Scene in Early History Plays." *MP,*
62(1964), 1-12.

"Whereas other playwrights tended to copy or simplify,
Marlowe and Shakespeare kept close to the native traditions and turned familiar dramatic situations to more
effective use than their models." The origin of con-
frontation scenes may be traced to such forerunners as
the scenes of struggle between the Virtues and Vices
in *The Castle of Perserverance* or the Medieval debate.
Shakespeare's history plays are mentioned frequently
throughout this study.

412. ————. "Characterization in Shakespeare's Early
History Plays." *ELH,* 31(1964), 241-58.

The characters in Shakespeare's *1* and *2H4* plays are
static, undergo no moral change of character and derive
from the abstractions of the morality plays emboding
concepts of vice and virtue. Beginning with *R3,* however, Shakespeare moves from the crude morality char
acters toward real human beings whose actions are
artistically motivated.

The Romances

413. Alintekannimal, Varughese Varughese. "Resolution and
Reconciliation in Shakespeare's Final Comedies."
DAI, 25(1964), 3320 (U. of Denver).

Shakespeare was concerned with the ultimate realities
of life at the final stage in his career. The last
plays are based upon reconciliation, forgiveness, and
regeneration and are in the Medieval Christian tradition.

414.   Babula, William. "Shakespeare's Romances and Early
       English Tragicomic Patterns." *DAI*, 31(1971), 726-A
       (Berkeley).

       Unlike the Medieval dramatist who presented an ideal
       order of life on the stage, Shakespeare portrays a
       tragicomic ending which upholds a vision of life that
       is providential. Emphasis is upon justice and judgment
       in the cycle dramas and judgment and mercy in the
       moralities. Shakespeare's last plays have a structure
       similar to the early native plays.

415.   Dunn, Catherine M. "The Function of Music in Shake-
       speare's Romances." *SQ*, 20(1969), 391-405.

       Dunn analyzes the concept of the tripartite division
       of music formulated by Boethius and applies these ideas
       to Shakespeare's plays. *Musica Mundana* represents the
       order and proportion of the heavens and the elements.
       Musica Humana denotes the rapport existing between the
       body and faculties of the soul and also is associated
       with the widespread belief in music's curative powers.
       Per., *Cym.*, *WT*, and *Tmp.* are discussed from the point
       of view of *Musica Mundana* and *Musica Humana*.

416.   Felperin, Howard. *Shakespearean Romance*. Princeton:
       Princeton U. Pr., 1972. 319 pp.

       See Chapter One (3-54) for a discussion of romantic
       themes which influenced Shakespeare. Topics include
       self-realization through love, the quest, and atonement.
       Shakespeare's last plays seem to be influenced by re-
       ligious drama and the Christian story of redemption.
       Felperin comments upon Shakespeare's deliberate irony
       when employing Medieval models for characters and
       their actions.

417.   Fergusson, Francis. "Romantic Love in Dante and Shake-
       speare." *SR*, 83(1975), 253-66.

       Fergusson discusses the concepts of romantic love or
       courtly love by tracing ideas through the Provençal
       poets up to Shakespeare's day. He sees the romantic
       love theme in all of Shakespeare's romantic comedies,
       but Shakespeare's last plays particularly employ this
       theme.

*   Gesner, Carol. *Shakespeare and the Greek Romance:
       A Study of Origins*. See 133.

418. Leech, C. "The Structure of the Last Plays." *ShS*,
     11(1958), 19-30.

     The structure of the last plays is basically derived
     from Medieval and Renaissance commentators on Terence.
     Leech agrees with F.W. Baldwin on the five-act struc-
     tural aspects of the plays. Other parts of the essay
     deal with time, cyclic action, and the allegorical
     nature of the last plays.

419. Muir, Kenneth. *Last Periods of Shakespeare, Racine,
     and Ibsen.* Detroit: Wayne State U. Pr., 1961. 117 pp.

     The section on Shakespeare (31-60) makes several
     observations concerning Medieval ideas. Muir notes
     that the last plays convert the Wheel of Fortune theme
     into the Wheel of Providence. Patience, sin, and re-
     demption replace the arbitrary working of Fortune.

*   Patchell, Mary F. *The Palmerin Romances in Elizabethan
     Prose Fiction.* See 261.

420. Pettet, Ernest C. *Shakespeare and the Romance Tradition.*
     New York: Haskell House, 1975. 208 pp.

     Of interest is Pettet's brief discussion (Chapter One)
     of the romance tradition. Some attention is paid to the
     native Medieval romance and its influence upon Shake-
     speare.

421. Salinger, L. G. "Time and Art in Shakespeare's
     Romances." *RenD*, 9(1966), 3-35.

     The tradition of courtly love and pastoral tragic
     comedy cannot fully explain Shakespeare's romances.
     Salinger argues that the Euripidean romance and Med-
     ieval exemplary romance play a significant role in
     Shakespeare's last plays. From the Euripidean romance,
     Shakespeare got ideas concerning mistakes of identity,
     misunderstanding, disguise, and coincidence. From the
     Medieval tradition, Shakespeare received the idea of
     families divided and reunited, tribulation and wander-
     ings of characters, concepts of faith and patience, and
     the Christian idea of Providence. Salinger cites
     miracle plays and folk-tales in dealing with the Medie-
     val exemplary romance.

422. Tillyard, E. M. W. *Shakespeare's Last Plays.*
     London: Chatto and Windus, 1958. 85 pp.

The introduction brings up the topic of Shakespeare's
debt to Fletcher for melodramatic elements and the
treatment of various romantic scenes. Tillyard disagrees
with Ellis-Fermor concerning Shakespeare's debt to
Fletcher. Tillyard also stresses the idea that Shakespeare's treatment of romantic material was derived
from Medieval romances. *The Huon of Bordeaux* is a
source for Shakespeare's Oberon.

423. Wincor, Richard. "Shakespeare's Festival Plays." *SQ*,
      1(1950), 219-242.

      Wincor associates *Per.*, *Cym.*, and *Tmp.* with festival
      plays which celebrate the return of spring after a
      barren winter. The author refers to Medieval folk
      festivals, the Robin Hood plays, *Sir Gawain and the
      Green Knight*, and Redford's *Wyl and Science* and finds
      the pattern of Mock Death and Cure in these works and
      interprets Shakespeare's last plays with this thematic
      device.

The Tragedies

424. Babula, William. *Wishes Fall Out as They're Willed:
      Shakespeare and the Tragicomic Archetype.* (Eliz-
      abethan and Renaissance Studies 48) Salzburg: Inst.
      für Englische Sprache und Literatur, U. of Salzburg,
      1975.

      The archetypal pattern of tragicomedy comes from Med-
      ieval cycles and Tudor moralities and underlies Eliz-
      abethan tragicomedy as well as Shakespeare's *AWW*, *MM*,
      and *Per.*

425. Barroll, J. L. "Structure in Shakespearean Tragedy."
      ShS, 7(1974), 345-78.

      Barroll has an extensive examination of the rise and
      fall concept of the Wheel of Fortune in Medieval lit-
      erature. He shows that the character of Shakespeare's
      protagonist is tested by his response to external
      agencies rather than a simplistic fortune concept.

426. Battenhouse, Roy W. *Shakespearean Tragedy: Its Art
      and Its Christian Premises.* Bloomington: Indiana
      U. Pr., 1968. 466 pp.

      Shakespeare's tragedies should be read from the
      perspective of Medieval moral theology. The book
      focuses upon the homiletic tradition and contains

numerous, brief references to allegory, moralities, Medieval comedy and tragedy, and Medieval rhetoric. *Rom.* is discussed from the point of view of Medieval astrology and courtly love ideas.

427. Bradbrook, M. C. *Themes and Conventions of Elizabethan Tragedy.* Cambridge: Cambridge U. Pr., 1957. 267 pp.

The introduction comments upon Medieval and Renaissance audiences. The actors' habit of talking to the audience (frequently seen in Renaissance plays) is a tradition which stems from the moralities. The Renaissance audience was at home with allegory, and the rhetoric they enjoyed was similar to that emphasized in the Middle Ages.

428. ————. *English Dramatic Form.* New York: Barnes and Noble, 1965. 205 pp.

In Part Two Bradbrook shows how the drama of Marlowe and Shakespeare rested upon two Medieval traditions: processional civic pageants and courtly games found in Chaucer's poetry. Lavinia in *Tit.* is described in a series of images taken from street pageants which depict the pageantry of woe. The book also comments upon the relation between Shakespeare's comedies and Chaucer's dream poetry.

429. Bradley, Andrew Cecil. *Shakespearean Tragedy.* Cleveland: Meridian Books, 1955. 448 pp.

Of interest are Bradley's brief comments in Chapter One. Although Shakespearean tragedy goes beyond Medieval aspects of tragedy, it also includes Medieval elements. Medieval tragedy is a narrative rather than a drama; it involves illustrious men ruled by fortune; and the characters are frightened and awed by an inscrutable power. Shakespeare incorporates these ideas in his tragedies.

430. Broude, Ronald. "Vindicta Filia Temporis: Three English Forerunners of the Elizabethan Revenge Play." *JEGP,* 72(1973), 489-502.

The revenge play comes to us by the way of political morality plays. Broude discusses *The Three Laws, Respublica,* and *Horestes* in regard to reformation politics and refers to *Tit.* and *Ham.* in passing. Shakespeare's revenge plays have ties to Medieval literature.

431. Campbell, Lily Bess. *Shakespeare's Tragic Heroes:*
      Slaves of Passion. New York: Barnes and Noble,
      1930. 296 pp.

      Shakespearean tragedy relies upon but is a further
      development of Medieval concepts related to tragedy.
      Chapter One, "The Mirrors of Fortune," and Chapter
      Two, "The Value of Imitation in Teaching," compare
      and relate Shakespearean drama to that of the Middle
      Ages. The depiction of the tragic Fall of Princes
      continued into the Renaissance, but instead of blaming
      fickle Fortune, the playwrights stressed that man's
      punishment was due to his passions. The Medieval
      habit of teaching by *exempla* was still popular during
      the Renaissance.

432. Coursen, Herbert R., Jr. *Christian Ritual and the*
      World of Shakespearean Tragedies. Lewisburg, Pa.:
      Bucknell U. Pr., 1976. 441 pp.

      Coursen's purpose is to show the extent that Christian
      sacraments are employed by Shakespeare in his plays.
      R2, Ham., Oth., Lr., Mac., and *Tmp.* are analyzed in
      depth in regard to the sacraments. These plays reflect
      Christian doctrines, particularly in reference to con-
      fession, repentance, and communion.

433. Craig, Hardin. "Shakespeare's Depictions of Passions."
      PQ, 4(1925), 289-301.

      Shakespeare's knowledge of the psychology of passions
      comes from the native development of English drama. He
      was particularly indebted to older drama for gestures
      and facial appearances which represent an inner passion
      such as love, hate, and anger. The audience was well
      aware of these gestures from viewing late morality plays,
      and Shakespeare's depiction of passions is within the
      established tradition.

*   ————. "Morality Plays and Elizabethan Drama."   See
          83.

434. Creeth, Edmund. *Mankynde in Shakespeare.* Athens:
      U. of Georgia Pr., 1976. 192 pp.

      Mac., Oth., and *Lr.* have the closest affinities to
      the early moralities. Creeth argues that there is a
      corresponding design between the above plays and *The*
      Castle of Perseverance, Wisdom Who Is Christ, and *The*
      Pride of Life. Shakespeare adapts the temptation plot
      to tragedy.

435. Cunningham, J. V. "Tragedy in Shakespeare." *ELH*, 17 (1950), 36–46.

The essay attempts to define the types of tragedy in Shakespeare's plays. Cunningham argues that tragedy is associated with the Wheel of Fortune in *R3*, while the Fall of Princes concept can be seen in the major tragedies. Other aspects of his essay deal with Senecan elements of tragedy.

436. ————. *Woe and Wonder*. Toronto: Burns and Mac-Eachern, 1951. 129 pp.

The first chapter defines aspects of tragedy and their effects upon the audience. The "Medieval tradition of psychological analysis" provides the concepts which are needed to understand Shakespearean tragedy. Instead of emphasizing pity, a classical influence, Cunningham employs the term wonder, a term more fertile than pity which includes the concepts of amazement, fear, pity, sorrow, and surprise. He illustrates the above ideas in *Ham.* and *Lr.* Chapters Three and Four relate the Donation tradition to Elizabethan tragedy and show how the Medieval writers Aquinas, Diomedes, Isidore of Seville, Boethius, Chaucer, and Lydgate modify the Donation tradition. Shakespearean tragedy relied upon the Donation tradition as modified by the Middle Ages. Chapter Five discusses Aristotelian and Thomist views of sin as background material for Shakespearean drama. The former stresses that transgression results from confusion, while the latter emphasizes moral and ethical precepts which have been violated. He reads *Oth.* in the Aristotelian tradition but finds *Mac.* influenced by Thomist concepts.

437. Dickey, Franklin M. *Not Wisely But Too Well: Shakespeare's Love Tragedies*. San Marino: The Huntington Library, 1957. 202 pp.

Dickey studies Medieval and Renaissance attitudes toward violent and excessive love. He shows that excessive love is unnatural and effeminate and frequently associated with violence and murder by referring to the works of Gower and Lydgate. Antony, Cleopatra, Goneril, and Regan exemplify this doctrine. In Chapter Ten, "The Tragedy of Antony and Cleopatra," Dickey compares both Medieval and Renaissance attitudes toward Cleopatra. Chaucer finds Cleopatra an example of love true unto death, but most Medieval Cleopatras were evil. Lydgate and Boccaccio see her as a moral *exemplum*.

Shakespeare's Cleopatra is in the tradition of the
Middle Ages and illustrates the *contemptu mundi* theme.

438. Fairchild, Arthur H. R. "Shakespeare and the Tragic
     Theme." *UMS*, 29(1944), 1-145.

     Fairchild reviews Medieval criticism of Shakespeare
     in a general way and adds pertinent comments of his
     own. He finds Shakespeare's plays a "combination of
     Elizabethan conceptions and Medieval survivals." The
     subjects discussed include chivalry which is reflected
     in honor, valor, loyalty, courtesy, and munificence.
     Hamlet's philosophical idealism is linked with the sur-
     viving ideals of chivalry which were largely ineffective
     with the new order of practicality, expediency, and
     Machiavellian opportunism as reflected in the Court
     of Elsinore.

439. Fansler, Harriott Ely. *The Evolution of Technic in
     Elizabethan Tragedy.* Chicago: Row, Patterson and
     Co., 1914. 183 pp.

     Chapter One emphasizes the Medieval heritage of Eliz-
     abethan drama with particular reference to Shakespeare.
     Fansler assesses the Medieval miracle and morality
     plays from a tragical point of view and shows surviving
     elements of this tragedy in *Mac.* She illustrates sim-
     ilar tone and dialogue between Herod and Macbeth. Other
     subjects include the idea of completeness which the
     Medieval cycles possessed and the Renaissance playwrights
     inherited. She also comments upon aspects of Medieval
     comedy, such as the ranting and raving of Herod. Comic
     elements are apparent in Medieval drama but not so
     apparent in Shakespearean plays.

440. Farnham, Willard. "The Mirror for Magistrates and
     Elizabethan Tragedy." *JEGP*, 25(1926), 66-78.

     Farnham's thesis is that while pure chance, undeserved
     punishment and ironical destruction still have their
     place in Shakespeare, the tendency in Renaissance
     tragedy is toward cause and effect and individual re-
     sponsibility. As such Renaissance tragedy manifests
     a reaction from the Medieval concept of fortune and
     mutability. Death and worldly defeat meant little
     to the Medieval writers, and mortal life was not valued
     so highly as in the Renaissance. The Renaissance con-
     cept of value in life sharpened the sense of tragedy
     in death. The negation of mortal values appears to
     starve tragedy, while love of life fertilizes tragedy.

441. ————. *The Medieval Heritage of Elizabethan Tragedy.*
Berkeley: U. of California Pr., 1936. 487 pp.

This book is the standard work on the influence of
Medieval tragedy upon the Renaissance. Farnham discusses
Shakespearean drama repeatedly throughout the book in
terms of Medieval concepts. The subjects discussed are
the contempt of the world theme, Boccaccio's Fall of
Princes concepts, further elucidation of the Fall of
Princes by Chaucer and Lydgate, the influence of the
moralities and mysteries and the theme of Fortune in
Medieval and Renaissance works. Farnham says that *JC*
"has the rise-and-fall structure reminiscent of Fortune's
revolving wheel." *R2* contains the Medieval idea of
Fortune's buckets, the Dance of Death, and a similarity
to *De Casibus* tragedy. Most of Shakespeare's tragedies
are associated with the Medieval Gothic element, a
term which contrasts with Greek tragedy.

442. ————. "The Medieval Comic Spirit in the English
Renaissance," pp. 429-37 in *Adams Memorial Studies,*
ed. James McManaway et al. Washington: The Folger
Shakespeare Library, 1948.

The Medieval comic spirit in the form of the Gothic
grotesque made a distinct impression upon the English
Renaissance. The glorification of the fool and elevation
of the common and sometimes irreverent to the sublime are
some of the ideas of the Gothic grotesque. The "fool
in *Lear* is by long odds the best of such Shakespearean
gargoyles used to emphasize tragic seriousness in the
style of the Gothic grotesque." The grave-digging
scene in *Ham.* and the glorification of Falstaff are
also in the Medieval comic spirit tradition.

443. ————. *Shakespeare's Tragic Frontier.* Berkeley: U.
of California Pr., 1950. 264 pp.

In his first chapter Farnham relates evil in *Oth.* and
Lr. to the dramatic character types in the Medieval
moral play. "Iago is a Renaissance descendant of the
Medieval Vice." Farnham sees Othello as a Medieval
Mankind who is duped by the power of evil. In *Lr.*
"evil works by brutal, direct action." Other references
are scattered throughout this work which relate Shakespeare to Medieval ideas. For example, in Chapter Two
Farnham says "before the writing of *Othello*, Shakespeare
had usually conceived tragedy as a pyramid of rising
and falling corresponding more or less to the full turn
of Fortune's Wheel in Medieval tragical storytelling."

After *Oth.* Shakespeare still used the Medieval concept
of Fortune, but positions corresponding to Fortune's
Wheel are different. In addition, Senecan elements are
clearly noticeable.

444. Foy, Ted C. "Shakespeare's Use of Time: A Study of
      Four Plays." *DAI*, 35(1975), 2220-21A (Delaware).

      Shakespeare adopts Medieval Christian assumptions of
      time which have a providential plan that works itself
      out. Self-centered characters try to manipulate time
      and become bound to Fortune's Wheel. Foy refers to
      Ant., *Lr.*, *Tro.*, and *Err.* in developing the above ideas.

445. Hankins, John E. "The Pains of the Underworld: Fire,
      Wind, and Ice in Milton and Shakespeare." *PMLA*,
      71(1956), 482-95.

      Shakespeare's concept of the afterworld follows the
      Medieval visions of Drythelm, Alberic, Tundale, and the
      Monk of Evesham. Medieval punishments by wheels of fire
      and molten metals are stressed throughout the plays.
      Lr. (IV, vii, 47), *Tim.* (III, i, 54-55) and *Oth.* (V,
      ii, 273-80) are specific instances of the Medieval in-
      fluence.

446. Hays, Michael L. "Shakespeare's Use of Medieval
      Romance Elements in his Major Tragedies." *DAI*,
      34(1974), 5102-03A (Michigan).

      Shakespeare used Medieval romance elements to char-
      acterize the *dramatis personae*, occasion events, and
      establish the atmosphere and structure of the play.
      Certain thematic elements such as feudal matters,
      courtly love ideas, and knightly concepts are seen in
      Oth., *Lr.*, and *Mac.*

447. Hewitt, Douglas. "The Very Pomper of the Divell--
      Popular and Folk Elements in Elizabethan and Jacobean
      Drama." *RES*, 25(1949), 10-23.

      The effect of *Ham.*, *Lr.*, or *Mac.* on the audience of
      Shakespeare's day came partly from an appeal to themes
      and feeling instilled into the audience by tradition
      and folk-beliefs. Hewitt shows that the hero in the
      Mummers Play was in many ways similar to Shakespeare's
      tragic hero. The community identified with him in
      terms of correspondence between different planes of
      existence. The mummer's hero removed sterility and
      evil from the village and brought revival to life.

448. Lawlor, John. *The Tragic Sense in Shakespeare*.
      London: Chatto and Windus, 1960. 183 pp.

      Shakespeare's conception of tragedy as it relates to
      the Medieval ideas of fortune is discussed in Chapter
      Two (77-87). Lawlor writes that the Medieval fortune-
      formula is simple, but Shakespearean drama based upon
      it is complex. He discusses the concept of pathos as
      it relates to the Medieval formula by referring to
      Chaucer, Dante, and Boethius and comments upon *Rom.*
      in relation to the above ideas.

449. Lord, John B. "Sources of the Technique of Comic
      Scenes in Shakespearean Tragedy." *RS*, 32(1964),
      228-39.

      Lord relates Medieval comedy and tragedy to *Rom.*, *Lr.*,
      Ham., *Mac.*, and *Ant.* He gives a brief survey of comic
      aspects in Medieval drama and shows surviving elements
      of the comic spirit in five Shakespearean tragedies.
      After *Tit.* Shakespeare's tragedies are not based on
      "the classical idea which excludes comedy from tragedy
      but on the Medieval English idea which combines them."

450. Morgenson, J. M. R. *The Origins of English Tragedy*.
      Oxford: The Clarendon Pr., 1967. 196 pp.

      This work studies the various forms of Tudor tragedy
      with an emphasis upon philosophical and political
      concepts. Shakespearean tragedy is regarded as a con-
      tinuous development whose origins are found in Med-
      ieval religious and secular drama.

451. Ornstein, Robert. *The Moral Vision of Jacobean
      Tragedy*. Madison: The U. of Wisconsin Pr., 1960.
      229 pp.

      Chapter One is a general discussion of various ideas
      concerning Jacobean tragedy. Ornstein comments upon
      De Casibus tragedies and finds they lack the moral
      qualities to accurately express man's condition on
      earth. Medieval epics, however, contain a "haunting
      sense of tears in things, used by the Elizabethans."
      He also comments upon the presence of Thomist philosophy
      during the Elizabethan Age.

*   Page, Susan Carolyn Ulichney. "The Emergence of the
      Humanist Tragic Hero: A Study in the Dramatization
      of the *Psychomachia* in the Morality Plays and in
      Selected Plays of Shakespeare." See 255.

452.   Ribner, Irving. *Patterns of Shakespearean Tragedy.*
        London: Methuen and Co., Ltd., 1960. 201 pp.

        Ribner stresses the importance of the Medieval
        heritage as vehicles for Elizabethan thought and
        tragedy. One controlling influence upon Shakespeare
        is the concept of the "ordered universe." This
        ritualistic technique is seen in *Tit.* as well as the
        H6 Triad. *Jn.* embodies the rise and fall concepts
        employed by *De Casibus* tragedy. *JC* is based upon
        the moral order of the morality play in that it is a
        full-scale tragedy of moral choice. Ribner reads *Oth.*
        as a play in the morality tradition where the hero
        must discern the difference between good and evil.
        Further, the didactic and homiletic elements of Medieval
        drama afforded the tools by which Shakespeare shaped a
        "complex of action to reflect the universal role of
        man in conflict with evil." *Lr.* is discussed in terms
        of the morality tradition also. *Tim.* is viewed in
        terms of feudal concepts, while *Ant.* reflects the
        tradition of Medieval *exempla.*

453.   Rossiter, A. P. *Angel with Horns.* New York: Theatre
        Arts Books, 1961. 316 pp.

        Rossiter presents a series of studies covering a
        dozen of Shakespeare's plays with a concentration upon
        the tragedies. He has infrequent comments concerning
        Shakespeare and Medieval tragedy, and he cautions
        against oversimplifying Shakespeare by relating him
        only to a classical or Medieval background. The book
        includes essays annotated in the history section on
        R3.

454.   Roth, Robert. "Another World of Shakespeare." *MP,*
        49(1951-52), 42-61.

        Roth reviews and criticizes Willard Farnham's *Shake-
        speare's Tragic Frontier.* Of interest is Roth's remark
        that one limitation to Farnham's study is the linking
        of the Medieval ideas of capricious fortune to the
        Renaissance view of tragedy. Roth does not condemn
        Farnham's study but indicates that any discussion based
        upon such premises is not necessarily valid.

455.   Schwartz, Elias. "The Idea of a Person and Shake-
        spearean Tragedy." *SQ,* 16(1965), 39-47.

        Shakespeare's tragic characters should be understood
        in terms of scholastic concepts of Christian and Tho-

mistic philosophy rather than Aristotelian philosophy. The characters do not represent moral qualities as in Greek drama but reflect personality as derived from the Augustinian tradition.

* Spencer, Theodore. *Death and Elizabethan Tragedy*. See 306.

456. Spivak, Bernard *Shakespeare and the Allegory of Evil*. New York: Columbia U. Pr., 1958. 508 pp.

This important study links Iago to the morality tradition. Spivak has individual chapters on "The Family of Iago," "The Psychomachia," "The Morality Play," "The Emergence of the Vice," "The Change and Decline of the Morality Convention," "The Hybrid Play," "The Hybrid Image in Farce," "The Hybrid Image in Serious Drama," "The Hybrid Image in Shakespeare," and "Iago Revisited." The notes and bibliography are extensive. Spivak pays particular attention to Richard III, Aaron the Moor and Iago as hybrid types of the Vice. Iago, for example, is a mixture of two theater types: the Medieval Vice and the Renaissance atheist. His behavior is dictated by an archaic "allegorical motive lacking psychological explanation." *Oth.* is seen as a hybrid drama bound on one side by Medieval allegory and on the other by Renaissance realism.

457. VanDyke, Joyce. "The Decomposition of Tragic Character in Shakespeare." *DAI*, 41(1980), 1620A (Virginia).

Shakespeare's tragic action is similar to the complex personae on the morality stage. The author discusses "composite character" in Shakespeare's early plays and heroic character in early tragedy. Some contrast to morality drama is also shown. The work concentrates on *Mac., Lr.,* and *Cor.*

458. Wells, Henry W. "Senecan Influence on Elizabethan Tragedy: A Re-examination." *SAB*, 19(1944), 71-84.

Wells limits the Senecan influence upon Elizabethan tragedy by indicating that many of those qualities which are credited to Seneca can be found in the Medieval mystery and morality plays. "Bombast, fustion, violence and brutality are to be found throughout both mystery and morality plays." A thorough study of the morality tradition would reveal far more violence than what has been commonly accepted.

459. Withington, Robert. "Vice and Parasite: A Note on
      the Evolution of the Elizabethan villain." *PMLA*,
      49(1934), 743-751.

      "Buffoonery and rascality--two outstanding qualities
      of the morality play 'Vice'--led under differing in-
      fluences, to the Elizabethan clown and villain."
      Withington emphasizes both comic and tragic aspects
      in the Vice in Shakespearean drama, and he contends that
      Shakespeare's Vice is a blend of Medieval and classical
      concepts.

MEDIEVAL INFLUENCE UPON PARTICULAR PLAYS

All's Well That Ends Well

* Beck, Erwin, Jr. "Prodigal Son Comedy: the Continuity
  of a Paradigm in English Drama, 1500-1642." See 22.

460. Bradbrook, M. C. "Virtue is the True Nobility." *RES*,
     1(1950), 289-301.

     Bradbrook sees a number of Medieval ideas in *AWW* such
     as literature should promote good actions. In addition,
     the allegorical mode of thought was still prevalent in
     Shakespeare's day though Shakespeare did not use it as
     lavishly as did the Medieval writers. Helena's counter-
     part is the patient Griselda of earlier literature.
     The essay also comments upon the history of the ruling
     caste in the fifteenth century and suggests that Shake-
     speare is using the metaphor of the sick king in *AWW*.
     Another section traces the Medieval tradition of the
     three classes of nobility: Christian, natural, and
     civil. The author points out Dante's conception of
     nobility in his *Convivio* and shows that he denies
     civil nobility while emphasizing grace and virtue.
     Shakespeare's conception of true nobility comes from
     the Medieval tradition as seen in Dante.

* ———. *Shakespeare and Elizabethan Poetry*. See 43.

* Charlton, H. B. "The Dark Comedies." See 368.

* Cunningham, Dolora G. "The Doctrine of Repentance as a
  Formal Principle in Some Elizabethan Plays." See 89.

* Feldman, Sylvia D. *The Morality Patterned Comedy of
  the Renaissance*. See 370.

* Glazier, Phyllis Gorfain. "Folkloristic Devices and
  Formal Structure in Shakespearean Drama." See 135.

461. Godshalk, W. L. "*All's Well That Ends Well* and the
      Morality Play." *SQ*, 25(1974), 61-70.

      Shakespeare's *AWW* takes a "new approach to the moral-
      ity" which gives the form a new sophistication. Shake-
      speare's play is a type of anti-morality genre, a
      refutation of the morality ethic. *AWW* becomes "darkly
      humorous" and in a sense a comic morality play.

*   Gorfain, Phyllis. "Remarks Toward a Folkloristic
      Approach to Literature: Riddle in Shakespearean
      Drama." See 140.

462. Hunter, G. K. ed. *Arden Edition of All's Well That Ends
      Well*. London: Methuen, 1979. 152 pp.

      In the introduction Hunter comments upon Shakespeare's
      adaptation of Boccaccio's *Decameron*.

*   Hunter, Robert Grams. *Shakespeare and the Comedy of
      Forgiveness*. See 377.

463. Lawrence, W. W. "The Meaning of *All's Well That Ends
      Well*." *PMLA*, 37(1922), 418-469.

      The essay discusses the "clever wife theme" in Med-
      ieval literature and comments that *AWW* is associated
      with this convention. Lawrence explores various jigs,
      ballads, and tales of Boccaccio and Chaucer while
      establishing the case that Shakespeare was well acquaint-
      ed with the prose narratives of the Middle Ages.

464. Layman, B. J. "Shakespeare's Helena, Boccaccio's
      Giletta, and the *Riddles of Skill and Honesty*."
      EM, 23(1972), 39-53.

      Shakespeare was aware of Boccaccio's tale of Giletta
      of Nerbona in the *Decameron*. Shakespeare's Helena in
      AWW is a blend of virtue and virtuousity, an extension
      of Boccaccio's character of Giletta.

*   Siegel, Paul N. "Shakespeare and the Neo-Chivalric
      Cult of Honor." See 295.

465. Smallwood, R. L. "The Design of *All's Well That Ends
      Well*." *ShS*, 25(1972), 45-61.

      From his source in Boccaccio, Shakespeare invented
      new characters, modified the plot, greatly developed
      the hero and heroine, and nearly inverted the con-
      clusion.

*   Toole, William B. *Shakespeare's Problem Plays.* See
  329.

Antony and Cleopatra

466.   Barroll, J. Leeds. "Antony and Pleasure." *JEGP*,
  57(1958), 708-20.

  Shakespeare uses food as a metaphor for sexuality
  and associates Cleopatra with gluttony. Barroll refers
  to food and lechery in Chaucer, Langland, and Guillaume
  de DeGuileville and determines that lust and lechery
  followed gluttony in Medieval works. Frequent references
  are made to Lust, Lechery, Sloth, and Gluttony in the
  morality plays. Shakespeare fuses morality abstractions
  with real characters in his play.

467.   ————. "Enobarbus' Description of Cleopatra." *TSE*,
  37(1958), 61-78.

  Shakespeare borrows concepts from the morality plays.
  Cleopatra is a symbol of the Vice Voluptas, and her role
  is to bring about Antony's fall.

*   ————. "Shakespeare and Roman History." See 14.

468.   Bell, Arthur H. "Time and Convention in *Antony and
  Cleopatra.*" *SQ*, 24(1973), 253-64.

  Bell sees the movement of time as being identical
  with the movements of Fortuna. He also sees Antony
  in the early scenes of the play as a courtly lover.

*   Chew, Samuel. *The Pilgrimage of Life.* See 63.

*   Craig, Hardin. "Morality Plays and Elizabethan
  Drama." See 83.

*   Cunningham, Dolora G. "The Doctrine of Repentance as
  a Formal Principle in Some Elizabethan Plays." See 89.

469.   ————. "The Characterization of Shakespeare's
  Cleopatra." *SQ*, 6(1955), 9-17.

  Of interest are Cunningham's remarks that Cleopatra's
  efforts to die better than she lived are analogous to
  the familiar steps in the discipline of repentance inherited from the Middle Ages. Cunningham sees the play
  providing a traditional scheme of Christian ethics, one
  which has ties to the Medieval world.

470. Danby, John E. "The Shakespearean Dialectic."
      Scrutiny, 16(1949), 196–213.

      Danby believes that earlier criticism which linked
      Ant. with the Medieval change of Fortune and the down-
      fall of a sinner (*exemplum* idea) is unfortunately too
      simple a reading of the play. Likewise, the criticism
      which extols the lovers by indicating that they tran-
      scend time and death is too simplistic. The true read-
      ing of the drama takes into account the dialectical
      nature of Rome and Egypt, the destructive impulse of
      man, and the creative spirit.

*   Dessen, Alan. *Elizabethan Drama and the Viewer's Eye.*
      See 100.

*   Dickey, Franklin M. *Not Wisely But Too Well: Shake-
      speare's Love Tragedies.* See 437.

471. Donno, Elizabeth Story. "Cleopatra Again." *SQ,*
      7(1956), 227–33.

      Donno argues against Cunningham's thesis that
      Cleopatra dies in the discipline of repentance in-
      herited from the Middle Ages. Donno finds no basis
      for any Christian ethic in *Ant.*

472. Doran, Madeline. "High Events as These: The Language
      of Hyperbole in *Antony and Cleopatra.*" *QQ,* 72
      (1965), 26–51.

      Shakespeare is writing in the tradition of the
      nobility of true lovers. High statement and hyperbolic
      treatment are a part of Medieval love poetry.

473. Dronke, Peter. "Shakespeare and Joseph of Exeter."
      N&Q, 27(1980), 172–74.

      A twelfth century Trojan epic by Joseph of Exeter is
      perhaps a source for Enobarbus' description of Cleopatra.

474. Hamilton, D. B. "Antony and Cleopatra and the Tradition
      of Noble Lovers." *SQ,* 24(1973), 245–51.

      Chaucer's and Lydgate's characterization of Cleopatra
      is positive and Shakespeare used this tradition of
      noble lovers to communicate the "higher spiritual di-
      mensions of Antony and Cleopatra." Shakespeare was not
      locked into the debased tradition for his character
      portrayals.

*   Lord, John B. "Sources of the Technique of Comic Scenes
      in Shakespearean Tragedy." See 449.

475. Mack, Maynard. *"Antony and Cleopatra*: The Stillness
      and the Dance," pp. 79–114 in *Shakespeare's Art:
      Seven Essays.* ed. Milton Crane. Chicago: U. of
      Chicago Pr., 1973.

      Shakespeare's *Ant.* owes much to the Medieval tragic
      formula of the Fall of Princes, the mirror for magis-
      trates tradition, and the *De Casibus* tradition.

476. Macmullan, Katherine Vance. "Death Imagery in
      Antony and Cleopatra." SQ, 14(1963), 339–410.

      The death images associated with Antony and Cleopatra
      are in the *danse macabre* tradition. Also Macmullan finds
      dance of death concepts in *Jn., Rom.,* and *Oth.* The
      death concepts in Shakespeare's plays are related to
      surviving Medieval literary motifs.

477. Nosworthy, J. M. "Symbol and Character in *Antony and
      Cleopatra." ShN,* 6(1956), 4.

      Nosworthy interprets *Ant.* in allegorical terms which
      are associated with fire and sun images. Cleopatra is
      the Phoenix and from the ashes of her mortal love rose
      a love immortal.

*   Ribner, Irving. *Patterns of Shakespearean Tragedy.*
      See 452.

478. Rice, Julian C. "The Allegorical Dolabella." *CLAJ,*
      13(1970), 402–07.

      Shakespeare's characterization of Dolabella is such
      that he becomes the definition of his name--beautiful
      grief. Rice sees an influence from the morality plays
      where the names of characters described their essential
      quality.

479. Schanzer, Ernest. *"Antony and Cleopatra and The Legend
      of Good Women." N&Q,* 205(1960), 335–36.

      Shakespeare apparently learned of Cleopatra's
      marriage to Ptolemy from Chaucer. Passages from *MV*
      and *MND* are cited which indicate that Shakespeare
      was acquainted with Chaucer's story.

480. Thomas, Mary Olive. "Cleopatra and the 'Mortal
      Wretch.'" *SJW,* 150(1963), 174–83.

Thomas views Cleopatra's love as a mixture of
caritas and *concupiscentia* and believes that Shak-
speare treats love as did twelfth century mystics, as
a mixture of the holy and the profane. The asp is
a symbol of the "Classical Nourishing Earth, the
Medieval Lust, and the Renaissance Charity."

481. Williamson, Marilyn. "Antony and Cleopatra in the
      Late Middle Ages and Early Renaissance." *MichA*,
      5(1972), 145-51.

Contrary to popular belief, pre-Shakespearean writers
treated the Antony and Cleopatra story with great
diversity. Williamson discusses how Dante, Boccaccio,
Chaucer, Lydgate, and Gower treated the love story.

As You Like It

482. Addis, John. "Fortune: Chaucer and Shakespeare."
      N&Q, 9(1872), 339.

Shakespeare's domestic use of Fortune in *AYL* (I, ii,
28) and in *Ant.* (IV, xv, 44) where he speaks of Fortune
as a housewife may have come from Chaucer's *Book of the
Duchess*. Chaucer speaks of Fortune as turning her false
wheel "Now by fire, now at table." (Morris, I, 645).

483. Barber, C. L. "The Use of Comedy in *As You Like It.*"
      PQ, 21(1942), 353-67.

"Shakespeare's affinities in comedy are Medieval
rather than modern." Barber compares Shakespeare's
comic method to Medieval fool humor in that Shakespeare
evokes the ideal in life and then makes fun of it because it does not square with life as it ordinarily is.
Likewise Medieval fool humor depicts what is not ideal
in man despite the apparent official perfection of the
long-robed dignitaries. Barber agrees with Coghill
that Shakespearean comedy is not a diversion from
serious themes but an alternative mode of developing
them.

484. Bennet, J. W. "Jaques 'Seven Ages.'" *SAB*, 18(1943),
      168-74.

Bennett rejects the idea that Shakespeare was drawing
upon a passage in Bartholomaeus Angilicus for Jaques'
speech and shows parallels between Shakespeare's description of the ages and a second century work by
Pollus entitled *Onomasticon*.

485. Bowers, R. H. "A Medieval Analogue to *As You Like It*,
      II. vii. 137-166." *SQ*, 3(1952), 109-12.

      An unpublished Medieval poem "Of the Seven Ages" is
      an analogue to Jaques' "All the world's a stage" speech.
      The Medieval poem contains sixty lines in rhyming coup-
      lets and is a dispute between a good angel, the Devil,
      and a character representing Everyman.

*   Charlton, H. B. *Shakespearean Comedy*. See 367.

486. Chew, S. C. "This Strange Eventful History," pp. 157-
      82 in *Adams Memorial Studies*. ed. James McManaway.
      Washington: The Folger Shakespeare Library, 1948.

      Chew examines Jaques' speech on the ages of man in
      regard to numerous Medieval ideas. The ages of man are
      linked with the pilgrimage of life and can be found in
      The Castle of Perseverance and other morality plays.
      The essay points out a connection between the Wheel of
      Fortune and Jaques' speech since both depict ideas of
      rising and falling. In addition, Chew discusses the
      various designs on woodcuts and stained glass in the
      Middle Ages which frequently portrayed the ages of man.
      By using the ages of man concept, Shakespeare was follow-
      ing an established tradition.

487. Cohen, Herman. "The Seven Ages of Man." *TLS*, 30
      January 1930, p. 78.

      Jaques's speech on the seven ages of man is traced to
      Geoffrey of Lynn's *Promptorium Paryorum*, a work written
      about 1440 and translated into English in 1586.

*   Costello, William T. *The Scholastic Curriculum at
      Early Seventeenth-Century Cambridge*. See 79.

*   Cox, Ernest H. "Shakespeare and Some Conventions of
      Old Age." See 82.

488. Dale, Judith. "*As You Like It* and Some Medieval
      Themes." *Words*, 2(1966), 54-65.

      In discussing the *locus amoenus* concept in classical
      and Medieval literature (*Roman de la Rose* and *The Book
      of the Duchess*), Dale points out that Shakespeare bor-
      rowed the conventional nature topoi of Medieval liter-
      ary accounts for his Forest of Arden. Also she suggests
      that *AYL* contains the debate between Fortune and Nature
      and the *amour courtois* convention.

*   Doebler, John. *Shakespeare's Speaking Pictures.*
        See 103.

489.   Draper, John W. "Jaques' 'Seven Ages' and Bartholomeaus
        Anglicus." *MLN*, 54(1939), 273-76.

        The essay reviews various analogues to Jacques'
        "Seven Ages" and argues that Shakespeare's concept of
        the ages of man comes from the Medieval writer Barthol-
        omaeus Anglicus de Glanvilla. His works were translated
        by Stephen Batman in 1582 and thus were readily acess-
        ible to Shakespeare.

490.   Draper, R. P. "Shakespeare's Pastoral Comedy." *EA*,
        11(1958), 1-17.

        Much of this study is an attempt to define the term
        pastoral comedy, but Draper makes scattered references
        to the Medieval influence upon this genre. Both Phebe
        and Silvius in *AYL* have a distinct quality reminiscent
        of the allegorical figures in a morality play. They
        are a part of a convention of literary types associated
        with Youth and Age. Touchstone and Audrey are a comic
        dramatization of the *pastourelle*. Much of the tension
        of the play is built around the mock-chivalric world of
        Touchstone and the chivalric world of Duke Senior.

*   Erskine, John. *The Elizabethan Lyric.* See 113.

491.   Frankis, P. J. "The Testament of the Deer in Shake-
        speare." *NM*, 59(1958), 65-68.

        The description of the dying deer in *AYL* (II, i, 33-
        49) is a distinct borrowing from Medieval writings. The
        theme is present in late Medieval English lyrics such as
        MS Rowlinson C. 813 found in the Bodelian library.
        Frankis does not argue that Shakespeare read this
        particular poem, but the convention may have reached
        him through Medieval romances or folk-beliefs.

492.   Gilbert, Allan H. "Jaques' 'Seven Ages' and Censorinus."
        MLN, 60(1940), 103-05.

        Gilbert essentially agrees with Draper's comment that
        Shakespeare's source for the "seven ages of man" is
        Bartholomaeus, but he also suggests that Shakespeare
        may have been acquainted with Censorinus' *De die
        natali liber*.

493.   Hankins, John E. *Shakespeare's Derived Imagery.*
        Lawrence: U. of Kansas Pr., 1953. 281 pp.

Hankins attempts to find sources for a number of
Shakespeare's images. Chapter Two deals with the
probable sources for Jaques' speech on the "Seven
Ages of Man." The book cites Bartholomew and Vincent
de Beauvais as possible Medieval influences.

494. MacQueen, John. *"As You Like It* and Medieval Literary
Tradition." *FMLS,* 1(1965), 216-229.

The antithesis of Nature and Fortune is the rhetorical
basis upon which Shakespeare developed his play, and this
formula is also the basis of some of the best Medieval
poetry. By using the forest of Arden, Shakespeare used
the European "mixed forest" found in Chaucer's *The Book
of the Duchess.* Arden represents Nature, the sole
refuge for the victims of an unjust Fortune. Rosalind
and Orlando are Nature's children, but they are opposed
by Fortune who causes disharmony. At the end of the
play, Nature and Fortune are reconciled, with Fortune
assuming a subordinate position. The theophany, the
appearance of Hymen at the end of the play, is also a
part of the Medieval conception of Nature. Some similarities are shown between Shakespeare's play and *The
Book of the Duchess, Parliament of Foules,* "The Wife
of Bath's Prologue," "The Knight's Tale," *Troilus and
Criseyde,* and "The Monk's Tale." Other Medieval works
mentioned are *The Testament of Cressid* and *The Romance
of the Rose.*

495. Peacock, Edward. "Fortune: Chaucer and Shakespeare."
N&Q, 9(1872), 339.

Shakespeare's association of the Wheel of Fortune with
a spinning wheel and housewife (*AYL,* I, ii, 28) may
well be taken from Chaucer's description of Fortune in
The Book of the Duchess.

* Pettet, E. C. *Shakespeare and the Romance Tradition.*
See 381.

496. Quiller-Couch, Sir Arthur. *Shakespeare's Workmanship.*
London: T. Fisher Unwin, Ltd., 1918. 368 pp.

This book touches upon sources and thematic aspects
of many Shakespearean plays and refers to the *Tale of
Gamelyn* as having influenced *AYL.* The name of the
faithful retainer Adam comes from *The Canterbury Tales.*

* Russell, William M. "Courtly Love in Shakespeare's
Romantic Comedies." See 384.

497.   Seronsy, C. "The Seven Ages of Man Again." *SQ*,
        4(1953), 364-65.

        The essay attempts to explain the origin of Jaques'
        speech by pointing to the Medieval song *Humanae Miseriae
        discursus* found in Thomas Lodge's *A Margarite*. The
        song contains the various states of man: infancy, youth,
        sorrow attending great wealth, vain pursuit of learning,
        and hazardous character of all trades and professions.

498.   Shaw, J. "Fortune and Nature in *As You Like It*." *SQ*,
        6(1955), 45-50.

        Shaw's emphasis is upon Fortune as a blind goddess
        who is depicted as turning the wheel, while Fortune's
        rival, Nature, is represented with the gifts of the body
        and mind, notably beauty, strength, nobility, and
        courage. Shaw believes that a close examination of
        the play will reveal that all the characters can be
        defined in terms of the conflict between Fortune and
        Nature.

*   Stevenson, David L. *The Love-Game Comedy*. See 312.

499.   Thaler, A. "Shakespeare, Daniel, and *Everyman*." *PQ*,
        15(1936), 217-18.

        The Duke's speech in Arden (*AYL*, II, i, 12-14) may
        have been influenced by the Medieval morality *Everyman*
        (556-58).

500.   ———. "Shakespeare and *Everyman*." *TLS*, 18 July
        1936. p. 600.

        See note above.

501.   Thorndike, A. H. "The Relation of *As You Like It* to
        the Robin Hood Plays." *JEGP*, 4(1901), 59-69.

        In addition to Lodge's *Rosalynde*, Shakespeare has
        consciously added elements from the Robin Hood plays
        to *AYL*. The open-air atmosphere found in scenes II, i,
        and IV, ii has no counterparts in *Rosalynde*. These
        scenes are remarkably similar to situations in the
        Robin Hood plays which originated the last part of
        the fifteenth century. The spirit of repentance and
        forgiveness which pervades *AYL* is similar to thematic
        counterparts in the Robin Hood plays. Furthermore,
        the mixture of songs, hunting, feasting, and rejoicing
        over deer owe an obvious debt to late Medieval plays.

502. Tolman, Albert H. "Shakespeare's Manipulation of His
     Sources in *As You Like It.*" *MLN,* 37(1922), 65-76.

     The essay compares Lodge's *Rosalynde* to *AYL* and
     further comments briefly upon Shakespeare's borrowing
     from the Robin Hood ballads. Shakespeare catches the
     woodland atmosphere that is present in the ballads.
     Tolman's remarks are addressed primarily to Act II,
     scene v, especially the song "Under the greenwood
     tree."

The Comedy of Errors

503. Brooks, Harold. "Themes and Structure in *The Comedy of
     Errors,*" pp. 55-71 in *Early Shakespeare.* ed. John
     Russel Brown. London: Edward Arnold Pub., 1967.

     Medieval writings influenced Shakespeare in numerous
     ways. The comic servants are descendants of the Vice
     and the characters in the miracle cycles. Shakespeare's
     habit of balancing groups of people is a characteristic
     of the moralities and the Tudor interludes. In addition,
     the Medieval romance with its emphasis upon adventure,
     marvel, enchantment, and the sentiment of love served
     as the background to many Shakespearean comedies. The
     theme of marital debate found throughout the comedies
     also has many parallels in Medieval writings.

504. Charlton, H. B. "Shakespeare's Recoil from Romanticism."
     BJRL, 15(1931), 35-59.

     Shakespeare's "recoil" from romance was due to the
     difficulties which he faced in attempting to harmonize
     drama and romance and the blending of classical and
     Medieval ideas. In *Err.* he was unable to break away
     from Medieval concepts of chivalry, pity for the un-
     fortunate, and surviving concepts of the Medieval romance.

505. Clubb, Louise G. "Italian Comedy and *The Comedy of
     Errors.*" *CL,* 19(1967), 240-51.

     Err. resembles aspects of Italian comedy, particularly
     commedia gravi. One of the important themes in this
     type of comedy is the blending of Medieval ideas of
     fortune and providence to form a type of comedy which
     may be described as a metaphor of life. Clubb refers
     to the plays of Oddi, Borghini, and Castelletti in
     relation to fortune and providence and shows similar
     ideas in Shakespeare's plays.

*   Coghill, Nevill. "The Basis of Shakespearean Comedy:
        A Study in Medieval Affinities." See 369.

506.   Reddington, John P. "On the Compositional Genetics of
        The Comedy of Errors." *SQ*, 19(1968), 88-89.

        The essay argues that Baldwin overstates the case for
        Shakespeare's knowledge of Biblical and patristic
        literature.

*   Pettet, E. C. *Shakespeare and the Romance Tradition*.
        See 381.

Coriolanus

*   Dessen, Alan. "The Logic of Elizabethan State Violence:
        Some Alarms and Excursions for Modern Critics, Editors,
        and Directors." See 102.

507.   Elton, William. "Two Shakespearean Parallels." *SAB*,
        22(1947), 115-16.

        Elton cites that Menenius' fable of the belly and the
        members (*Cor*. I, i, 95-159) has a possible Medieval
        parallel in the morality *Le Ventre, Les Jambes, Le
        Coeur, et Le Chef*.

*   Knights, L. C. *Shakespeare's Politics: Some Reflections
        on the Nature of Tradition*. See 197.

*   ————. *Further Explorations*. See 198.

508.   Maxwell, J. C. "Animal Imagery in *Coriolanus*." *MLR*,
        42(1947), 417-21.

        Maxwell finds eighty-five animal references in *Cor*.
        and comments that Shakespeare related animals to the
        traditional hierarchy and correspondences in the realm
        of nature, a theory inherited from the Middle Ages.
        Maxwell also illustrates that animal imagery in Shake-
        speare is associated with the beast fables.

509.   Ribner, Irving. "The Tragedy of *Coriolanus*." *ES*,
        34(1953), 1-9.

        Ribner points out that a number of the tragedies are
        influenced by the morality play tradition. Coriolanus'
        fault is excessive pride, the most terrible of the
        Medieval Seven Deadly Sins. Unlike *Oth*. and *Lr*., *Cor*.
        is a story of a great hero whose impulses are towards

the good; but because he has been corrupted by pride,
Coriolanus does not achieve repentance or salvation.

* Siegel, Paul N. "Shakespeare and the Neo-Chivalric
  Cult of Honor." See 295.

* VanDyke, Joyce. "The Decomposition of Tragic
  Character in Shakespeare." See 457.

Cymbeline

* Bryant, J. A. *Hippolyta's View: Some Christian
  Aspects of Shakespeare's Plays.* See 50.

510. Colley, John Scott. "Disguise and New Guise in
  Cymbeline." *ShakS*, 7(1974), 233-52.

  Colley discusses the use of costuming in early English
  drama and suggests that Shakespeare's use of costuming
  in *Cym.* is for emblematic purposes. Posthumus' character, for example, is like a "puppet in a strange mor-
  ality-romance puppet show." The roles of Imogen and
  Cloten are similarly analyzed.

* Dessen, Alan. *Elizabethan Drama and the Viewer's Eye.*
  See 100.

* ———. "The Logic of Elizabethan Stage Violence:
  Some Alarms and Excursions for Modern Critics,
  Editors, and Directors." See 102.

* Erskine, John. *The Elizabethan Lyric.* See 113.

* Gorgain, Phyllis. "Remarks Toward a Folkloristic
  Approach to Literature: Riddles in Shakespearean
  Drama." See 140.

* Hengerer, Joyce H. "The Theme of the Slandered Woman
  in Shakespeare." See 162.

* Hunter, Robert Grams. *Shakespeare and the Comedy of
  Forgiveness.* See 377.

511. Kelly, Andrew James, S.J. "*Cymbeline* Unravelled: A
  Study of Shakespeare's Allegory of Redemption." *DAI*,
  37(1976), 2861A (Princeton).

  Shakespeare's *Cym.* is read allegorically. The three

narratives in the play dramatize the "fall and redemption of an Everyman Figure." The relation between
the three plots reflects the "archetypal pattern of
human sin."

*   Kolin, Philip C. "The Elizabethan Stage Doctor as a
       Dramatic Convention." See 199.

512.   Lawrence, William Witherle. "The Wager in *Cymbeline*."
       PMLA, 35(1920), 391-431.

       Lawrence examines the main plot in *Cym.* in the light
       of various Medieval and Elizabethan conventions. The
       source of the Imogen-Posthumus-Iachimo plot is similar
       to Boccaccio's ninth novella of the second day in his
       Decameron. Also the author reviews literature of the
       Middle Ages which involves a wife's constancy in re-
       lationship to severe tests. In addition, there are
       comments upon the Medieval convention of "a virtue
       exaggerated is a virtue magnified." The romantic obser-
       vances and conventions stem from Medieval concepts of
       chivalry.

513.   Munro, John. "Some Shakespearean Matters." *TLS*, 27
       September 1947. p. 500.

       Munro objects to the theory that the story of Belarius
       in *Cym.* is Shakespeare's own creation and points out
       that the Belarius story is related to romance characters.
       He cites Guillaume de la Baire in the early provencal
       verse romance by that name, and he also sees some re-
       lationship to a character in the *Decameron* (II, viii,
       1348-53).

514.   Nosworthy, J. "The Sources of the Wager Plot in
       Cymbeline." *N&Q*, 192(1952), 93-96.

       Shakespeare was indebted to Boccaccio's ninth novel
       of the second day in the *Decameron*. Nosworthy argues
       that a debased tale of this story called *Frederyke of
       Jennen* may be the source of the wager plot in *Cym.*

515.   Rogers, H. L. "The Prophetic Label in *Cymbeline*."
       RES, 11(1935), 296-99.

       The passage in *Cym.* (V, iv, 138) which states that
       the miseries of Britain shall end when severed branches
       grow again on a tree was derived from Medieval accounts
       of a famous death-bed vision of St. Edward the Confessor
       who died in 1066. The account of this confession is

found in William Caxton's *The Golden Legend* and in
Holinshed. Rogers believes that Shakespeare's source
for the passage quoted above may well have been
Holinshed, and he compares the passage in Holinshed
with that of Shakespeare.

*   Stokes, James David. "Roots of the English History
      Play." See 408.

516.   Thrall, William Flint. "*Cymbeline*, Boccaccio, and
      the Wager Story in England." *SP*, 28(1930), 639-51.

Thrall advances the proposition that the *Decameron*
may not be Shakespeare's source for the wager plot in
Cym. A version of the wager story appeared in Germany
in the fifteenth century called *Four Merchants* which
was later translated into English in 1518 and entitled
Frederick of Jennen. Thrall points out similarities
between this translation and Shakespeare's play, and
he argues that the position held by Sir Edmund Chambers,
J. Q. Adams, and Tucker Brooke is wrong.

517.   Wright, Herbert G. "How did Shakespeare Come to Know
      the *Decameron?*" MLR, 50(1955), 45-48.

Shakespeare read the French translation of the
Decameron by Antoine le Macon and used the work as
source material for *AWW* and *Cym*. The wager-theme in
Cym. is particularly indebted to the *Decameron*. Wright
shows that Shakespeare had some knowledge of French by
referring to some half dozen plays where French words
occur.

Hamlet

518.   Baker, J. E. "The Philosophy of Hamlet," pp. 455-70
      in *Parrot Presentation Volume*. ed. Hardin Craig.
      New York: Russell and Russell, 1935.

Hamlet's philosophy is of the Medieval Catholic
realist tradition which had inherited the concept of
Platonic dualism. Hamlet's contempt for the world
and his emphasis upon the impermanence of the physical
echo Medieval Christian sentiment.

519.   Baldwin, Peter, Brother, F.S.C. "*Hamlet* and *In*
      Paradisium." *SQ*, 3(1952), 279-80.

Baldwin observes that the antiphon, *In Paradisium*,
is sung by the choir as the body is carried out of the

church. This antiphon belonged to church ritual during the Middle Ages, and perhaps Shakespeare may have had this hymn in mind when Horatio eulogizes the departed Hamlet.

520.   ————. *"Hamlet* and *In Paradisium."* *SQ*, 3(1952), 208.

Horatio's line "and flights of angels sing thee to thy rest" is a Medieval commonplace. Baldwin refers to similar phrases in the *Divine Comedy* and *Everyman*.

521.   Battenhouse, Roy W. "Hamlet's Apostrophe on Man." *PMLA*, 66(1951), 1073–1113.

The Hamlet problem is examined in light of Renaissance philosophy and Medieval theological teachings. Hamlet's philosophy is not related to Thomism as Tillyard and Semper propose but to the Medieval blending of Platonic and Stoic ideas.

*   Beck, Margaret M. "The Dance of Death in Shakespeare." See 23.

522.   Belsey, Catherine. "The Case of Hamlet's Conscience." *SP*, 76(1979), 127–48.

Belsey explores the revenge theme in *Ham.* from two viewpoints: the morality tradition and the protestant science of causistry. She discusses Wrath as the Vice and refers to *The Castle of Perseverance* and *The World and the Child*. *Ham.* is read as "ultimately ambiguous."

523.   Item deleted.

524.   Budd, F. E. "Shakespeare, Chaucer, and Harsnett." *RES*, 11(1935), 421–29.

Shakespeare's allusions to Nero as a fisherman and as a murderer of his mother can be traced only to Chaucer. Budd dismisses the classical writers as well as Lydgate, Higden, and Boccaccio as possible writers of source material for Shakespeare's allusions to Nero. Passages in *Ham.* (III, ii, 407–10) and *Jn.* (V, ii, 152–53) are remarkably similar to the "Monk's Tale" (3665–3676). Also the Host's words to the Monk concerning a troublesome wife resemble some of Goneril's remarks to Albany (*Lr.* IV, ii, 12–18).

*   Campbell, Lily B. "Theories of Revenge in Renaissance England." See 57.

*   Chew, Samuel. *The Pilgrimage of Life.* See 63.

*   Conley, C. H. "An Instance of the Fifteen Signs of Judgment in Shakespeare." See 75.

*   Costello, William T. *The Scholastic Curriculum at Early Seventeenth-Century Cambridge.* See 79.

*   Coursen, Herbert R., Jr. *Christian Ritual and the World of Shakespeare's Tragedies.* See 432.

525. Cox, Ernest H. "Another Medieval Convention in Shakespeare." *SAB*, 16(1941), 249-53.

      Cox illustrates that the popular Medieval *ubi sunt* theme is used by Hamlet in the graveyard scene. Also, Hamlet's listing of long-gone heroes such as Caesar and Alexander is another familiar Medieval habit which continued in the Renaissance.

*   Cunningham, J. V. *Woe and Wonder.* See 436.

*   Fairchild, Arthur H. R. "Shakespeare and the Arts of Design." See 114.

*   ———. "Shakespeare and the Tragic Theme." See 438.

526. Falk, Doris V. "Proverbs and the Polonius Destiny." *SQ*, 18(1967), 23-36.

      Polonius' advice to Laertes, the "wise father" tradition extends back to the old English "Faeder larcwidas" and also is found in the thirteenth-century Albertanus of Brescia's advice to his three sons. Some of the same tradition can be seen in Peter Idley's *Instructions*. The convention is also seen in Cato's book *Dido M. Catonis ad filium Suun*. Falk determines that such advice was insincere and represented hackney conventions.

527. Felperin, Howard. "O'erdoing Termagant: An Approach to Shakespearean Mimesis." *YR*, 1974, 372-91.

      In Hamlet's speech (III, ii, 7-25) the Medieval idea of drama as timeless moral play survives in the speech.

At the very center of *Ham.*, one finds a primitive Elizabethan revenge tragedy. It has morality affiliations--
dumb show, emblematic settings, generalizing rhetoric,
virtue-figures, and a highly theatrical Vice.

528.   Guifolyle, Cherrell. "'Ower Swere Sokor': The Role
        of Ophelia in *Hamlet.*" *CompD*, 14(1980), 3-17.

The author finds parallels between Ophelia and Mary
Magdalene. Ophelia's name links her with succor, and
Shakespeare portrays her as a suffering, sacrificial
figure--similar in some aspects to the purer half of
Magdalene. Magdalene legends are similar in detail
to Ophelia's mad scene. Guifolyle refers frequently
to the Digby *Mary Magdalene.*

529.   Hankins, John E. "Hamlet's 'God Kissing Carrion': A
        Theory of the Generation of Life." *PMLA*, 54(1940),
        507-16.

Hankins traces both classical and Medieval writers who
refer to the sun's ability to generate life. Thomas
Aquinas, Duns Scotus, Vincent de Beauvais write about
the ability of the sun to promote human generation.
Thus when Hamlet tells Polonius not to let his daughter
walk in the sun, there is some rationale behind the
saying if we call to mind the Medieval and classical
sources.

530.   Hibbard, G. R. "Critical Studies." *ShS*, 33(1970),
        137-159.

Of interest is Hibbard's review of Medieval influences
upon Shakespeare. The study of *Ham.* and its Medieval
heritage is one of the "most impressive essays in
Wickham's *Shakespeare's Dramatic Heritage.* But Hibbard
notes that Wickham's essay on *Mac.* and the Medieval
world is driven "rather hard."

531.   Hockey, Dorthy C. "Wormwood, Wormwood!" *ELN*, 2(1965),
        174-77.

Hamlet's words of grief take on fuller meaning if
they are associated with concepts related to herbals
as found in the Middle Ages. Certain herbs would com-
fort the heart and cure despair and disillusion.
This is an interesting study relating certain folk
rituals to Shakespeare.

532. Howard, D. R. *"Hamlet* and the Contempt of the World."
     SAQ, 58(1959), 167-75.

   Howard examines the themes of the *de contemptu mundi*
   tradition--"the transiency of life, the corruption of
   nature, the evils of society, and the peril of the
   afterlife"--and relates these elements to *Ham*. In
   addition, detailed background information on this theme
   is shown in the literature of the Middle Ages.

*   Lanier, Sidney. *Shakespeare and His Forerunners*.
     See 207.

*   Lord, John B. "Sources of the Technique of Comic
     Scenes in Shakespearean Tragedy." See 449.

533. Lawrence, W. J. "The Ghost in *Hamlet*." *NC*, 95(1924),
     370-77.

   The ghost in *Ham*. does not have its roots in classical
   conceptions of ghosts but rather in the plays of Medieval times. Lawrence stresses the objectivity of the
   ghost and deprecates those who view the ghost as sub-
   jective. Shakespeare's treatment of the ghost is in
   accord with popular, native English drama.

534. Milward, Peter J. "The Homiletic Tradition in Shake-
     speare's Plays." *ShStud*, 5(1966-67), 72-87.

   Milward deals mainly with the homiletic tradition
   in the sixteenth century, particularly as it applies
   to *Ham*. He has a general discussion on Shakespeare's
   debt to Medieval homilies.

535. Montgomery, Marshall. "Lydgate's *Fall of Princes* and
     Hamlet." *TLS*, 16 October, 1924. p. 651.

   Shakespeare borrowed the Gonzago story "writ in very
   choice Italian" from Lydgate's version of *De Casibus*.

536. Montgomerie, William. "Folk-Play and Ritual in *Hamlet*."
     Folklore, 67(1956), 214-27.

   A number of events in *Ham*. are associated with native
   folk play and traditional ritual. The comments concern
   the play within the play, and Montgomerie demonstrates
   that the mummers play, morris songs, and Robin Hood
   plays are a part of the background of *Ham*.

537. O'Brien, Gordon W. *"Hamlet* IV, v, 156-57." *SQ*,
     10(1959), 249-51.

Laertes' speech of grief over Ophelia's mad condition
is examined in light of Medieval and Renaissance treatises
explaining humors. For the most part the essay refers
to Stephen Batman's translation of Bartholomaeus
Anglicus' *De Proprietatibus Rerum* while explaining
Laertes' speech.

*   Page, Susan Carolyn Ulichney. "The Emergence of the
      Humanist Tragic Hero: A Study in the Dramatization
      of the Psychomachia in the Morality Plays and in
      Selected Plays of Shakespeare." See 255.

538. Pitts, Rebecca, E. "This Fell Sergeant, Death."
      SQ, 20(1969), 486-91.

      Hamlet's dying words on death (V. ii. 343-51) should
      be understood in light of Medieval Christian tradition.
      Pitts shows parallels between Hamlet's words and the
      Medieval treatise, *The Lamentation of the Dying Creature.*

*   Potter, Robert. *The English Morality Play.* See 265.

539. Quinlan, Maurice J. "Shakespeare and the Catholic
      Burial Services." *SQ*, 5(1954), 303-06.

      Quinlan builds upon Peter Baldwin's essay "Hamlet
      and *In Paradisium*" which suggests that Shakespeare was
      well acquainted with a familiar Medieval hymn. Quinlan
      believes that Hamlet saw something amiss in the pageantry
      of the burial service.

540. Robbins, William. *"Hamlet* as Allegory." *UTQ*, 21
      (1952), 217-23.

      Robbins suggests that one way of viewing *Ham.* is
      as an allegory of human nature and human existence.
      He explores the possibility of balancing the Ghost,
      Hamlet, and the King with the Queen, Ophelia and
      Horatio. The former represent obsession, uncompromising
      idealism, while the latter can be viewed as hedonism,
      dutiful simplicity, and balanced and passion-free
      judgment. The essay does not argue for any specific
      Medieval influence but indicates that *Ham.* is in the
      tradition of allegorical writings.

541. Robertson, D. W., Jr. "A Medievalist Looks at *Hamlet,*"
      pp. 312-31 in *Essays in Medieval Culture* by D.W.
      Robertson, Jr., Princeton: Princeton U. Pr., 1980.

This study gives a fresh approach to the reading of *Ham.* in that Robertson does not see Hamlet as admirable. The reading associates the character of Hamlet with Sloth, Malice, Envy and a host of other Medieval vices. All in all Hamlet is dethroned and a thoroughly despicable character.

542. Santayana, G. *Essays in Literary Criticism.* New York: Charles Scribner's Sons, 1956. 414 pp.

In the section on *Ham.* (120-136), Santayana remarks that the disconcerting mixture of comic and ignoble elements in many of the passages in *Ham.* are a survival of remnants of a traditional force which was inherited from the Middle Ages. Piety and obscenity and rant and simplicity could be jumbled together without offense. Hamlet's remarks on the ghost, calling him a mole, a truepenny, is a case in point.

543. Semper, I. J. "'Yes, by St. Patrick.'" *TLS*, 3 August 1946. p. 367.

The probable source for Hamlet's invocation is the *Golden Legend*, a work translated by Caxton in 1483 and appearing in Shakespeare's day in numerous versions.

544. ————. "On the Dignity of Man." *Month*, 199(1955), 292-301.

Hamlet's lines on the dignity of man show that Shakespeare was consciously using Medieval Thomistic philosophy.

* Spencer, Theodore. *Death and Elizabethan Tragedy.* See 306.

545. Thaler, Alwin. "'In my Mind's Eye, Horatio.'" *SQ*, 7(1956), 351-54.

Shakespeare may have borrowed the phrase "In my mind's eye" from Chaucer's "Man of Law's Tale."

546. Thomas, Sidney. *The Antic Hamlet and Richard III.* New York: King's Crown Pr., 1943. 92 pp.

Richard III and Hamlet are dissemblers and descendants of the Vice tradition. Richard is a combination of Vice Dissimulation and the villain of melodrama, while Hamlet is a transformation of the Vice. Thomas shows parallels between the language of the Vice (love of puns)

and Hamlet and the brutality and savagery of language
that each uses. Chapter Four discusses the general
classical and Medieval ideas which influenced Shakespeare with Thomas noting that the Medieval influence
has been scarcely realized.

547. Thompson, R. Ann. "'Our revels now are ended': An
      Allusion to 'The Franklin's Tale'?" *Archiv*.
      121(1975), 317.

      Shakespeare's words echo Chaucer's "and fare our
      revel all was ago" found in "The Franklin's Tale."

*   Toole, William B. *Shakespeare's Problem Plays*. See
      329.

548. Tracy, Robert. "The Owl and the Baker's Daughter:
      A Note on *Hamlet*, IV. v. 42-43." *SQ*, 17(1966),
      83-86.

      The author traces the use of owl imagery in Medieval
      and classical works to determine that it is a symbol
      of false chastity. The Baker's daughter is associated
      with harlotry. The enigmatic image blends with the
      larger aspects of the play in that it deals with
      perception and reality.

                            I Henry IV

549. Auden, W. H. "The Fallen City: Some Reflections on
      Shakespeare's *Henry IV*." *Encounter*, 13(1959), 21-31.

      Falstaff is a symbol of the Lord of Misrule, the
      worldly person, and the Devil. Hal's alliance with
      Falstaff must be rejected just as Everyman must turn
      from the world and the Devil. Shakespearean drama is
      patterned after the morality play structure.

550. Berkeley, David and Edison, Donald. "The Theme of
      Henry IV, Part 1." *SQ*, 19(1969), 25-31.

      The commonly accepted manner of interpreting *1H4* as
      the education of a prince and the tripartite clarifica-
      tion of the idea of honor is wholly inadequate. The
      main theme of the play is the "politic concealment
      and exhibition of seminally transmitted virtue."
      Medieval legend and philosophical concepts emphasized
      a hierarchial structure in society and place great
      emphasis upon a hereditarily determined station for
      an individual. A series of events would clarify or

assess the individual's hereditary worth. The essay discusses *Havelok* and several tales of Malory's *Morte d'Arthur* and shows that Shakespeare's treatment of of blood ties and awareness of family continuity are treated similarly.

*   Campbell, Josie P. "Farce as Function in Medieval and Shakespearean Drama." See 56.

551. Cochran, Carol M. "Flyting in Pre-Elizabethan Drama in Shakespeare, and in Jonson." *DAI*, 35(1974), 1616A (New Mexico).

Dramatic flyting involves a battle of wits in which contestants try to excel each other in imaginative abuse. Cochran examines "representative plays" from the Medieval mysteries to *Gammer Gurton's Nedle* in an attempt to find out what flyting is doing in drama. She shows Shakespeare's use of this tradition in *1H4* and *Ado*.

*   Curtin, Madelyn Elaine Douglas. "Mistaking the Word and Simple Syllogisms: Form and Function in Shakespeare's Wordplay." See 91.

552. Dessen, Alan C. "The Intemperate Knight and the Politic Prince: Late Morality Structure in *1 Henry V*." *ShakS*, 7(1974), 147-71.

Shakespeare employed a dramatic mode inherited from the morality tradition. The characters, issues, and relationships are structured according to patterns that are didactic and allegorical. Some parallels in structure and theme between *1H4* and *Trial of Treasure* and *Enough* are discussed.

*   ————. "The Logic of Elizabethan Stage Violence: Some Alarms and Excurxions for Modern Critics, Editors, and Directors." See 102.

553. Holland, Norman N. *The Shakespearean Imagination*. New York: Macmillan Co., 1964. 338 pp.

In Chapter Seven Holland shows the morality influence in *1H4*. Prince Hal is the Christian hero who must overcome Vice (Falstaff) and the devils (Douglas, Percy, and Glendower). Falstaff is a descendant of the Vice and follows several traditions associated with him. The Vice carries the body of a condemned soul back

to Hell. Likewise, Falstaff packs Hotspur off the
stage. The Vice also carried a false dagger which
he used to clown around on the stage. Likewise,
Falstaff threatens Hal with a dagger in jest. In
addition, we learn that Falstaff has sold his soul
to the devil on "Good Friday last for a cup of Maderia
and a cold capon's leg."

554. Levin, Lawrence L. "Hotspur, Falstaff, and the Emblem
      of Wrath in *1 Henry IV*." *ShakS*, 10(1977), 43-65.

      Levin reads the play in terms of the homiletic,
      dramatic, and literary tradition of the Psychomachia
      and finds striking parallels between Falstaff and
      Hotspur. In Act II Falstaff "represents an ironic,
      comic personification of the sin of wrath whose tragic
      incarnation is manifested in Hotspur."

*   Matte, Nancy Lightfoot. "The Ars-Moriendi in Selected
      Shakespearean History Plays." See 401.

555. Oliver, Leslie Mahin. "Sir John Oldcastle: Legend or
      Literature?" *Library*, 5th Series, 1(1947), 179-83.

      Oliver takes issue with Wilson that Falstaff had
      become a heretic and was transmuted in the popular
      mind into the body highwayman. Falstaff's creation is
      due to Shakespeare's imagination which was grounded
      in the chronicles such as Fabyan's, Walsingham's,
      Foxe's or possibly Bole's.

*   Potter, Robert. *The English Morality Play*. See 265.

*   Reese, M. J. *Shakespeare: His World and His Work*.
      See 270.

556. Shaw, John. "The Staging of Parody and Parallels in
      Henry IV." *ShS*, 20(1967), 61-73.

      Shakespeare relies on the technique of theological
      prefiguration, a device of Medieval mystery plays to
      portray typological relationships. Iconic imagery is
      stressed throughout Shaw's study.

*   Siegel, Paul N. "Shakespeare and the Neo-Chivalric
      Cult of Honor." See 295.

*   Stone, Charles Veneable. "Dramas of Christian Time:
      Temporal Assumptions and Dramatic Form in the Med-
      ieval Mystery Cycle, the Morality Play, and Shake-

speare's Second Tetralogy." See 313.

2 Henry IV

557. Bacon, Wallace A. "The Margery Bailey Memorial
      Lectures I: The Diseased State in *Henry IV, Part
      Two.*" *SM*, 40(1973), 75-100.

      2H4 is read as a morality play which emphasizes
      illness and purgation. The diseases of the state are
      also reflected in the condition of Falstaff's body as
      well as the relationship between Falstaff and the king.

*   Matte, Nancy Lightfoot. "The Ars-Moriendi in Selected
      Shakespearean History Plays." See 401.

558. Mendilow, A. A. "Falstaff's Death of Sweat." *SQ*,
      9(1958), 479-83.

      The description of Falstaff's death is in the tradition
      of the literature describing the plague. Shakespeare
      borrows the medical description of classical and Med-
      ieval treatises dealing with the suffering victims of
      the plague, such as high fever, thirst, anxieties,
      laments, moans, and the frothing mouth in depicting
      Falstaff's death.

*   Stone, Charles Veneable. "Dramas of Christian Time:
      Temporal Assumptions and Dramatic Form in the Med-
      ieval Mystery Cycle, the Morality Play, and Shake-
      speare's Second Tetralogy." See 313.

1 & 2 Henry IV

559. Barber, C. L. "From Ritual to Comedy: An Examination
      of *Henry IV.*" *EIE*, (1954), 22-51.

      The essay points out the analogies between the two
      parts of *H4* and the customary misrule of traditional
      saturnalian holidays. The saturnalian pattern came
      to Shakespeare from the theatrical institution of
      clowning, the clown of the morality plays, and festival
      occasions associated with holidays such as May Day,
      Whitsuntide, Midsummer Eve, and Harvest Home. In
      creating the comedy of *1 & 2H4*, Shakespeare fused two
      main saturnalian traditions: the clowning customary
      on the stage, and the folly associated with festive
      occasions. With respect to clowning and the use of
      double plots, Barber indicates that it was a practice

which can be found in many Medieval plays such as
the *Second Shepherd's Play*.

560. Benham, A. R. "Shakespeare's *Henry IV* and the Spirit
of the Fifteenth Century in England." *PQ*, 2(1923),
224-28.

    1H4 and *2H4* are a commentary upon the restlessness
of fifteenth century politics. Shakespeare shows waning
aspects of chivalry and feudalism in his play and deals
with these changing social conditions in a comic manner.
Benham also contrasts Medieval and Renaissance commer-
cial ideals. The Middle Ages stressed the artistry of
the product, while the Renaissance emphasized the profit
or loss of an item.

561. Boughner, Daniel C. "Traditional Elements in Falstaff."
JEGP, 43(1944), 417-28.

    Boughner denies the influence of the English stock
character and the Vice of the morality plays upon
Shakespeare's creation of Falstaff. Falstaff is based
upon the Italian soldier of Renaissance comedy who is
indebted to the *miles gloriosus* of Latin comedy.

562. ———. "Vice, Braggart, and Falstaff." *Anglia*, 72
(1954), 35-61.

    Boughner modifies his earlier article by presenting
a survey of cowardly bullies in Medieval and early
Renaissance drama which may have influenced Shakespeare's
depiction of Falstaff. The essay discusses *Mankind,
Wisdom, The Castle of Perseverance, The Nature of Four
Elements* as background material for *1 & 2H4*.

563. Draper, Charles L. "Falstaff's Bardolph." *Neophil*,
33(1953), 222-26.

    Bardolph is similar to Falstaff in that both are
remnants of decadent chivalry. Prowess and virtue
have been reduced to magniloquence and braggadocio.

564. Draper, John W. "Falstaff, 'A Fool and Jester.'"
MLQ, 7(1946), 453-62.

    In the beginning of his essay, Draper relates
Falstaff's character to the "boastful fighter of the
Medieval ritual play." His humor is due to his
relation to the Vice of the morality play and to the
Elizabethan fool.

565. Empson, William. "Falstaff and Mr. Dover Wilson." *KR*, 15(1953), 211-62.

   Empson directs caustic comments in many directions
   in this essay by attacking Dover Wilson's remarks on
   Falstaff and by discrediting criticism which links
   Hal and Falstaff to Medieval ideas of Vice, dying
   chivalry, and decadent feudal order.

566. Hemingway, Samuel B. "On Behalf of That Falstaff."
   SQ, 3(1952), 307-11.

   The criticism of Falstaff has been one sided and inaccurate, and the essay classifies the many articles
   concerning Falstaff into three schools: (1) Stoll who
   claims that Shakespeare is following Medieval and Renaissance stage traditions and conventions; (2) Morgan
   and Bradley who see Falstaff as the creation of Shakespeare's mind; (3) John D. Wilson who attempts to
   synthesize the two opposing schools of thought. The
   shortcomings of the interpretations mentioned above
   are discussed.

*   Kruegel, Sister Mary Flaula. "An Ideological Analysis
   of Honor in William Shakespeare's *Richard II*, *1* and
   2 Henry IV, and *Henry V*." See 400.

567. Landt, D. B. "The Ancestry of Sir John Falstaff."
   SQ, 18(1967), 69-76.

   Landt argues against those who see Sir John Falstaff
   as a stock character or the Vice and determines that
   Falstaff is a product of Shakespeare's transformative
   powers. Falstaff's origin can be found in North and
   Holinshed's *The Famous Victories of Henry the Fifth*.
   Shakespeare's debt in the creation of Falstaff is due to
   borrowing the dialogue from several character in the
   source play, notably that of Old Castle, Dericke,
   Poins, and the Prince himself.

568. Law, Robert Adger. "Structural Unity in the Two Parts
   of *Henry the Fourth*." *SP*, 24(1927), 223-242.

   Law's essay adds to those already written which
   stress the importance of the morality play as an
   underlying structure behind *1 & 2H4*. Law comments
   briefly concerning the Vice in the play and argues
   extensively that *2H4* "sets forth the conflict between
   Sir John and the Chief Justice, after the manner of the
   moralities, for the soul of Prince Hal." In addition,

Law points out that the characters in *2H4* are similar
to those in the morality: Rumour, Pistol, Shallow,
Silence, Fang, Snare, Feeble, Wart, and Mouldy appear
to step right out of the morality play.

*   Levenson, Geraldine Bonnie. "'That Reverend Vice':
A Study of the Comic-Demonic Figure in English Drama
and Fiction." See 209.

569. McCutchan, J. Wilson. "Similarities Between Falstaff
and Gluttony in Medwall's *Nature*." *SAB*, 24(1949),
214-19.

The author places passages involving Gluttony and
Falstaff side by side and determines that they resemble
each other in the following ways: a fondness for food
and drink followed by sleeping; a disregard for the
passing of time; the habit of napping on chairs and
benches; both carried a bottle as a weapon in warfare;
a determination not to come within range of gunfire;
and a proclivity to taverns with their promise of
food and entertainment.

570. McNeal, Thomas N. *"Henry IV, Parts I and II* and
Speght's First Edition of Geoffrey Chaucer." *SAB*,
21(1964), 87-93.

After the completion of *1H4* and during the composition
of *2H4*, Shakespeare read and was influenced by Speght's
Chaucer. The appearance of the names Gower and Skogan
not in *1H4* but present in *2H4* is part of the evidence
for McNeal's conclusion. The rest of the essay attempts
to evince that Shakespeare in *1H4* wrote about people
whom Chaucer had some connection with in his day.
Further, Shakespeare read Chaucer carefully in order
to acquire a historical outlook of the times.

571. Merrix, Robert Paul. "Structural Satire in Shakespeare's Henry Plays." *DAI*, 27(1966), 1784-A
(U. of Cincinnati).

The alternating comic plot in Elizabethan drama is
ubiquitous and multiform and occurs as a risible
element in the early mystery plays. In later trans-
itional dramas, the secularized Vice and his lieutenants
become comics but continue to impose moral judgments
on their serious or historical counterparts. In the
Elizabethan history play the comic part achieves
perfection in satire by undercutting traditional

verities. Merrix traces the origins of the comic plot used by Shakespeare to the early mystery plays. In addition, the essay shows that Shakespeare used familiar allegorical characters who were borrowed from the old morality plays.

572. Monahan, J. "Falstaff and His Forebears." *SP*, 18(1921), 353-61.

This source study explains that the comic actions of the characters in *1 & 2H4* are to be found in the *Famous Victories of Henry the Fifth, Containing the Honorable Battle of Agincourt*. Shakespeare's Falstaff is really a composite of Sir John Oldcastle and Derrick the clown of the earlier play. The dialogue of each character is traced in the earlier play to show parallel phrases in Shakespeare's plays.

*   Morrison, George Peter. "Shakespeare's Lancastrian Tetralogy in the Light of the Medieval Mystery Cycles: A Theory for Unity." See 402.

573. Pratt, Samuel M. "Shakespeare and Humphrey Duke of Gloucester." *SQ*, 16(1965), 210-16.

Pratt compares Medieval versions of Humphrey Duke of Gloucester with Shakespeare's version in *1 & 2H4*. By referring to *The Mirror of Magistrates* and humorous ballads written about Humphrey, Pratt determines that Shakespeare followed the pattern set by these early writers by making Humphrey an important and appealing figure. In effect, Shakespeare contributes to the myth surrounding Humphrey as an unselfish servant of the law and a figure of heroic proportions.

*   Ribner, Irving. "Morality Roots of the Tudor History Play." See 404.

574. Schell, E. T. "Prince Hal's Second Reformation." *SQ*, 21(1970), 11-16.

The structural pattern of *1H4* and *2H4* is derived from the moralities and from the life of Henry V as seen in *The Famous Victories of Henry V*. Medieval clothing influence is seen in Hal's symbolic robe which is "reminiscent of the robe Mankind dons and doffs" to show repentance and conversion.

*   Scott-Giles, C. W. *Shakespeare's Heraldry*. See 292.

575. Shirley, J. "Falstaff, an Elizabethan Glutton."
      PQ, 17(1938), 271-87.

      Shirley reviews the various concepts of Falstaff as
      a wit, clown, parasite, and Tudor soldier and then
      argues that Falstaff should be seen in the tradition
      of the glutton. Falstaff's character is similar to
      Gula, the Gluttony of the Seven Deadly Sins of the
      patristic tradition. References are made to *The
      Castle of Perseverance*, Medwall's *Nature*, and Wager's
      The Life and Repentance of Mary Magdalene.

576. Spivak, Bernard. "Falstaff and the Psychomachia."
      SQ, 8(1957), 449-59.

      Spivak traces the growth of literature that deals
      with the Devil's struggle of man's soul from early
      Christian writers through the Middle Ages into the
      Renaissance. Spivak shows the importance of homiletic
      allegory while dealing with the conflict of vices
      and virtue. Shakespeare's Falstaff is a combination
      of those figures who have represented vice in hom-
      iletic literature and in the morality plays. His
      humorous nature comes from the comic aspects of the
      morality plays, but we also see in Falstaff the
      faint echo of the Vice's evil. The shadow of serious
      moral judgment hovers above him, and Falstaff succumbs
      to the moral severity which is always present in the
      traditional stage image of the morality vices.
      Background material for the above analysis comes from
      The Castle of Perseverance, the Digby play of *Mary
      Magdalene*, Lydgate's *Assembly of the Gods* and *Wisdom*.

577. Stoll, E. E. "Falstaff." *MP*, 12(1914), 65-108.

      As is his custom, Stoll takes to task many previous
      critics who have written about Falstaff. The romantic
      school of criticism is particularly attacked as is the
      Medieval school which finds Falstaff an offspring of
      the Vice. Stoll also insists that the chivalric ideal
      is upheld by Falstaff, while others believe that he is
      the agent by which chivalry is satirized. Some comments
      are directed toward the Medieval type of satire found
      in Falstaff's lines, but this satire is not directed
      toward chivalry. Stoll sees a similarity between the
      satire found in Falstaff's dialogue and that seen in
      the *"Prologue of the Wife of Bath."*

*   Turner, Robert Y. "Characterization in Shakespeare's
      Early History Plays." See 412.

578. Wilson, John Dover. *The Fortunes of Falstaff*.
      Cambridge: Cambridge U. Pr., 1943. 143 pp.

      Wilson sees both Prince Hal and Falstaff in terms of
      "The machinery of the old morality." Falstaff's
      function in the play is comic and necessary for the
      reformation of Hal. As such Falstaff is a supplanted
      Medieval Vice.

Henry V

579. Adler, Alfred. "Falstaff's Holy Dying, Pagan as well
      as Christian." *MLN*, 61(1946), 72.

      Falstaff's death follows the tradition of the
      folklore pattern for a buffoon who associates with
      nobility.

580. Barber, Charles. "Prince Hal, Henry V and the Tudor
      Monarachy," pp. 67-75 in *The Morality of Art*. ed.
      D.W. Jefferson. London: Routledge and Kegan Paul,
      1969.

      Prince Hal attempts to strike a balance between
      opposed attitudes represented by Hotspur and Falstaff.
      Barber links old-fashioned chivalry to Falstaff, while
      Hotspur represents questioning cynicism.

581. Braddy, Haldeen. "The Flying Horse in *Henry V.*"
      SQ, 5(1954), 205-07.

      Shakespeare did not invent the incident of the flying
      horse in *H5* (III, vii, 11-17) but relied upon an episode
      in Froissart's *Chronicle*.

582. Erickson, Peter B. "'The Fault My Father Made': The
      Anxious Pursuit of Heroic Fame in Shakespeare's
      Henry V." *MLS*, 10(Winter 1979-80), 10-25.

      Of concern is Erickson's reference to Shakespeare's
      chivalric ideology. In *H5* chivalric ideology is
      militarily successful but fails as far as Henry's moral
      and psychological identity is concerned.

583. Holmes, Martin. "A Heraldic Allusion in *Henry V.*"
      N&Q, 195(1950), 333.

      Holmes refers to the following Shakespearean refer-
      ence: "Fire answers fire, and through their paly flames/
      Each battler sees the other's umbered face." Holmes
      indicates that umbra is associated with heraldry.

584. Jorgensen, P. "The Courtship Scene in *Henry the V.*"
      MLQ, 11(1950), 180–88.

      The contemptuous attitude toward the rough soldier is
      to be found in the courtly love tradition. In the early
      Renaissance, authors expressed contempt toward the
      English soldier. However, by the 1580s a collection of
      tales entitled *Riche His Farewell to Militarie Profession*
      began to give prominent and favorable attention to the
      English soldier. Other dramas followed and continued
      to establish this tradition. Shakespeare's presentation
      of Henry V as a plain soldier should be interpreted in
      this favorable light.

*   Kruegel, Sister Mary Flaula. "An Ideological Analysis
      of Honor in William Shakespeare's *Richard II*, *I* and
      II Henry IV, and *Henry V.*" See 400.

*   Matte, Nancy Lightfoot. "The Ars-Moriendi in Selected
      Shakespearean History Plays." See 401.

585. McElroy, George. "Forebears of Falstaff." *ON*,
      23 January 1965, 24–25.

      McElroy briefly describes the morality background of
      Falstaff and finds that the trilogy of Henry V shows
      Prince Hal caught between two opposing values. Hotspur
      represents honor in a Medieval military sense, while
      Falstaff mocks honor and the virtue associated with it.
      Hal's character emerges and evolves as we see him in
      relation to these opposing values.

*   Morrison, George Peter. "Shakespeare's Lancastrian
      Tetralogy in the Light of the Medieval Mystery
      Cycles: A Theory for Unity." See 402.

586. R., V. "*Henry V.*, Act IV. Chorus:--." *N&Q*,
      4(1911), 84.

      Lydgate's *Troy Book* is cited as evidence that
      "umber'd face" means "vizarded face."

*   Scott-Giles, C. W. *Shakespeare's Heraldry.* See 292.

*   Stone, Charles Veneable. "Dramas of Christian Time:
      Temporal Assumptions and Dramatic Form in the Medieval
      Mystery Cycle, the Morality Play, and Shakespeare's
      Second Tetralogy." See 313.

I Henry VI

*   Dessen, Alan. "The Logic of Elizabethan Stage Violence:
    Some Alarms and Excursions for Modern Critics, Editors,
    and Directors." See 102.

*   Scott-Giles, C. W. *Shakespeare's Heraldry.* See 292.

Henry VI Triad

*   Barry, Patricia S. *The King in Tudor Drama.* See 15.

*   Hawkins, Richard H. "Some Effects of Technique Developed
    in the Native English Drama on the Structure of
    Shakespeare's Plays." See 160.

*   Jones, Emrys. *The Origins of Shakespeare.* See 179.

*   Matthews, Honor. *Character and Symbol in Shakespeare's
    Plays.* See 225.

*   Ribner, Irving. *Patterns of Shakespearean Tragedy.*
    See 452.

*   Sheriff, William E. "Shakespeare's Use of the Native
    Comic Tradition in his Early English History Plays."
    See 407.

Henry VIII

587. Berry, Edward I. *"Henry VIII* and the Dynamics of
      Spectacle." *ShakS,* 12(1979), 229-46.

      Of interest is Berry's comment on the way *H8* integrates
      the *De Casibus* tradition into the drama. Shakespeare's
      use of this older tradition is handled in a sophisticated
      way.

588. Felperin, Howard. "Shakespeare's *Henry VIII:* History
      as Myth." *SEL,* 6(1966), 225-46.

      Felperin points out *felix culpa, contemptu mundi* and
      De Casibus concepts throughout *H8.* Richard's speech
      (V, i, 18-22) should be seen as a sober *exemplum* after
      the manner of those in *A Mirror for Magistrates* and
      serves a didactic function "illustrating the wages of
      political wrongdoing." Shakespeare united the Medieval
      tragic formula of the fall from high degree with

Christian myth and supplies traditional and orthodox
answers to political and moral inquiry.

*   Hogan, Jerome William. "The Rod and the Candle:
      Conscience in the English Morality Plays, Shakespeare's
      Macbeth and Tourneur's *The Atheist's Tragedy*."
      See 167.

589. Kermode, Frank. "What is Shakespeare's *Henry VIII*
      About?" *DUJ*, 9(1947), 48–55.

      H8 is a "Late morality showing the state from which
      great ones may fall; the manner of their falling, be
      they Good Queen, Ambitious Prelate, Virtuous Prelate,
      or merely Great Man; and the part played in their falls
      for good or ill by a King who, though human, is *ex
      officio* the deputy of God, and the agent of divine
      punishment and mercy." Kermode sees a relationship
      between the King and the role of Mercy in the earlier
      moralities. There is an extended discussion about the
      type of "falls" in *H8*. Wolsey illustrates the *De
      Casibus exemplar* while Katharine is neither good nor
      evil; her fall shows the capricious actions of Fortune.
      It is the Medieval concept of Fortune and tragedy which
      provides unity and coherence in the play.

*   Scott–Giles, C. W. *Shakespeare's Heraldry*. See 292.

                        Julius Caesar

590. Brewer, D. S. "Brutus' Crime: A Footnote to *Julius
      Caesar*." *RES*, 3(1952), 51–54.

      Brewer supplements and corrects John Dover Wilson's
      remarks concerning Shakespeare's view of Brutus and
      Julius Caesar. The Renaissance generally saw Julius
      Caesar as a monstrous tyrant and Brutus as an admirable
      character. Medieval literature, however, had sympathy
      for Julius Caesar and regarded Brutus as a murderer.
      Brewer reviews Dante's *Inferno* (XXXIV, 61–67), Chaucer's
      "The Monk's Tale"(3885–3900), Gower's *Confessio Amantis*
      (Prologue, I, 714) and Lydgate's *Fall of Princes* (Books
      II and VI) to establish the Medieval viewpoint.

*   Conley, C. H. "An Instance of the Fifteen Signs of
      Judgment in Shakespeare." See 75.

591. Fisher, L. A. "Shakespeare and the Capitol."
    MLN, 22(1907), 177-82.

    Fisher argues that Caesar's death took place in the
Senate house. To Shakespeare "Capitol was only another
name for the Senate house." References to Medieval
works such as Chaucer's "The Monk's Tale" support the
idea that the Capitol and Senate house were thought of
as being the same.

592. Fowler, W. W. *Roman Essays and Interpretations.*
    Oxford: The Clarendon Pr., 1920. 287 pp.

    Fowler notes that Shakespeare's opinion of Caesar was
very favorable, a concept inherited from the Middle
Ages. Augustine's pupil Orosius devoted a whole chapter
to extolling Caesar and deploring his enemies. It is
this tradition that Shakespeare follows.

593. Owen, Trevor. "Julius Caesar in English Literature from
    Chaucer through the Renaissance." *DAI*, 21(1966),
    3847-A (U. of Minnesota).

    The Medieval Caesar is a hero, a model and symbol for
others whose fall is brought about by his enemies and the
caprice of Dame Fortune. Shakespeare's conception of
Julius Caesar reflects the richness of the references
appearing in the English writings of the later Middle
Ages. Shakespeare's Caesar is overwhelmingly Medieval
but traces of the Renaissance Caesar appear too, a
view which holds that he is an erring individual
because of his weaknesses and sins.

*   Ribner, Irving. *Patterns of Shakespearean Tragedy.*
    See 452.

594. Schanzer, Ernest. "The Problems of *Julius Caesar*."
    SQ, 6(1955), 297-308.

    This essay reviews the scholarship concerning *JC*
and comments upon the various critical conclusions.
The Medieval viewpoint sees Caesar as boastful and
strutting as well as a hero brought low by enemies
and fortune. Schanzer argues that Shakespeare's
Caesar has no grounds in the Medieval tradition since
his character is divided, complex, and ambiguous.

595. Tolman, Albert H. "Studies in *Julius Caesar*," pp.
    122-45 in *Falstaff and Other Shakespearean Topics.*
    New York: The Macmillan Co., 1925.

Concerning the character of Caesar, Tolman believes Caesar's boastfulness comes from the tradition of the boastful ruler in native drama. Caesar is akin to the braggart Herod, a stock figure in the scripture plays. Tolman cites *Ham.* (III, v, 10–16) as evidence that Shakespeare was acquainted with such a figure.

*   Whitaker, Virgil K. *Shakespeare's Use of Learning.* See 344.

King John

*   Dessen, Alan. *Elizabethan Drama and the Viewer's Eye.* See 100.

*   Jones, Emrys. *The Origins of Shakespeare.* See 179.

*   Ribner, Irving. "Morality Roots of the Tudor History Play." See 404.

*   ————. *Patterns of Shakespearean Tragedy.* See 452.

*   Scott-Giles, C. W. *Shakespeare's Heraldry.* See 292.

King Lear

*   Bhattacharya, M. M. *Courtesy in Shakespeare.* See 31.

596.   Bryant, P. E. "Nuncle Lear." *ESA,* 20(1977), 27–41.

Bryant discusses *Lr.* in terms of the morality play. *Lr.* reflects the "moral absolutes" of Christian moralities. Further, the madness imagery is similar to that expressed by the mad Nebuchadnezzar of Medieval works.

597.   Camden, Carroll. "An Absurdity in *King Lear.*" *PQ,* 11(1932), 408–09.

Tannebaum had previously mentioned that Shakespeare's account of the tearing out of the eyes of Gloucester was scientifically inaccurate and absurd. Camden points out that the event is in accord with the account of eyeball removal as explained by the Medieval scientist Thomas Vicary in *The Anatomy of the Bodie of Man.* In addition, Camden indicates that other dramatists used eyeball tearing accounts in their plays. Shakespeare's scene is not absurd.

598. Campbell, Oscar J.   "The Salvation of Lear."   *ELH*,
     15(1948), 93-109.

> *Lr.* is a sublime morality play with Lear's problem
> and his career resembling those of the central figure
> who is called Mankind in the typical morality play.
> The action in Shakespeare's play is a version of man's
> search for true and everlasting spiritual values which
> Lear finds just before Death's awful summons. In his
> version of the summoning of Mankind, Shakespeare places
> a stoical unwise man in the place of a Christian
> sinner; Lear's redemption, therefore, should not be
> seen in orthodox theological terms but as a mixture of
> Stoic insight and Christian humility. Lear, like the
> Mankind of the morality and the homiletic tradition,
> devotes all of his energies to the accumulation and
> worship of ephemeral possessions and to the pursuit of
> satisfaction. Campbell argues that Lear undergoes a
> series of purgatorial experiences which awakens him to
> his vanity, renders him humble, and causes him to
> discover the enduring love of Cordelia.

599. Cauthen, I. B., Jr.   "'The Foule Flibbertigibbet' in
     King Lear: III, iv, 113; IV, i, 60."   *N&Q*, 5(1958),
     98-99.

> Shakespeare may have been indebted to *The Castle of
> Perseverance* rather than Harsnett for the word flibber-
> tigibbet.   The word appears three times in the morality
> and is associated with the devil and a gossiping person.
> Shakespeare uses the word in a similar way.

*   Coursen, Herbert R., Jr.   *Christian Ritual and the World
     of Shakespeare's Tragedies*.   See 432.

*   Craik, T. W.   "The Tudor Interlude and Later Elizabethan
     Drama."   See 86.

*   Creeth, Edmund.   *Mankynde in Shakespeare*.   See 434.

*   Cunningham, J. V.   *Woe and Wonder*.   See 436.

600. Danby, John F.   *Shakespeare's Doctrine of Nature: A
     Study of King Lear*.   London: Faber and Faber, 1949.
     234 pp.

> In the first chapter "The Chronicle Play and the Drama
> of Ideas," Danby asserts that Shakespeare's drama is
> tied more to the Medieval pulpit than to the morality

play. The ideas in the homiletic tradition were more
important than the abstractions in the morality play.
He also argues that the chronicle play with its emphasis upon realism was able to present moral and ethical
principles more effectively than the morality play.

601. Delany, Paul. *King Lear* and the Decline of Feudalism."
      PMLA, 92(1977), 429-40.

      Delany asserts that the "feudal aristocratic society
      of Medieval England was in an upheaval. Edmund is a
      proponent of the "bourgeois state."

*   Dessen, Alan. "The Logic of Elizabethan Stage Violence:
      Some Alarms and Excursions for Modern Critics,
      Editors, and Directors." See 102.

602. Doran, Madeleine. "Elements in the Composition of
      King Lear." *SP*, 30(1933), 34-58.

      The study primarily shows Shakespeare's treatment of
      older material. By referring to Holinshed and the old
      King Leir story, Doran makes brief reference to Med-
      ieval legends of King Lear.

603. Elton, William. *"King Lear* and the Gods: Shakespeare's
      Tragedy and Renaissance Religious Thought." *DAI*,
      28(1967), 302-A (Ohio State U.).

      Elton examines the widespread interpretation of *Lr.*
      as a morality play in which the protagonist is ultimately
      saved. Another aspect which Elton studies is the cosmic
      significance of *Lr.* as a play which "conveys a sense
      of divine justice." He determines that the characters
      are grouped as the virtuous (Cordelia and Edgar), the
      atheistic (Edmund, Goneril, and Regan), and the super-
      stitious (Gloucester). The numerous Christian refer-
      ences in *Lr.* are employed by Shakespeare for his
      Christian-conditioned audiences.

604. Everett, Barbara. "The New *King Lear.*" *CritQ*,
      2(1960), 325-39.

      Some consideration is given to Cordelia as the impetus
      for divine love and Lear's journey as a quest for his
      understanding and redemption. Everett sees a type of
      hybrid allegory at work, but she rejects a morality
      play reading of *Lr.*

* Farnham, Willard. "The Medieval Comic Spirit in the
English Renaissance." See 442.

605. Fraser, Russell. *Shakespeare's Poetics in Relation to
Lear*. London: Routledge and Kegan Paul, 1962.
184 pp.

Discussing the images in *Lr.*, Fraser notes that Shakespeare follows the native traditions of his time. The
Seven Deadly Sins, the combat between the Virtues and
the Vices, the Triumph of Truth, the vagaries of fortune,
and the character of Pride and Luxury are conventional
ideas found throughout the play. Fraser remarks that
Shakespeare uses characters on stage without acting
in much the same way as did the morality plays.

* Gallagher, Ligera Cecile. "Shakespeare and the
Aristotelian Ethical Tradition." See 128.

606. Gaull, Marilyn. "Love and Order in *King Lear*."
ETJ, 19(1967), 333-42.

The Medieval courtly love concept is important for an
understanding of the relationship between Lear and
Goneril and Regan. In the courtly love convention, the
love goddess conquers her love servant as long as the
sexual relationship is not consummated. Once consummated
the woman is bereft and the conquered one. Gaull sees
a similarity between this concept and Lear and his
daughters. Goneril and Regan protest their love in
terms similar to a courtly lover. Once Lear is seduced
of his kingdom, he is cast aside and conquered by his
daughters. There is a basic opposition between divine
order and the courtly love convention.

607. Gorfain, Phyllis. "Contest, Riddle, and Prophecy:
Reflexivity through Folklore in *King Lear*." *SFQ*,
41(1977), 239-54.

Gorfain analyzes the rich native tradition particularly
the use of prophecy, contest, and riddle; and she
suggests how these elements add insight into the play.

* ————. "Remarks Toward a Folkloristic Approach to
Literature: Riddles in Shakespearean Drama." See 140.

608. Greenfield, Thelma N. "The Clothing Motif in *King Lear*."
SQ, 5(1954), 281-86.

The author presents an interesting study of the clothes
pattern in *Lr.* which is important to the structure and
the meaning of the play. Gorgeousness and nakedness
and draped and undraped figures are related to the clothing motif in Medieval literature. The clothing motif in
miracle and morality plays is discussed extensively.
Greenfield comments at length upon the allegorical use
of clothing in Henry Medwall's *Nature* and then uses the
play as a springboard for the discussion of the clothing
motif in *Lr.* Pride in Medwall's *Nature* wears fine
garments and is condemned; clothing denotes worldly
interest but nakedness denotes innocence, especially
after one received God's grace. In *Lr.* the debate
elements concerning clothing appear in numerous and
complicated ways, and Shakespeare's use of this motif
enriches the familiar allegorical overtones borrowed
from the Medieval world.

609. Greg, W. W. "The Date of *Lear* and Shakespeare's Use
      of Earlier Versions of the Story." *Library,* 20
      (1940), 377-400.

The second section of Greg's study deals with parallel
lines in the old *King Leir* story and Shakespeare's *Lr.*
Greg lists some twenty passages which indicate that
Shakespeare read *King Lear* rather closely. Shakespeare
used *The Mirror for Magistrates* for the name of Albany,
and he employed versions of the Lear story by Geoffrey
of Monmouth, Wace, and Layamon.

610. Hamilton, Donna B. "Some Romance Sources for *King Lear:*
      Robert of Sicily and Robert the Devil." *SP,* 71
      (1974), 173-92.

Robert of Sicily's poem (1375) contains a number of
motifs found in *Lr.* Both emphasize grace through loss
and both find identity through suffering.

611. Hawkes, Terence. "The Fool's 'Prophecy' in *King Lear*."
      N&Q, 205(1960), 330-32.

The fool's prophecy (III, ii) in *Lr.* is in the
tradition of Merlin prophecies stemming from the Middle
Ages, and the immediate Shakespearean source probably
was Caxton. Hawkes believes that Shakespeare parodies
such prophecies and that the audience was fully aware
of the Merlinesque tradition.

*   Hays, Michael L. "Shakespeare's Use of Medieval Romance
       Elements in his Major Tragedies." See 446.

612.   Helton, Tinsley. "Shakespeare's Divine Comedy." *WSL*,
       1(1964), 11–16.

       Shakespeare's spiritual journey parallels Dante's.
       Helton discusses the vision of good and evil seen in
       both authors with particular application to *Lr*.

613.   Heubert, Ronald. "The Paganism of *King Lear*." *DR*,
       56(1976), 429–47.

       The metaphysical universe of *Lr*. is an imaginative
       reconstruction of pagan Celtic beliefs. Shakespeare's
       three major divisions of supernatural powers in *Lr*.
       "conform to the three layers of the Celtic spirit world."

614.   Hunter, Robert G. *Shakespeare and the Mystery of God's
       Judgments*. Athens: U. of Georgia Pr., 1977. 208 pp.

       Lr. as well as other Shakespearean tragedies, is
       concerned with the nature of free will and providential
       design. Hunter's analysis of Shakespeare is preceded
       by an examination of Medieval miracle plays in regard
       to their treatment of will and the sense of redemption.

615.   Jones, James Horace. "Shakespeare's Transformation of
       His Sources in *King Lear*. *DAI*, 25(1964), 4630–31
       (U. of Indiana).

       Jones compares the Medieval versions of King Lear
       beginning with Geoffrey of Monmouth's *History of the
       Kings of Britain* with Shakespeare's *Lr*. Jones notes
       that in Monmouth's version, Cordelia answers the love-
       test question with a riddle. Lear understands the
       riddle only after he has undergone a number of laments
       and lessons, one of which is that love founded upon
       mutable worth is vain. While Shakespeare's version
       has some echoes of Christian thought, it is not as
       religious as Medieval versions of the story.

*   Keilstrup, Lorraine M. "The Myth of Cain in the Early
       English Drama." See 185.

616.   Kernan, Alvin B. *The Playwright as Magician: Shake-
       speare's Image of the Poet in the English Theater*.
       New Haven: Yale U. Pr., 1979. 204 pp.

Of interest is the section in which Kernan read *Lr.*
as a drama "obviously structured in the morality play
manner." Though his discussion remains general, he
sees the Gloucester subplot and the reunion of Cordelia
and Lear as morality staged episodes.

617. Kernodle, G. F. "The Symphonic Form of *King Lear*,"
      pp. 185-91 in *Elizabethan Studies and Other Essays
      in Honor of George F. Reynolds*. Denver: U. of
      Colorado Pr., 1945.

      Lr. is deeply based upon Medieval habits of thinking
      and the unity and structure of the play is derived from
      Medieval drama. Kernodle discusses the concept of
      hierarchy as imposing a type of unity in *Lr.* In
      addition, the artistic principle of correspondence or
      parallelism is derived from Medieval drama. Also, the
      two-fold beginning of *Lr.* (the stories of Lear and
      Gloucester) comes from the custom of presenting the
      characters to the audience before they were put in
      action. The two-fold prologue in the *Second Shepherd's
      Play* is a typical parallel in Medieval drama.

*   Knights, L. C. *Shakespeare's Politics: With Some
      Reflections on the Nature of Tradition*. See 197.

618. Lascelles, Mary. "*King Lear* and Doomsbury." *ShS*,
      26(1973), 69-79.

      Native murals about Doomsday paintings which depict
      souls awaiting judgment help to explain Lear's state
      of mind on the heath. The Medieval plate "Words of
      Mercy and Seven Deadly Sins at Trotton" stresses the
      principle that those who are in a position of power
      are responsible for those under them. Lear's recogi-
      tion is that he has not been faithful.

619. Law, R. A. "Holinshed's Leir Story and Shakespeare's"
      SP, 47(1950), 42-50.

      Law compares and contrasts Holinshed's sources and
      his story of *King Leir* to Shakespeare's *Lr.* Other
      sources mentioned are the prose of *Brut*, *The Mirror
      for Magistrates*, and Caxton's *Chronicles of England*.

620. Leech, Clifford. "Shakespeare and the Idea of
      Fortune." *UTQ*, 35(1955-56), 213-228.

      However much Shakespeare may have used the morality
      modes of action, he is not giving us a morality play.

Lear stands "everyman fashion" between Cordelia and her
sisters: though like a morality play character he
abandons Cordelia and adheres to her sisters and then
returns to Cordelia, the result is only a temporary
blessing. None of Shakespeare's tragedies ends in the
same happy manner of a morality play.

*   Lord, John B. "Sources of the Technique of Comic
Scenes in Shakespearean Tragedy." See 449.

*   Loske, Olav. "The Story and the Play." See 216.

621.   Mack, Maynard. "'We Came Crying Hither': An Essay on
Some Characteristics of *King Lear*." *YR*, 54(1964-65),
161-86.

Mack believes that Lear's words, "we came crying
hither," denote the *de contemptu mundi* theme expressed
by Innocent III, a common Medieval idea.

622.   ————. *King Lear in Our Time*. Berkeley: U. of
California Pr., 1965. 126 pp.

Mack cites many parallels between *Lr*. and the morality
play tradition and argues that the whole legacy of
Medieval culture permeates the play. The opening scene
depicts those who represent Vice and those who stand
for Virtue. Edmund is associated with the Appetite
figure of the morality play. *Exempla* and homiletic
concepts are a part of the play's structure.

623.   Meier, Hans H. "Middle English Styles in Translation:
A Note on *Everyman* and Caxton's *Reynard*," pp. 13-30
in *From Caxton to Beckett*, ed. by Jacques Alblas and
Richard Todd. Amsterdam: Rodopi, 1979.

Of interest is the commentary and comparison between
Everyman and *Lr*. Structural similarities are noted with
an emphasis upon "simple architectural" aspects of
both dramas.

624.   Nojima, Hidekatsu. "Exit the Fool," pp. 84-100 in
*English Criticisms in Japan: Essays by Younger
Japanese Scholars on English and American Literature*.
ed. Earl Miner, Tokyo: Tokyo U. Pr., 1972.

The author presents a brief history of the fool in
native English drama and asserts that the fool in *Lr*.
is "equivalent to the function of the Vice in morality
plays."

*   Owst, G. R. *Literature and Pulpit in Medieval England*.
      See 254.

625. Parr, Johnstone. "A Note on the 'Late Eclipses' in
      King Lear." *SAB*, 20(January 1945), 46–48.

      Parr clarifies a passage in *Lr*. (I, ii, 98–141) in
      which Gloucester speaks of the "late eclipses." Shake-
      speare adapted material from Medieval astrological
      pamphlets and "by making the effects suit his plot,
      fashioned the astrologer's material into something
      quite his own."

626. ————. "Edmund's Nativity in *King Lear*." *SAB*,
      21(October 1946), 181–85.

      While referring to Medieval and Renaissance aspects of
      astrology, Parr explains how Edmund's birth under the
      sign of Ursa Major and under the influence of Venus and
      Mars coincides with his evil career.

627. Perkinson, R. "Shakespeare's Revision of the Lear
      Story." *PQ*, 22(1943), 315–29.

      Perkinson compares and contrasts Shakespeare's trial
      scene in *Lr*. with those found in stories of Medieval
      times such as *The Mirror for Magistrates*, the chronicle
      of *King Leir*, and other versions of the Lear story.
      The author also examines Shakespeare's characterization
      and dramatic art.

*   Potter, Robert. *The English Morality Play*. See 265.

628. Pratt, Norman T. "From Oedipus to Lear." *CJ*, 61
      (1965–66), 49–57.

      Of particular interest concerning the Medieval influ-
      ence on *Lr*. is Pratt's discussion and additions to O.
      J. Campbell's view of *Lr*. as a morality play and Lily
      B. Campbell's interpretation of *Lr*. as a tragedy of
      exempla. Pratt points out that O.J. Campbell's view
      is an attempt to graft Renaissance Stoicism upon tra-
      ditional Christian piety. Pratt determines that Lear's
      experiences are purgatorial and eventually lead to a
      level of salvation. The play ends with an affirmation
      of a continuing, self-asserting moral order. Pratt
      argues that in Shakespearean tragedy the misfortunes
      of men are traced not to chance but to sinful action
      resulting from the passions. Renaissance tragedy is
      oriented more toward the conflict between reason and

and unreason, temperance and passion, and Medieval
modifications of classical philosophy.

629. Presson, R. K. "Boethius, King Lear and 'Maystresse
Philosophie.'" *JEGP*, 64(1965), 406-24.

Presson's concern is to show a number of analogies
between *Lr.* and Boethius' *The Consolation*. The comparisons include the various reactions "to the situation
adversity creates," "the mutability of events," the
employment of "tempest imagery," and "the Boethian
conception of Nature."

630. Price, T. R. "*King Lear*, A Study of Shakespeare's
Dramatic Method." *PMLA*, 9(1894), 165-81.

Of possible interest is Price's treatment of the
Lear story as it relates to Celtic myth and the relationship of this myth to the story of Gloucester
and his two sons.

631. Ribner, Irving. "Shakespeare and Legendary History:
Lear and *Cymbeline*." *SQ*, 7(1956), 47-52.

This essay defines a historical play and a historical
romance by making the point that both plays draw from
the legend of King Brut and his descendants. The
political problem is primary in *Lr.*, and this is the
criteria by which a history play is judged. Political
intrigue in *Cym.* is secondary and thus the play should
be under the genre of a historical romance.

632. ————. "The Gods are Just." *TDR*, 2(1958), 34-54.

The character, action, symbol, and the poetry in *Lr.*
are shaped by the theme of regeneration. Shakespeare
"availed himself of the morality play tradition which
was so much a part of his dramatic heritage." Ribner
also comments upon the didactic and homiletic tradition of Medieval drama which afforded Shakespeare
the tools for his play. Ribner discusses the concept
of Christian humanism which survived from the Middle
Ages and refers to the historical stories of Lear as
they relate to Shakespeare's dramatic purposes. The
morality influence can particularly be seen in the
distinctive philosophies of the two sets of characters
in *Lr.*, one is good and the other is markedly evil.

633. Rusche, Harry. "Edmund's Conception and Nativity in
King Lear." *SQ*, 20(1969), 161-64.

Rusche adds additional comments to Parr's article
"Edmund's Nativity in *King Lear*" by stressing that
Edmund's conception under the sign of the Dragon's
Tail (according to Ptolemy) is an important sign which
does influence the character's actions. He also points
out that the union of Mars and Venus is not always an
unfavorable sign, especially in its ascendancy.

634. Salter, K. W. "*Lear* and the Morality Tradition."
       N&Q, 199(1954), 109-10.

Salter interprets *Lr.* as a morality play and sees a
parallel between Albany's speech (IV, ii, 46) and a
passage in *Everyman* (47-50). The line in question refers to humanity preying on itself like monsters from
the deep.

*   Schell, Edgar T. "The Pilgrimage of Life: The Imitation
       of an Action in Renaissance Drama." See 287.

635. Schoff, Francis G. "*King Lear:* Moral Example or
       Tragic Protagonist." *SQ*, 13(1963), 157-72.

The play offers no evidence to support the idea that
it is a morality or an *exemplum*. Furthermore, no morality figures appear in the play. The protagonist is
in the grips of evil, an event that may happen to
anyone.

636. Sewall, R. *The Vision of Tragedy*. New Haven: Yale
       U. Pr., 1959. 178 pp.

The discussion of *Lr.* (68-79) makes several notable
observations. Sewall applies the Medieval concept of
hierarchy to the tragic process in the play. As the
drama begins, order is imperiled; we then find a period
of hierarchy broken and finally hierarchy restored.
Also the play is in the morality tradition if seen from
Edmund's point of view--laying evil to the charge of
sinful will.

637. Siegel, Paul N. "Adversity and the Miracle of Love
       in *King Lear*." *SQ*, 6(1955), 325-36.

Siegel relates concepts of adversity in the play to
the continuing influence of Boethius' *De Censolatione
Philosophiae*. The reconciliation of the misfortunes
by chance and by divine providence is the basis of
the play.

638. Smith, Roland M. *"King Lear* and the Merlin Tradition."
     MLQ, 7(1956), 153-74.

    The atmosphere and local color in *Lr.* come from works
Shakespeare read that depicted the reign of King Arthur
and the marvels of Merlin. Smith refers to the "wild
man" tradition in Medieval literature and shows passages
in *Lr.* which are similar. Some twenty passages are
cited throughout the play which depict elements associated with the Merlin tradition.

639. Stuart, Betty K. "Truth and Tragedy in *King Lear." SQ,*
     18(1967), 167-80.

    Unlike Campbell, who sees *Lr.* as a Christian allegory,
Stuart argues that ideas of sin and moral regeneration
are in the play, but these concepts hold for any age.
Shakespeare used Christian-like terminology to make his
audience grasp the meaning more readily. The emphasis
in the play is upon waste and shame and not upon some
affirmation of life. Dramas in the allegorical tradition refer to eternal happiness or to some blessed
state in the afterlife, but *Lr.* is noticeably silent
concerning this.

640. Turner, Darwin T. *"King Lear* Re-examined." *CLAJ,*
     3(1959), 27-39.

    Turner reads the play as a study in the redemption of
man by relating *Lr.* to Dantesque concepts of moral
theology.

*   VanDyke, Joyce. "The Decomposition of Tragic Character
     in Shakespeare." See 457.

641. Watkins, Walter B. C. *Shakespeare and Spenser.*
     Princeton: Princeton U. Pr., 1950. 339 pp.

    In his discussion of the play (75-110), Watkins writes
that *Lr.* is not a morality play like Faustus, but it
has the same effect because of the unusual measure of
symbolical stylization, which makes possible universal
emotional power and meaning. Consciously or uncon-
sciously Shakespeare attempts to fuse the "native
Medieval tragedy and the Senecan derivative." Watkins
also notes the presence of the *contemptu mundi* theme in
Lr. Like Everyman, Lear becomes naked and is deprived of
everything except good deeds on his way to the grave.

*   Welsford, Enid. *The Fool: His Social and Literary
       History.* See 338.

642.   Young, A. R. "The Written and Oral Sources of *King
       Lear.*" *SEL,* 15(1975), 309-19.

       Young reviews the folk-tale tradition underlying the
       play and finds that Shakespeare departs from the con-
       ventional pattern of a father who mistakenly rejects
       his daughter. The tragic ending is intended to produce
       a sense of injustice.

                          Love's Labor's Lost

643.   Anderson, J. J. "The Morality of *Love's Labour's Lost.*"
       ShS, 24(1971), 55-82.

       Some influence of the morality tradition is apparent
       in *LLL* though Shakespeare combines the comic and moral
       aspects of the play in a less serious manner than Med-
       ieval writers. Other discussions include the Nine
       Worthies and the *ubi sunt* theme.

644.   Ashton, John W. "Conventional Elements in John a Kent
       and John a Cumber." *PMLA,* 40(1934), 752-61.

       Ashton discusses folk elements, magic, and super-
       natural aspects (particularly characters) in Monday's
       works and relates some of these folklore concepts to
       Shakespeare's plays. *LLL* and *MND* contain Medieval
       magical ideas.

645.   Babcock, Weston. "Fools, Fowls, and Perttaunt-Like in
       Love's Labour's Lost." *SQ,* 2(1951), 211-19.

       Shakespeare's use of the term "Perttaunt-Like" is
       an allusion to Chaucer's Dame Partlet. The term is
       associated with sexual connotations as well as concepts
       relating to a scolding and domineering wife.

*   Brooks, Harold F. "Marlowe and Early Shakespeare."
       See 48.

*   Courthope, W. J. *A History of English Poetry: The
       Development and Decline of the Poetic Drama.* See 80.

*   Cunningham, W. J. "The Doctrine of Repentance as a
       Formal Principle in Some Elizabethan Plays." See 89.

*   Hanford, James H. "The Debate Element in Elizabethan
      Drama." See 150.

*   Hassel, R. Chris, Jr. *Faith and Folly in Shakespeare's
      Romantic Comedies*. See 376.

*   Hawkins, Richard H. "Some Effects of Technique De-
      veloped in the Native English Drama on the Structure
      of Shakespeare's Plays." See 160.

646. Lennam, T. "The Ventricle of Memory: Wit and Wisdom
      in *Love's Labour's Lost*." *SQ*, 24(1973), 54-60.

      Shakespeare was influenced by the moral pattern of
      the "wit" moralities, principally *The Marriage of Wit
      and Science*.

647. Maxwell, J. C. "Chaucer in the Queen Mab Speech."
      N&Q, 7(1960), 17-18.

      Claudian's *De Sextu Consulatu Honorii Augusti*,
      Praefatio, 3-10 and Chaucer's *The Parliament of Foules*,
      99-105 are possible sources for *LLL* (II, i, 82-86).
      Maxwell prefers the Chaucerian passage since Shake-
      speare's soldier is closer to Chaucer's knight than
      to the *nauita* of Claudian.

648. McLay, Catherine M. "The Dialogue of Spring and Winter:
      A Key to the Unity of *Love's Labour's Lost*." *SQ*,
      18 (1967), 119-27.

      The song dialogues in *LLL* are similar to the Medieval
      tradition of the debate of the seasons. Throughout the
      play the seasonal metaphors are used to suggest themes
      associated with life, death, and rebirth. While winter
      is usually associated with death, Shakespeare actually
      refers to life beyond death, a theme which was to emerge
      in the late Medieval romances. The spring dialogue be-
      ginning with "When daisies pied and violets blue"
      should be seen as a paradoxical inversion since spring
      is associated with cuckoldry rather than rebirth.
      McLay quotes Huizinga's *The Waning of the Middle Ages*
      to suggest that blue symbolized infidelity, cuckoldry,
      and folly.

649. Merrill, Elizabeth. "The Dialogue in English
      Literature." *YSE*, 42(1911), 1-131.

      Of interest are the remarks concerning the dialogues

in *LLL* (V, ii) and *1H4* (V,i) as being remarkably similar to dialogues in Medieval literature.

650. Ogle, M. B. "The Classical Origin and Tradition of Literary Conceits." *AJP*, 34(1913), 125-52.

Ogle traces the tradition of the formula for praising a lady through Medieval literature to the Alexandrian poets and examines Shakespeare's use of the formula. Shakespeare satirizes the tradition in the sonnets and *LLL* but appears to adopt the convention for all of his heroines. The formula involves the description of a lady's hair, ruby lips, rosy cheeks and dark eyes.

*   Pettet, E. C. *Shakespeare and the Romance Tradition.* See 381.

651. Presson, Robert K. "The Conclusion of *Love's Labour's Lost.*" *N&Q*, 7(1960), 17-18.

The conclusion of *LLL* where the suitors must accept a year's postponement of marriage prospects is remarkably similar to the end of Chaucer's *The Parliament of Foules*. Both works are terminated by birds contrasting two seasons with their songs.

652. Shibata, Toshihiko. "On the Palinodial Ending of *Cynthia's Revels.*" *ShStud*, 10(1972), 1-15.

This essay primarily focuses upon *Cynthia's Revels*, but some commentary is concerned with *LLL*. Shakespeare employed the Medieval convention of palinode as moral necessity.

*   Stevenson, David L. *The Love-Game Comedy.* See 312.

*   Thompson, K. M. "Shakespeare's Romantic Comedies." See 387.

*   Vyvyan, John. *Shakespeare and the Rose of Love: A Study of the Early Plays in Relation to the Medieval Philosophy of Love.* See 390.

*   Wickham, Glynne. "Medieval Comic Traditions and the Beginnings of English Comedy." See 392.

Macbeth

653. Adam, R. J. "The Real Macbeth: King of Scots, 1040–
     1054." *HT*, 7(1957), 381–87.

     Adam writes that the historical Macbeth was a better
     man than the man he killed, for Macbeth brought a
     certain degree of equity and culture to the throne.

654. Allen, Michael, J. B. "Macbeth's Genial Porter."
     ELR, 4(1974), 326–36.

     Sections of this essay explicate the Medieval re-
     ligious background. Allen argues that the porter can
     be seen as the bad angel who is viewed as betraying
     Macbeth's soul to hell.

655. Camden, Carroll. "The Mind's Construction in the Face."
     PQ, 20(1941), 400–12.

     Camden considers Macbeth's speech in light of Medieval
     physiognomy. In referring to the works of Giles of
     Carbeil, the legendary Albert, Arnold of Villanova, and
     Nicholas Oresme, he shows the popularity of the science
     of physiognomy in the Middle Ages. Shakespeare was
     acquainted with this science.

656. Coffin, Tristram. "Folk Logic and the Bard: Act I
     of *Macbeth*," pp. 331–42 in *Medieval Literature and
     Folklore Studies: Essays in Honor of Francis Lee
     Utley*. eds. Jerome Mandel and Bruce A. Rosenberg.
     New Brunswick: Rutgers U. Pr., 1971.

     The six passages in Act I—iii, 130–141; iv, 48–53;
     v, 1–30; v, 39; v, 60–71; and vii—are not consistent
     with each other but can be explained in terms of the
     semi-literary legend which held that Macbeth had
     planned Duncan's death regardless of the witches and
     urging of Lady Macbeth

*   Coffman, George R. "Some Trends in English Literary
      Scholarship with Special Reference to Medieval
      Backgrounds." See 70.

*   Cormican, L. A. "Medieval Idiom in Shakespeare:
      Shakespeare and the Medieval Ethic." See 77.

*   Coursen, Herbert R., Jr. *Christian Ritual and the
      World of Shakespeare's Tragedies*. See 432.

657.   Craig, Hardin.   "Motivation in Shakespeare's Choice
       of Materials."   *ShS*, 4(1951), 26-34.

       Shakespeare's source materials gave him a pattern or
       design which gave structure to his plays.   Craig shows
       the morality pattern in *Mac.* and attributes the
       structure of the play to chronicles concerning Duncan
       and Macbeth.   In the "morality pattern of *Macbeth*, we
       see the aberration of a hero, under delusions of the
       powers of evil, pursue a career of crime and wickedness,
       violent to the last degree and continued until such
       time as his course of evil was arrested."

*   ————.   *English Religious Drama of the Middle Ages*.
       See 84.

*   Creeth, Edmund.   *Mankynde in Shakespeare*.   See 434.

*   Cunningham, J. V.   "Tragedy in Shakespeare."   See 435.

658.   Curry, Walter Clyde.   "Tumbling Nature's Germens."
       SP, 29(1932), 15-28.

       See 660.

659.   ————.   "The Demoniac Metaphysics of Macbeth."   *SP*,
       30(1933), 395-426.

       See 660.

660.   ————.   *Shakespeare's Philosophical Patterns*.   Baton
       Rouge: Louisiana State U. Pr., 1937.   215 pp.

       The first chapter illustrates the role of scholasticism
       upon the Renaissance with succeeding chapter relating
       Medieval philosophy to *Mac.*   The second chapter "Tumbl-
       ing Nature's Germens" explicates a passage in *Mac.*
       (IV, i, 56-65) in light of Medieval metaphysical phi-
       losophy.   Curry considers "nature's germens" to be
       similar to the concept held by Augustine referred to
       as *rationes seminales*.   The term is associated with
       seeds of matter which demoniac powers, such as the
       Weird Sisters, are capable of manipulating.   In "The
       Demonic Metaphysics of *Macbeth*," Curry traces demoniac
       powers to Medieval ontology.   The Renaissance inherited
       the concept of evil from the Middle Ages which can be
       divided into two areas: the subjective concept of sin
       (original sin); and the objective world of sin (the
       malignant activity of demons).

661. Doebler, Bettie Anne. "'Rooted Sorrow': Verbal and
      Visual Survivals of an *Ars* Commonplace." *TSLL*,
      22(1980), 358-68.

      Doebler surveys woodcuts, paintings, and tracts which
      make up the *ars moriendi* tradition. Lady Macbeth's
      mind was closely rooted to the sin of despair. The
      bleakness of despair was for "Shakespeare's audience
      on a profound level an experience of the absence of God."

*   Doebler, John. *Shakespeare's Speaking Pictures*. See
      103.

*   Fansler, Harriott Ely. *The Evolution of Technic in
      Elizabethan Tragedy*. See 439.

662. Fisher, Anne Adele. "A Reading of *Macbeth* in the Light
      of Earlier Native Drama." *DAI*, 39(1979), 4268-A
      (Toronto).

      Fisher shows the influence of the mystery and mor-
      ality tradition on *Mac.* The study discusses particular
      conventions, broad themes, characterizations, and plot
      structure, and it concentrates on the decision making
      process "technically called counsel and of despaire."

*   Golden, Martha Hester. "The Iconography of the English
      History Play." See 136.

*   Gorfain, Phyllis. "Remarks Toward a Folkloristic
      Approach to Literature: Riddles in Shakespearean
      Drama." See 140.

663. Harcourt, John B. "I Pray You, Remember the Porter."
      SQ, 12(1961), 393-402.

      The second half of this essay links Shakespeare's
      porter to the ragmuffin, the devil, and Ribald of
      Medieval literature and shows similarities between
      scenes from *Mac.* and those found in mystery plays.
      Harcourt observes: "emerging from the specific sit-
      uations of Shakespeare's plot are certain larger meanings
      that could be suggested through the associative value
      of materials inherited from the late Medieval dramatic
      tradition."

*   Hays, Michael L. "Shakespeare's Use of Medieval
      Romance Elements in his Major Tragedies." See 446.

*   Hogan, Jerome William. "The Rod and the Candle:
       Conscience in the English Morality Plays, Shakespeare's
       Macbeth and Tourneur's *The Atheist's Tragedy*. See 167.

664.   Hunter, E. R. *"Macbeth* as a Morality." *SAB*, 12
       (1937), 217-235.

       Shakespeare may have seen morality plays in his youth,
       and Hunter presents evidence of surviving morality ideas
       and techniques in *Mac.* and *MV*. The study emphasizes the
       conflict of the "vice and virtue in *Macbeth*" and "the
       coming of death." Shakespeare shows the futility of
       Macbeth's evil bargain, the futility of life, and the
       hopelessness of death.

*   Knights, L. C. *Poetry, Politics, and the English
       Tradition*. See 195.

*   Kolin, Philip C. "The Elizabethan Stage Doctor as a
       Dramatic Convention." See 199.

*   Lord, John B. "Sources of the Technique of Comic
       Scenes in Shakespearean Tragedy." See 449.

665.   McGee, Arthur R. *"Macbeth* and the Furies." *ShS*,
       19(1966), 55-67.

       In examining the use of the supernatural element in
       Mac. and in particular the witches, McGee reconstructs
       classical, Medieval, and Renaissance concepts of Hell,
       evil, and beliefs in devils which the Elizabethans
       would be familiar with while viewing the play. The
       Medieval concept relates to hogs or demons who drag
       men down to everlasting punishment in Hell.

666.   Morris, Harry. "Macbeth, Dante, and the Greatest
       Evil." *TSL*, 12(1967), 23-37.

       Morris cites closeness of imagery and symbolism which
       suggests that Shakespeare was more than vaguely familiar
       with Dante. Shakespeare names Macbeth's crimes in the
       same way Dante does in his ninth circle: kinsmen, sub-
       ject, guest, and lord. There is a similarity between
       the Porter's scene, "This place is too cold for Hell"
       (II, iii, 19) and Canto XXXIII, where Dante meets
       Friar Alberigo.

*   Owst, G. R. *Literature and Pulpit in Medieval England*.
       See 254.

*   Pollard, Alfred W. *English Miracle Plays, Moralities,
     and Interludes.* See 264.

667. Rea, J. D. "Notes on Shakespeare." *MLN,* 35(1920),
     377-78.

     The passage in which Macbeth rouses the murderers to
     kill Banquo (III, i, 91-103) is probably taken from
     Erasmus' colloquy *Philodoxus.* Rea shows striking
     similarities both in wording and ideas.

*   Rosier, James Louis. "The Chain of Sin and Privation
     in Elizabethan Literature." See 279.

*   Schell, Edgar T. "The Pilgrimage of Life: The
     Imitation of an Action in Renaissance Drama." See 287.

668. Spivack, Charlotte. *"Macbeth* and Dante's *Inferno."*
     NDQ, 28(1960), 50-52.

     Spivack considers *Mac.* in the light of Medieval
     Christian heritage, for the play contains "the dual
     Dantesque theme of the equivocal nature of evil and
     its double-dealing consequences."

669. Swaminathan, S. R. "The Image of Pity in *Macbeth."*
     N&Q, 215(1970), 132.

     The description of Pity as a newborn babe is reminis-
     cent of Medieval Christian art in that the soul is
     symbolized by a naked infant.

670. Taylor, Pauline. "Birnam Wood: 700 A.D.--1600 A.D."
     MLN, 29(1924), 244-47.

     Taylor traces Shakespeare's source for "Birnham Wood"
     to an eighth century work *Liber Historiae Francorum.*
     Vincent of Beauvais borrowed from the eighth century
     work; Wyntoun incorporated Beauvais' account into his
     chronicles; Roece probably borrowed from Wyntoun;
     Holinshed borrowed from Boece, and Shakespeare went
     directly to Holinshed.

*   VanDyke, Joyce. "The Decomposition of Tragic Character
     in Shakespeare." See 457.

671. Wickham, Glynne. "Hell-Castle and its Doorkeeper."
     ShS, 19(1966), 68-74.

The vocabulary found in *Mac.* II, iii, is similar to
the wording in the Medieval miracle cycle "The
Harrowing of Hell." Shakespeare used the story as a
model for the scene mentioned above and possibly for
the whole play. Wickham shows parallels between
Shakespeare's porter and Belzabub of the Towneley
and York plays and the character Ribald who acts
as a porter.

Measure for Measure

672. A., E. S. "Measure for Measure, II, i. ('O thou
      wicked Hannibal')." *N&Q*, 5(1894), 363.

      Why should Hannibal be branded with obloquy? The
      essay suggests that Shakespeare may have been acquainted
      with the Townely mysteries since one of the fiends in
      Extractio Animorum is called Anabelle.

673. Battenhouse, Roy W. "Measure for Measure and the
      Christian Doctrine of the Atonement." *PMLA*, 61
      (1946), 1029-59.

      The essay reviews criticism which finds resemblances
      between *MM* and the Medieval moralities. Battenhouse
      points out many parallels between Medieval, Augustinian
      theology, and concepts of sin and redemption in *MM*. He
      has a discussion of the presence of the Seven Deadly Sins
      and the Four Daughters of God in Shakespearean comedy.

674. Bradbrook, M. C. "Authority, Truth, and Justice in
      Measure for Measure." *RES*, 18(1941), 385-99.

      Shakespeare's dramatic technique resembles that found
      in the late moralities. Bradbrook suggests that the
      play could be called "The Contention between Justice
      and Mercy, or False Authority Unmasked by Truth and
      Humility." Angelo is associated with authority and
      the law who usurps the Duke, a representative of
      Justice and Humility. Isabel illustrates qualities
      found in Truth and Mercy.

*   Charlton, H. B. "The Dark Comedies." See 368.

675. Coghill, Nevill. "Comic Form in *Measure for Measure.*"
      ShS, 8(1955), 14-26.

      This essay interprets *MM* by referring to the Medieval
      tradition of comedy as seen in Dante and Chaucer, a
      type which "begins with trouble, ends in joy and is

centered in love." The allegory found in *MM* includes the type seen in the morality plays but is older than that tradition. Coghill refers to the Christian scheme of salvation "which includes sin as a root-cause of sorrow, as it is also a cause of Christian joy as depicted in the *felix culpa* theme."

*   Cunningham, Dolora G. "The Doctrine of Repentance as a Formal Principle in Some Elizabethan Plays." See 89.

*   Fergusson, Francis. "Trope and Allegory: Some Themes Common to Dante and Shakespeare." See 119.

*   Galway, Margaret. "Flyting in Shakespeare's Comedies." See 373.

*   Janecek, Thomas John. "The Literary History of the Parliament of Heaven Allegory from Origination in Christianity to Culmination in the Renaissance Drama of England." See 177.

676.   Knights, L. D. "The Ambiguity of *Measure for Measure*." *Scrutiny*, 10(1942), 222.

The play deals with moral problems which are indicated by the recurrent use of the words "scope," "liberty," and "restraint," and the play has an obvious "relation to the old moralities." Shakespeare questions the relationship between natural impulse and individual liberty and self-restraint and public law. The essay focuses upon the relationship of the characters' restraint (Claudio's sexuality needs to be curbed) and the relationship of the state to the individual (Angelo's treatment of Claudio).

677.   Krieger, Mary. "*Measure for Measure* and Elizabethan Comedy." *PMLA*, 66(1951), 775-84.

Although Krieger stresses the importance of classical ideas as background material for *MM*, the didactic influence of the morality play is also significant.

678.   Lascelles, Mary. "'Glassie Essence,' *Measure for Measure*, II. ii. 120," *RES*, 2(1951), 140-42.

Lascelles explains the term "glassie essence" by referring to a thirteenth century work *Dialogus Miraculorum* by Caesarius of Hersterbach and believes Shakespeare's term is associated with man's soul.

679. Leavis, F. R. "The Greatness of *Measure for Measure.*"
      Scrutiny, 10(1942), 234-47.

      Leavis agrees with L.C. Knights' essay that *MM* bears
      some resemblance to the morality plays, but Shakespeare's
      use of morality material is far more subtle than Knights
      has indicated. Isabella, for one, does not have to
      represent "chaste serenity or self-regarding puritanism."

680. Leech, Clifford. "The Meaning of *Measure for Measure.*"
      ShS, 3(1950), 66-73.

      This essay cautions against those critical readings
      of the play which present a single point of view and
      allow little room for any other type of reading. Leech
      agrees with many critics that the play contains a
      morality-framework, much incidental satire, a deep
      probing into the springs of actions and a passionate
      sympathy with the unfortunate and hard-pressed.

681. McBride, Tom. "*Measure for Measure* and the Unreconciled
      Virtues." *CompD*, 8(1974), 264-73.

      The "parliament of Heaven" allegory is seen in the
      play's action. *MM* is concerned with the punishment of
      sinners. The Duke is similar to Christ in that both
      bring reconciliation between justice and mercy.

682. Muir, Kenneth. "Shakespeare and Erasmus." *N&Q*,
      3(1956), 424-25.

      Shakespeare was indebted to Erasmus' *Furies* for
      background material concerning the conduct of friars
      in *MM*.

*   Page, Susan Carolyn Ulichney. "The Emergence of the
      Humanist Tragic Hero: A Study in the Dramatization
      of the Psychomachia in the Morality Plays and in
      Selected Plays of Shakespeare." See 255.

683. Sale, Roger. "The Comic Mode of *Measure for Measure.*"
      SQ, 19(1968), 55-61.

      Sale argues against the theory put forth by Lascelles
      concerning the Christian allegorical reading of *MM*.
      The essay finds that Shakespeare's play resembles
      Jonsonian comedy with the Duke being a character sim-
      ilar to Brainworm.

684. Schanzer, E.   "The Marriage Contracts in *Measure for
      Measure*." *ShS*, 13(1960), 81–89.

      Shakespeare shows the contradictions inherent in the
      church with the marriage contract between Claudio and
      Juliet. Schanzer surveys Medieval and Renaissance
      marriage contracts and determines that both were sim-
      ilar, and a knowledge of marriage customs is necessary
      for the understanding of the play.

685. Smith, R. M.   "Interpretations of *Measure for Measure*."
      SQ, 1(1950), 208–18.

      In reviewing criticism of *MM*, Smith disagrees with
      those critics who interpret the play from the point
      of view of Medieval religious and moral concepts. The
      criticism of the play has emphasized the preconceived
      ideas of the scholars and has been too piecemeal and
      too egocentric.

686. Stevenson, D. L.   "Design and Structure in *Measure for
      Measure*." *ELH*, 23(1956), 256–78.

      The first part of the essay attacks those critics
      who stress homiletic and theological ideas in the
      play. Stevenson does not disparage critics who link
      the play to Medieval concepts per se, but he finds
      allegorical and religious interpretations to be weak.
      The dramatic design of the play hinges on irony and
      paradox, and it is with the conflict of justice and
      mercy that the "human potential for good and evil has
      been perceptibly extended."

*   Toole, William B. *Shakespeare's Problem Plays*. See 329.

*   Vyvyan, John. *Shakespeare and the Rose of Love: A
      Study of the Early Plays in Relation to the Medieval
      Philosophy of Love*. See 390.

The Merchant of Venice

687. Bratcher, James.   "The Lorenzo-Jessica Subplot and
      Genesis XXXIV," pp. 33–42 in *Shakespeare 1964*. ed.
      Jim W. Corder. Fort Worth: Texas Christian U. Pr.,
      1964.

      This is a rejoinder to Beatrice Brown's article "Med-
      ieval Prototypes of Lorenzo and Jessica." Bratcher
      contends that the source of the subplot is not found in

Medieval writings but rather the book of Genesis.

688. Bronstein, Herbert. "Shakespeare, the Jews, and
      The Merchant of Venice." *SQ*, 20(1969), 3-10.

      Shakespeare's knowledge of Jews did not come from
      Renaissance books or people of his own day but rather
      from Medieval writers such as Chaucer. The Jew of
      passion plays and Corpus Christi pageants also in-
      fluenced Shakespeare.

689. Brown, B. D. "Medieval Prototypes of Lorenzo and
      Jessica." *MLN*, 44(1929), 227-32.

      Brown refers to *MV* as a play rich in Medieval conno-
      tations. He traces the subplot of Lorenzo and Jessica
      to Medieval theological works. Stories which deal with
      the love of a Christian youth for a Jewish damsel occur
      in many collections of exempla from the thirteenth
      century. The author quotes at length from *MS Royal
      7D1*, a collection of *exempla* compiled by a Dominican
      friar in the thirteenth century and refers to the
      Gesta Romanorum, Alphabet of Tales, and *The Exempla of
      Jacques de Vitry* in establishing Shakespeare's debt to
      the native tradition.

690. Brown, J. R. "Introduction," pp. xi + lviii in *The
      Merchant of Venice, Arden Shakespeare.* Cambridge:
      Harvard U. Pr., 1955.

      Brown reviews criticism of the play and comments on
      Coghill's thesis that Shakespeare was indebted to the
      Medieval Processus Belial. The author does not see that
      the conflict between Justice and Mercy is the governing
      idea of the play, but it certainly represents part of
      the play. Other remarks concern the *exemplum* idea be-
      hind the three caskets. Brown attributes the episode
      of the three caskets to Shakespeare's acquaintance with
      the *Gesta Romanorum.*

691. Cardozo, Jacob. "The Background of Shakespeare's
      Merchant of Venice." *ES*, 14(1932), 171-86.

      This essay traces the origin of the pound of flesh
      story and the path by which Shakespeare could have re-
      ceived the story. Cardozo rules out the classical in-
      fluence and suggests that the tale arose in the Middle
      Ages. There are two possible areas of influence: the
      Central and Western European sphere which includes the
      continental Franco-German area and the Scandinavian-

English area; the Levantine sphere which includes
Persian, Turkish, and Moslem authorship. Although
the flesh-bond story was legendary, it became a
matter of record in Medieval romances.

692. Chew, S. C. *The Virtues Reconciled: An Iconographic
Study*. Toronto: The U. of Toronto Pr., 1947.
163 pp.

In presenting the general background of the Parliament of Heaven concept, Chew traces the development of
these ideas through Shakespeare's day. in *MV* Shakespeare changed symbols found in Medieval writings concerning Justice and Truth by having Shylock hold a
knife instead of a sword. The knife is a symbol of
treachery while the sword is associated with righteous-
ness and nobility. Other sections of this book refer
to Medieval ideas of Fortune, Seven Deadly Sins, and the
combat between Virtues and Vices.

* Coghill, Neville. "The Basis of Shakespearean Comedy:
A Study in Medieval Affinities." See 369.

* Doebler, John. *Shakespeare's Speaking Pictures: Studies
in Iconic Imagery*. See 103.

693. Fleissner, Robert F. "A Key to the Name Shylock."
AN&Q, 5(1966), 52-54.

The author reviews scholarship concerning the name
"Shylock" and agrees with those who stress that Shakespeare used a native English name. Fleissner traces the
name "Shylock" to a family that lived in Somerset in
1327.

* Gallagher, Ligera Cecile. "Shakespeare and the
Aristotelian Ethical Tradition." See 128.

* Glazier, Phyllis Gorfain. "Folkloristic Devices and
Formal Structure in Shakespearean Drama." See 135.

694. Gollancz, Israel. *Allegory and Mysticism in Shakespeare,
A Medievalist in The Merchant of Venice*. London:
George W. Jones, 1931. 68 pp.

The moral intention of Shakespeare's play is much
like that found in the moralities. The mystical
atmosphere of the Middle Ages influenced Shakespeare's
idea of heavenly spheres. Another distinct indebtedness

was the concept of the Four Daughters of God, a con-
trolling pattern found throughout the play. Gollancz
further notes that the meaning behind the caskets comes
from *exempla* literature.

*   Gorfain, Phyllis. "Remarks Toward a Folkloristic
       Approach to Literature: Riddles in Shakespearean
       Drama." See 140.

695.   Grebanier, Bernard. *The Truth about Shylock.* New York:
       Random House, 1962. 369 pp.

       Chapter Four "The Pound of Flesh Story" lists and
       summarizes all known analogues concerning the taking
       of flesh as payment for a debt. Grebanier stresses
       that it is improbable that Shakespeare was acquainted
       with the many versions of the story, yet during the
       Middle Ages the pound of flesh motif was popular.
       Accounts of this tale are seen in the *Gesta Romanorum,*
       Cursor Mundi, Tale of Johannes de Alta Silva, and
       Persian and Turkish tales.

*   Hassel, R. Chris, Jr. *Faith and Folly in Shakespeare's*
       Romantic Comedies. See 376.

696.   Holaday, Allan. "Antonio and the Allegory of Salvation."
       ShS, 4(1968), 109-18.

       Shakespeare exploits the Medieval Parliament of Heaven
       concept in *MV.* In Holaday's words, "Shakespeare in-
       tended the mataphor of the parliament, embedded in the
       play's center, to epitomize the drama. Recognition of
       its message would indeed equip his audience to compre-
       hend not only Portia's startling interest in Shylock's
       soul, but also the dramatist's concern with Antonio's
       salvation."

*   ————. "Shakespeare, Richard Edward, and the Virtues
       Reconciled." See 168.

*   Janecek, Thomas John. "The Literary History of the
       Parliament of Heaven Allegory from Origination in
       Christianity to Culmination in the Renaissance Drama
       of England." See 177.

*   Keilstrup, Lorraine M. "The Myth of Cain in the Early
       English Drama." See 185.

697. Kozikowski, Stanley J. "The Allegory of Love and Fortune: The Lottery in *The Merchant of Venice*."
Renascene, 32(1980), 105-15.

   The lottery scenes should be defined in terms of
   Tudor allegory. Background material concerning allegorical interpretation is presented along with analogues
   from various Elizabethan plays.

698. Lewalski, Barbara K. "Biblical Allusions and Allegory
in *The Merchant of Venice*." *SQ,* 13(1962), 327-43.

   In reviewing the criticism of Gollancz, Coghill, and
   Frye concerning the Medieval influence on the play,
   Lewalski shows the extent and manner in which Medieval
   and Biblical allegory influenced Shakespeare. A number
   of affinities between Shakespeare's allegorical method
   and Dante's are shown. She applies the four-fold allegorical method of interpretation to the play: (1) literal level or story; (2) an allegorical significance
   concerned with truth and relating to humanity as a
   whole; (3) a moral or tropological level which deals
   with moral development of the individual; (4) an ana-
   gogical level which points to the ultimate reality--
   the heavenly city. Only the four-fold method of interpretation recognizes the fundamental unity of the
   play.

*   Matthew, Honor. *Character and Symbol in Shakespeare's
   Plays*. See 225.

699. Obaid, Thoraya Ahmed. "The Moor Figure in English Renaissance Drama." *DAI,* 35(1975), 4446-A (Wayne State).

   Obaid examines the figure of the Moor in *MV* and *Tit*.
   Background information is given on the moor who is a
   product of Medieval and Renaissance experience.

*   Owst, G. R. *Literature and Pulpit in Medieval England*.
   See 254.

700. Rea, J. D. "Shylock and the Processus Belial." *PQ,*
8(1929), 311-13.

   The trial scene where Portia pleads the cause of
   mercy against judgment is a re-dramatizing of the Medieval Processus Belial with Shylock substituted for the
   Devil, Portia for the Virgin Mary, and Antonio for
   Mankind.

701. Roth, Cecil. "The Background of Shylock." *RES*, 9
      (1933), 148-56.

      Shylock was a figment of Shakespeare's imagination,
      but the essay speculates on the historical figure of
      Shylock as a real person. There was a real Shylock
      of the Medieval, Levantine tradition who lived in the
      Ghetto Nuovo area of Venice. He spoke excellent Italian,
      was a professional money-lender, and dealt in precious
      stones.

*   Russell, William M. "Courtly Love in Shakespeare's
      Romantic Comedies." See 384.

702. Siegel, Paul N. "Shylock the Puritan." *CUF*, 5(1962),
      14-19.

      Siegel makes the point that the Elizabethan audience
      associated Shylock with the Jew of Medieval legends.
      Cannibalistic images which are associated with Shylock
      throughout the play are suggestive of Medieval legend
      that Jews delighted in feasting on the flesh of murdered
      Christians. The essay demonstrates that Jewish money-
      lenders and Puritan usurers were kindred spirits in
      their villainy.

703. Sinsheimer, Hermann. *Shylock: The History of a
      Character of the Myth of the Jew*. London: Victor
      Gollancz Ltd., 1947. 147 pp.

      Shakespeare's characterization of Shylock is wholly
      in the Medieval tradition associated with Jews. The
      anti-Christian element and the usury theme clearly stem
      from the body of Medieval literature dealing with the
      Jews. The essay does not argue that Shakespeare used
      one particular work for his portrayal of Shylock but
      deals generally with the tradition. Scattered through-
      out the work are various references to Shakespeare and
      the last chapter (114-140) deals mainly with Shylock's
      Medieval elements.

704. Slover, George W. "A Comparative Study of the
      Symbolism in the Sources of *The Merchant of Venice*."
      MA Thesis, Indiana U., 1960.

      In addition to the study on source material, Slover
      reads *MV* from the point of view of the Medieval four-
      fold interpretation.

705. Tillyard, E. M. W. "The Trial Scene in *The Merchant of Venice.*" *REL*, 2(1961), 51-59.

Shakespeare exploits the Medieval theme of the conflict of Justice and Mercy by associating the trial scene with concepts related to the Four Daughters of God. Tillyard stresses the allegorical transformation of Portia from a girl to an abstraction associated with the theme of Mercy and Justice reconciled. Portia's concern in the trial scene is for the salvation of Shylock's soul as well as for Antonio's life. At the end of the scene, Portia abandons her allegorical role and becomes the girl she once was.

706. Vogt, G. "Gleanings for the History of a Sentiment: *Generositas, Virtus, Non Sanguis.*" *JEGP*, 24(1925), 102-24.

Vogt shows parallel treatment of the theme of true nobility and its relationship to virtuous acts in Chaucer and Shakespeare. Chaucer believed true nobility to be the fruit of virtuous and noble living, and Shakespeare used the same ideas in *MV* (II, ix).

707. Wilson, James L. "Another Medieval Parallel to the Jessica and Lorenzo Story." *SAB*, 23(1948), 20-23.

The story of Floripas in the Medieval romance *The Sultan of Babylon* is remarkably similar to the Jessica-Lorenzo story. Both daughters treat their fathers in a similar manner, and both stories involve the axiom that "it is better to be a Christian than non-Christian."

The Merry Wives of Windsor

708. Fleissner, Robert F. "The Malleable Knight and the Unfettered Friar: *The Merry Wives of Windsor* and Boccaccio." *ShakS*, 11(1978), 77-93.

The author compares Shakespeare's *Wiv.* to Boccaccio's tale of Friar Alberto and the Angel Gabriel. He finds "eight major correlations" between the two works.

* Galway, Margaret. "Flyting in Shakespeare's Comedies." See 373.

* Kolin, Philip C. "The Elizabethan Stage Doctor as a Dramatic Convention." See 199.

709. Munro, John. "Some Matters Shakespearean." *TLS,*
      13 September 1947. p. 472.

      Munro objects to Greg's emendation of "counting
      house" to "closet." Munro traces the "counting house"
      to *The Book of Courtasye* (1430) and determines that the
      "counting house" is a place where tallies, records of
      expenditure and income, and the cook's accounts were
      kept.

*   Russell, William M. "Courtly Love in Shakespeare's
      Romantic Comedies." See 384.

710. Steadman, John M. *Nature into Myth: Medieval and Ren-
      aissance Moral Symbols.* Pittsburgh: Duquesne U. Pr.,
      1979. 308 pp.

      Steadman discusses the emblematic descriptions of
      Falstaff in terms of the "humiliated lover" and as an
      exemplum of lust. The basket episode has antecedents
      in late Medieval and Renaissance literature, and Fal-
      staff's depiction in *Wiv.* echoes that tradition. See
      especially pages 117-130.

                    A Midsummer Night's Dream

711. Andreas, James. "From Festivity to Spectacle: *The
      Canterbury Tales,* Fragment I and *A Midsummer Night's
      Dream. UC,* 3(Fall 1980), 19-28.

      This essay explores the way in which Shakespeare
      employed romantic and farcical motifs in *MND, TGV,* and
      TNK. Shakespeare borrowed Chaucerian concepts and was
      influenced by "The Knight's Tale."

*   Barry, Patricia S. *The King in Tudor Drama.* See 15.

712. Bethurum, Dorothy. "Shakespeare's Comment on Med-
      ieval Romance in *Midsummer Night's Dream." MLN,*
      60(1945), 85-94.

      Shakespeare detected Chaucer's ironic treatment of
      the Medieval romance and heightened "the satire he
      found in Chaucer" by changing Emily to two girls and
      leaving Palamon and Arcite as they were. Like Chaucer,
      Shakespeare lightly satirizes the Medieval romance.
      Bethurum observes that there are many parallels between
      Chaucer's and Shakespeare's stories: the parody of
      lover's contending for a girl; the love versus friend-
      ship theme; and the change in fortune for the lovers.

Shakespeare's figures in the lovers' plot are simply
Chaucer's characters treated more realistically than
the romantic conventions would permit. Another point
of comparison is that both authors ridicule the convention of courtly love.

713. Blount, Dale M. "Shakespare's Use of Folklore, Fairies,
      and Magic in *A Midsummer Night's Dream* and *The
      Tempest.*" *DAI*, 30(1969), 679-80-A (Indiana).

      Chapter One examines the popular English tradition of
      fairies, magic, and witchcraft as seen in works from
      the twelfth century through the Jacobean age and relates
      a number of these ideas found in Medieval literature to
      Shakespeare's plays. Blount discusses the types of
      fairies, witches, and magic from the Middle Ages to
      the Renaissance. *MND* and *Tmp.* depict Shakespeare's
      extensive use of fairy and magic lore, and the folk-
      lore employed by Shakespeare is similar to that found
      in Medieval times.

714. Braddy, Haldeen. "Shakespeare's Puck and Froissart's
      Orthon." *SQ*, 7(1956), 276-280.

      Braddy suggests the possibility of Shakespeare's in-
      debtedness to the *Chronicles* of Froissart as a source
      for Puck (II, XXXVII, 353). Many points of comparison
      are shown between Puck and Orthon. Both characters,
      for example, serve as speedy messengers for their
      masters and transform themselves into animals.

*   Campbell, Josie P. "Farce as Function in Medieval and
      Shakespearean Drama." See 56.

715. Champion, Larry S. "*A Midsummer Night's Dream:* The
      Problem of Source." *PLL*, 4(1968), 13-19.

      Shakespeare adapted Chaucer's "The Knight's Tale" to
      the purpose of romantic comedy. The basic structure
      and sequence of events in both works run parallel to
      each other. Champion argues that Shakespeare "utilized
      Chaucer's tale in a much more extensive fashion than
      critics have previously articulated."

716. ————. *The Evolution of Shakespeare's Comedy: A
      Study in Dramatic Perspective.* Cambridge: Harvard
      U. Pr., 1970, 241 pp.

      See especially pp. 50-54 for a discussion of Shake-
      speare's indebtedness to Chaucer's "The Knight's Tale."

See also pp. 198-199 for a listing of criticism dealing
with the sources for *MND*.

*   Charlton, H. B. *Shakespearean Comedy*. See 367.

717.   Doran, Madeleine. *"A Midsummer Night's Dream:* A
       Metamorphosis." *RIP*, 46(1960), 113-135.

       Doran studies two aspects of the play: the character
       of Theseus and the relationship of source material to
       the play. Shakespeare owes much to Chaucer, Ovid, and
       Plutarch for the figure of Theseus and to the Ovidian
       myth for the classical background of the play. Specific
       borrowings from Chaucer's "The Knight's Tale" are
       Theseus' "keeping state" for the wedding of Hippolyta;
       the conquered bride; his riding to hounds; his change
       of service from Mars to Diana; his role as an arbiter
       in a romantic love story; and his amused and tolerant
       attitude toward the lovers.

718.   Fisher, P. "The Argument of *A Midsummer Night's Dream*."
       SQ, 8(1957), 307-10.

       Fisher briefly comments upon the relationship of
       saturnalian comedy and folklore in *MND*.

*   Hassel, R. Chris, Jr. *Faith and Folly in Shakespeare's
       Romantic Comedies*. See 376.

719.   Moore, John R. "The Transformation of Bottom." *IUS*,
       13(1926), 45-50.

       This study suggests a number of episodes found in
       Medieval and early Tudor drama as an analogue to Puck's
       "transformation" of Bottom. Moore objects to Apuleius
       as a source because Lucius transforms himself, while
       Bottom is transformed.

720.   Muir, K. "Pyramus and Thisbe: A Study in Shakespeare's
       Method." *SQ*, 5(1954), 141-53.

       Muir examines classical and Medieval sources for
       Shakespeare's *MND*. Muir believes that Shakespeare
       used several sources, among them Chaucer's *Legend of
       Good Women*, Gower's *Confessio Amantis*, and Lydgate's
       Reson and Sensuallyte.

721.   ————. "Shakespeare as a Parodist." *N&Q*, 199
       (1954), 467-68.

Shakespeare parodies Medieval and Renaissance
material in the Pyramus and Thisbe story.

722.   Olsen, P. *"Midsummer Night's Dream* and the Meaning of
       Court Marriage." *ELH,* 24(1957), 95-119.

The structure of *MND* is built upon the Medieval
conception of comedy: "the work begins with order
(act I), then passes through the cycle of a fall which
brings the domination of unbridled passion (acts II and
III). Finally the play stresses charity and morality
(acts IV and V). In addition, the fairy rulers are
cosmic projections of the same qualities which Theseus
and Hippolita embody in the world of the state. Their
plot forms a commentary upon the foibles of the lovers.
Shakespeare borrowed this technique (the usage of
various levels of reality) from Chaucer. Pluto and
Prosperina serve as analogues to January and May in
"The Merchant's Tale."

*   Russell, William M. "Courtly Love in Shakespeare's
         Romantic Comedies." See 384.

723.   Vlasopolos, Anca. "The Ritual of Midsummer: A Pattern
       for *A Midsummer Night's Dream.*" *RenQ,* 31(1978), 21-29.

MND is tied closely to folklore and ancient ritual.
The power of plants and their scheme within the play
are stressed. According to Medieval belief, the mugwort
"belongs to Saint John" in the Christian scheme of the
ritual. The author interprets chastity to mean "fruitful, generative monogamy."

*   Weld, John. *Meaning in Comedy: Studies in Elizabethan
         Romantic Comedy.* See 391.

724.   Young, David Pollock. "Something of Great Constancy:
       A Study of *A Midsummer Night's Dream.*" Diss.,
       Yale U., 1965.

Young's chapter "The Non-Dramatic Background" is a
general discussion of Shakespeare's manipulation of
classical and Medieval sources for *MND*.

Much Ado About Nothing

*   Hassell, R. Chris, Jr. *Faith and Folly in Shakespeare's
         Romantic Comedies.* See 376.

*   Hengerer, Joyce H. "The Theme of the Slandered Woman
        in Shakespeare." See 162.

*   Hunter, Robert Grams. *Shakespeare and the Comedy of
        Forgiveness.* See 377.

725.   Page, N. "My Lady Disdain." *MLN*, 49(1935), 494-99.

        By contrasting the role of women in the Middle Ages
        with that of the Renaissance, Page clarifies Beatrice's
        significance and position in *Ado*. A woman's role in
        Medieval times was generally subservient to a man's.
        The woman served her husband and her family. The Ren-
        aissance, however, brought forth the emancipated woman
        who chose her own marriage partner. Beatrice is not
        anti-matrimonial but merely discriminatory in her choice
        of a husband.

*   Presson, Robert K. "Some Traditional Instances of
        Setting in Shakespeare's Plays." See 382.

*   Russell, William M. "Courtly Love in Shakespeare's
        Romantic Comedies." See 384.

726.   Sexton, Joyce Hengerer. "The Theme of Slander in
        Much Ado About Nothing and Garter's *Susanna*." *PQ*,
        54(1975), 419-33.

        Shakespeare is using the theme of the slandered woman
        in *Ado*. The theme is a Medieval commonplace, but per-
        haps Shakespeare was influenced by Gower's *Mirrour de
        l'omme*. Psychological realism is not stressed, but
        rather the effects of slander on Hero and Claudia.
        Ado. is very close to a late morality play.

Othello

727.   Berger, Thomas L. "Shakespeare's Medieval World:
        Audience Response and Othello." *RORD*, 24(1981), 161.

        Berger presents an abstract of his reading of *Oth*.
        in terms of the Seven Deadly Sins of the moralities.

728.   Bethell, S. L. "Shakespeare's Imagery: The Diabolic
        Images in *Othello*." *ShS*, 5(1952), 62-80.

        Oth. appears to have three different levels of under-
        standing: the personal level which portrays a domes-
        tic tragedy; the social level which depicts conflict
        between atheistic machiavellism and the Medieval chival-

ric code; and the metaphysical level which depicts the
warfare of good and evil, much in the same way as that
seen in the morality play.

728a. Brennecke, Ernest. "'Nay, That's Not Next!' The
Significance of Desdemona's 'Willow song.'" *SQ*,
4(1953), 35-38.

This essay shows the significance of Desdemona's
song which was popularly performed since the time of
Henry VIII. The ballad allows Desdemona to speak
words too difficult in conversation.

729. Camden, Carroll. "Iago on Women." *JEGP*, 48(1949),
56-71.

The exchange of words between Iago and Desdemona
(II, i) is viewed in relation to Medieval and Ren-
aissance concepts of a woman's duties. Camden links
Iago's remarks to antifeminist literature and rejects
Rymer's remarks in his *Short View of Tragedy* that
Shakespeare was following the improvised witticisms
of the mystery plays.

* Coursen, Herbert R., Jr. *Christian Ritual and the
World of Shakespeare's Tragedies.* See 432.

* Craig, Hardin. "Morality Plays and Elizabethan Drama."
See 83.

* Creeth, Edmund. *Mankynde in Shakespeare.* See 434.

* Cunningham, J. V. *Woe and Wonder.* See 436

* Curtin, Madelyn Elaine Douglas. "Mistaking the Word
and Simple Syllogisms: Form and Function in Shakespeare's Wordplay." See 91.

* Dessen, Alan. "The Logic of Elizabethan Stage Violence:
Some Alarms and Excursions for Modern Critics, Editors, and Directors." See 102.

730. Doebler, Bettie Anne. "Othello's Angels: *Ars Moriendi*,"
pp. 172-85 in *Shakespeare's Speaking Pictures* by
John Doebler. Albuquerque: U. of New Mex. Pr., 1974.

The final scene in Act V of *Oth.* invokes the *ars
moriendi* tradition. The bed is an iconic stage prop
which was popularly shown by late Medieval pictures.

*   Farnham, Willard. *Shakespeare's Tragic Frontier.*
       See 443.

731.   Faver, M. D. "The Summoning of Desdemona: *Othello,*
       V. ii. 1-82." *AN&Q,* 9(1970), 35-37.

       This scene shows Shakespeare's imagination working
       along the same lines as the authors of *Everyman*
       and other earlier *ars moriendi* treatises. Desdemona
       and Othello are acting very similar to the character
       Death and his victim in the moralities.

732.   Fortin, Rene E. "Allegory and Genre in *Othello.*"
       Genre, 4(1971), 153-72.

       The convergence of the Iago-Othello roles results in
       an inversion of the morality pattern. Othello is identi-
       fied with the tempter and as the Bad Angel kills Des-
       demona, the Angel of Mercy figure. Fortin sees differ-
       ent levels of allegory at work in *Oth.*

*   Gallagher, Ligera Cecile. "Shakespeare and the Aris-
       totelian Ethical Tradition." See 128.

733.   Hawkes, Terence. "Iago's Use of Reason." *SP,* 58
       (1958), 160-69.

       Oth. is in the "stark morality tradition" with Iago
       as 'motiveless' evil and Desdemona as "simple good."
       Hawkes uses Aquinas' philosophy of *ratio inferior* and
       ratio superior in understanding Othello's seduction
       by Iago. Iago is the user of *ratio interior,* a method
       of deception similar to Satan's deception of Eve.

734.   Moore, John Robert. "Othello, Iago, and Cassio
       as Soldiers." *PQ,* 31(1952), 189-94.

       Of interest is Moore's comment that Iago is associated
       with the traditional role of honesty in the morality
       play.

735.   Morris, Harry. "No Amount of Prayer Can Possibly
       Matter." *SR,* 77(1960), 8-24.

       The concept of damnation so apparent in the morality
       plays influenced Shakespeare's writing of *Oth.* Although
       Othello begins as an innocent person, he succumbs to
       the wiles of a demon--Iago. Characters in the play are
       identified as being good or bad. Desdemona plays the
       role of an angel struggling to prevent Othello's soul
       from being damned.

736.   Poisson, Rodney. "Death for Adultery: A Note on
       Othello, III, iii, 394-96." *SQ,* 28(1977), 89-92.

Poisson examines numerous Elizabethan and some
Medieval references to show that death to the unfaithful
wife is the only alternative to enduring dishonor. For
example, Guinevere was sentenced to burn at the stake.

*   Ribner, Irving. *Patterns of Shakespearean Tragedy*.
      See 452.

737. Rice, Nancy Hall. "Beauty and the Beast and the Little
      Boy: Clues about the Origins of Sexism and Racism
      from Folklore and Literature: Chaucer's 'The
      Prioress's Tale,' *Sir Gawain and the Green Knight*,
      The Alliterative Morte Arthure, Webster's *The Duchess
      of Malfi*, Shakespeare's *Othello*, Hawthorne's ' Rap-
      paccini's Daughter,' and Melville's 'Benito Cereno.'"
      DAI, 36(1975), 875-A (Mass.).

      Virulence against women and blacks is surveyed in
      folklore and Medieval works such as *Gawain* and *Morte
      Arthure*. In Shakespeare's *Oth*. "racist attitudes
      compound a tragedy generated by sexism in society."

738. Ross, Lawrence J. "The Shakespearean *Othello*: A
      Critical Exposition on Historical Evidence." *DAI*,
      20(1959), 2302 (Princeton).

      Part of this study concludes that Shakespeare worked
      in the tradition of the morality play with the concepts
      of evil and good struggling for the soul of the hero.

739. ————. "Shakespeare's 'Dull Clown' and Symbolic
      Music." *SQ*, 17(1966), 107-28.

      The clown mentioned in *Oth*. (III, i) is examined from
      the viewpoint of Medieval and classical motifs of music.
      Ross interprets music in *Oth*. by emblems and Platonic
      and Boethium concepts.

740. Scragg, Leah. "Iago--Vice or Devil?" *ShS*, 21(1968),
      53-65.

      Scragg gives an account of the Vice in Medieval and
      Renaissance drama and shows that Iago's characteristics
      are derived from the morality plays. She particularly
      emphasizes that Iago is derived from the Devil by
      demonstrating that Iago's words and actions are similar
      to the various representations of the Devil of Medieval
      drama.

*   Spivak, Bernard. *Shakespeare and the Allegory of Evil*.
      See 456.

741. Stewart, Douglas J. "*Othello:* Roman Comedy as Night-
      mare." *EMQ,* 22(1967), 252-76.

      The study of *Oth.* is largely one-sided since the
      history of its criticism is basically a study of Iago.
      Although Spivak's *Shakespeare and the Allegory of Evil*
      contains a "brilliant account of Iago's progress from
      the Vice of the morality play, yet this type of study
      is patchwork and disproportionate." Stewart, therefore,
      contends that Iago is more than just a Vice. Shakespeare
      fused the comic slave of Plautus and Terence with the
      Vice concept. In addition, Shakespeare's indebtedness
      to classical comedy is extensive.

742. Stroup, T. P. "Shakespeare's Use of a Travel-Book
      Commonplace." *PQ,* 17(1938), 355-56.

      Stroup takes issue with scholars who point out that
      Othello's accounts of his travels to Desdemona (I, iii,
      128-45) are based upon classical sources. It is just
      as probable that Shakespeare used Medieval sources, such
      as Isidore of Seville's *Etymolgiae,* Caxton's *Mirror of
      the World,* and Vincent of Beauvais' *Speculum Historiale*
      and *Speculum Naturale.* Also the alliterative *Wars of
      Alexander* and various travel books by Mandeville and
      John de Plano Carpini may be the likely origin of
      Othello's speech.

743. Watson, Thomas L. "The Detractor-Backbiter: Iago and
      the Tradition." *TSLL,* 5(1963-64), 546-54.

      Although Iago is a much more complex and sophisticated
      detractor than his dramatic antecedents, he is a char-
      acter conceived and born in the tradition of the Vice
      and of the detractor found in morality plays.

744. West, Robert H. "Iago and the Mystery of Iniquity."
      RP, 917(1961), 63-69.

      West disagrees with Spivak's emphasis that Iago
      should be related to the Vice in the morality play.
      Iago represents evil of a more general nature; the type
      of evil that "we sense in us all."

Pericles

745. Baskerville, Charles. "Some Evidence for Early Romantic
      Plays in England." *MP,* 14(1916), 229-51.

      The study traces the growth of folk festivals and

early native drama in written and oral tradition and briefly comments upon remnants of early songs and rituals in *Per.*, *MND*, and *Cym.* The introduction of *Per.* is similar to songs found in folk festivals.

*   Douce, Francis. *Illustration of Shakespeare, and of Ancient Manners.* See 106.

746.   Evans, Betrand. "The Poem of *Pericles*," pp. 35–56 in *Essays in Criticism.* ed. B.H. Lehman et al. Berkeley: U. of California Pr., 1955.

Evans examines the role of Gower as chorus in *Per.* and argues that for the most part the chorus is superfluous. The first four speeches of Gower are associated with "Gower's poem with only certain episodes dramatized." The first three acts are really more poem than play, but the remainder of the drama shows a remarkable change. Gower's speeches then serve a dramatic purpose with more accent upon drama.

*   Glazier, Phyllis Gorfain. "Folkloristic Devices and Formal Structure in Shakespearean Drama." See 135.

747.   Goolden, P. "Antiochus's Riddle in Gower and Shakespeare." *RES*, 6(1955), 245–51.

The riddle in *Per.* (I, i, 64) is explicated in terms of the prose romance *Apollonious of Tyre* to determine that Shakespeare improved the clarity of the riddle by substituting a different speaker than the one found in the older stories. In Medieval versions, the speaker is King Antiochus, while in Shakespeare's version the daughter is the speaker. Medieval versions of the riddle are nearly incomprehensible, while Shakespeare's version is understandable because he reworked the clues of the riddle in order to gain clarity.

748.   Gorfain, Phyllis. "Puzzle and Artifice: the Riddle as Metapoetry in *Pericles*." *ShS*, 29(1976), 11–20.

Gorfain explores the intricacies of ritual and riddling in *Per.* with regard to folklore and anthropology.

749.   Hoeniger, F. D. ed. *Pericles.* London: Methuen and Co., Ltd., 1963. 188 pp.

Hoeniger shows the continuing use of the romance

Apollonius of Tyre throughout the Middle Ages and the
Renaissance. Godfrey de Viterbo, the *Gesta Romanorum*,
Chaucer, and Gower retold the famous story. Shakespeare's
source is Gower's tale in Book Eight of *Confessio Amantis*
and Twine's *The Patterns of Painefull Adventures*. By
introducing Gower at the beginning of *Per.*, Shakespeare
moralizes in a manner similar to his Medieval predecessors.
In addition, Hoeniger believes that the structure of
Per. parallels that found in certain miracle or saint's
plays as, for example, the Digby play of *Mary Magdalene*.

750.   ————. "*Pericles* and the Miracle Play," in *New Arden
        Shakespeare, Pericles*. London: Methuen and Co.,
        Ltd. lxxxviii-xci pp.

        The structural features of *Per.* have derived from the
        miracle plays. Hoeniger stresses the building of the
        action out of a number of loosely related episodes, the
        treatment of the work as a pageant, the tragic comic
        development, the emphasis upon supernatural powers, and
        the didactic features of the play.

751.   Kane, Robert J. "A Passage in *Pericles*." *MLN*, 68
        (1953), 483-84.

        The fate of King Antiochus and his daughter in *Per.*
        (II, iv) is suggested by John Gower, but additional
        source material may be found in *Antiochus IV* and *I* and
        II Maccabees.

752.   Knapp, Peggy Ann. "The Orphic Vision of *Pericles*."
        TSLL, 15(1974), 615-26.

        The romance "follows the lines of the plot of *Sir
        Orfeo* and reverberates its tone." Hence, the myth of
        Orpheus is important and determines the structure of
        Per.

753.   Marder, Louis. "The Riddle in *Pericles*." *ShN*, V
        (1955), 44.

        Marder reviews and adds additional comments on Golden's
        article "Antiochus's Riddle in Gower and Shakespeare,"
        and stresses that Shakespeare used the riddle found in
        the Medieval prose romance *Aplonious of Tyre*.

754.   Thorne, W. B. "The *Pericles* and the 'incest-fertility
        opposition.'" *SQ*, 22(1971), 43-56.

        The traditional folk opposition of the old father and

and the young suitor has been modified to accommodate
the incestuous daughter-father relationship. The same
type of structure is seen in *Shr.* and *TGV*.

The Phoenix and the Turtle

755. Bates, Ronald. "Shakespeare's '*The Phoenix and
      Turtle.*'" *SQ*, 6(1955), 19-30.

    Bates rejects Fairchild's hypothesis that Shakespeare
leaned heavily upon Chaucer's *Parlement of Foules* for
the first five stanzas of the poem. The comic and magi-
cal aspects of the poem derive from the rhyme scheme,
which is closely connected to the Old English riddle
poems. Also the essay analyzes Shakespeare's use of
birds and determines the bird of loudest lay is the
cock.

756. Cunningham, J. V. "'Essence' and *The Phoenix and Turtle*."
      JEGP, 19(1952), 265-76.

    The courtly love convention in Shakespeare's poem is
treated in terms of scholastic theology. Cunningham
deals mainly with the terminology of scholasticism and
also applies scholastic theory in interpreting *MM*, *TGV*,
and *1H4*.

757. Dronke, Peter. "*The Phoenix and the Turtle*." *OL*,
      23(1968), 199-220.

    The poem basically deals with the perfection and
imperfection of love, and Dronke explains this theme
in relation to Medieval and Renaissance concepts.
Finally, Shakespeare's poem is compared to Robert
Chester's "Loves Martyr."

758. Fairchild, Arthur. "*The Phoenix and Turtle*." *EStud*,
      33(1904), 337 84.

    This essay establishes parallels between Shakespeare's
poem and Chaucer's *The Parlement of Foules* and suggests
the importance of the Medieval court of love and emblems
to an understanding of the poem. In addition, both
Chaucer's and Shakespeare's concepts of birds are explored
in the poems.

The Rape of Lucrece

759. Battenhouse, Roy W. "'Lucrece' in Other Versions,"
      pp. 385-405 in *Shakespearean Tragedy*. Bloomington:
      Indiana U. Pr., 1969.

The essay discusses the possibility of Shakespeare's
debt to Chaucer for the story of Lucrece. Both Chaucer
and Shakespeare view Lucrece from a Medieval Christian
perspective. Chaucer's ironical handling of Lucrece
influenced Shakespeare.

760.   ———. "Shakespeare's Re-Vision of 'Lucrece,'" pp.
        3-41 in *Shakespearean Tragedy*. Bloomington:
        Indiana U. Pr., 1969.

This essay reads the poem from an Augustinian point
of view. The moral vision behind "Lucrece" is not
readily apparent, but its roots are found in the Bible
and St. Augustine. Further, the author states that
"the metaphor of a perspective glass suggests a concept
common in Medieval art—the distinction between a
work's surface of beautiful lie and a truth hidden
under this fiction."

761.   Borinski, Ludwig. "The Origin of the Euphuistic Novel
        and its Significance for Shakespeare," pp. 38-52 in
        Studies in Honor of T.W. Baldwin. ed. Don Cameron
        Allen. Urbana: U. of Illinois, 1958.

"Venus and Adonis" and "Lucrece" are the most
euphuistic of Shakespeare's works. Pettie, not Lyly,
is the source of this tradition. Pettie derived his
ideas from the debate tradition from Medieval literature,
Senecan rhetoric, and Aeneas Sylvius. The essay also
discusses four traditions which were important to
Shakespeare: Senecan tragedy, the concept of the Fall
of Princes, the Arcadian novel, and the euphuistic
novel.

762.   Patton, Jon F. "Essays in the Elizabethan She-Tragedies."
        DAI, 30(1970), 1534-A (Ohio State).

Chapter One surveys female complaints in classical and
Medieval literature, and Chapter Four relates "The
Rape of Lucrece" to the essential qualities of the She-
tragedies in the classical and Medieval origins of the
genre outside the *De Casibus* tradition. Patton argues
that the She-tragedies constitute a separate genre from
the *De Casibus* influence.

*   Schofield, William Henry. *Chivalry in English
        Literature*. See 291.

Richard II

763. Altick, Richard D. "Conveyor's and Fortune's Buckets
in *Richard II*." *MLN*, 61(1946), 179-180.

   R2 (IV, i, 317-18) refers to the word "conveyors"
   which Altick associates with the buckets of Fortune's
   Wheel. The image conveys the idea of rising and
   falling Fortune, a familiar and popular Medieval literary convention.

* Bergeron, David M. *English Civic Pageantry 1558-1642*.
   See 27.

764. Black, Matthew W. "The Sources of Shakespeare's
   Richard II," pp. 199-216 in *J.Q. Adams Memorial
   Studies*. ed. James G. McManaway. Washington: Folger
   Shakespeare Library, 1948.

   Shakespeare's sources for *R2* are Holinshed and Hall,
   two versions of the *Chronicque de la Traison et Mort
   de Richard Deux Roy Dengle-terre*, Creton's *Historie du
   Roy d'Angleterre Richard II*, the anonymous play *Thomas
   of Woodstock*, Daniel's *Civil Wars*, and the *Chronicles*
   of Froissart. While the list of works appears to be
   enormous, Black maintains that Shakespeare could have
   read the works in less than thirty hours. Shakespeare
   took Medieval picturesque incidents and certain aspects
   of character interpretation from Froissart.

* Coursen, Herbert R., Jr. *Christian Ritual and the
   World of Shakespearean Tragedies*. See 432.

* de Montmorency, J. E. G. "Gardens of Chaucer and
   Shakespeare." See 97.

* Dessen, Alan. "The Logic of Elizabethan Stage Violence:
   Some Alarms and Excursions for Modern Critics,
   Editors, and Directors." See 102.

765. Duls, Louisa DeSaussure. "The Complex Picture of
   Richard II Inherited by Sixteenth-Century Writers
   from Fourteenth and Fifteenth-Century Chronicle
   Sources." *DAI*, 23(1961), 4675 (U. of North Carolina).

   The wicked tyrant concept--the martyr king exploited
   by a shrewd politician--and the Yorkist view which de-

picts the weakness of Richard's government and Richard
as a victim of an ambitious pretender are the ambiguous and complex portrayals presented by the fourteenth-
century chronicles. Duls shows how the sixteenth
century writers, including Shakespeare, used aspects
of the earlier chronicles.

766.   Elliott, John R., Jr. *"Richard II* and the Medieval,"
       pp. 25-34 in *Renaissance Papers, 1965.* ed. English
       Department. Durham: U. of North Carolina Pr., 1966.

       Elliott examines Tillyard's ideas that *R2* is Shake-
       speare's "picture of the Middle Ages," and Richard's be-
       lief of the inviolability of kingship is a Medieval
       concept, and Elliott points out that the Tudors empha-
       sized that rebellion was evil and thus Richard's ideas
       of kingship are not necessarily Medieval. Also, the
       subjects' responsibility from a Medieval point of view
       is not to surrender to the unjust and unrighteous de-
       mands of a monarch but to insure that the ruler's
       powers were according to natural and divine laws. It
       is in this manner that *R2* embraces Medieval political
       tendencies.

767.   ————. "History and Tragedy in *Richard II.*" *SEL,*
       8(1968), 253-71.

       Of particular interest are the remarks concerning
       Richard's violation of Medieval political ideas. Shake-
       speare presents a Richard who habitually violates the
       legal restraints on the power of a king. The murder of
       political enemies, the arbitrary imposition of taxes,
       the denial of justice, and the renunciation of the
       essential rights of a lord indicate that Richard is a
       tyrant and a sinner whose foul enormities infect his
       entire realm by evil example.

768.   Freeman, Arthur. *"Richard II,* I, iii, 294-95." *SQ,*
       14(1963), 89-90.

       This essay takes issue with Coghill's essay "Shake-
       speare's Reading in Chaucer" by pointing out that Shake-
       speare did not borrow from Chaucer when using the term
       "frosty Caucasus." Freeman believes the source can be
       found in classical mythology.

*   Gallagher, Ligera Cecile. "Shakespeare and the Aris-
       totelian Ethical Tradition." See 128.

*   Kantorowicz, Ernst. *The Kings Two Bodies.* See 183.

*   Kruegel, Sister Mary Flaula. "An Ideological Analysis
      of Honor in William Shakespeare's *Richard II, I* and
      II Henry IV, and *Henry V.*" See 400.

769. Kwiokawa, Takashi. "*De Casibus* Theme and Machiavellism."
      ShStud, 7(1968-69), 61-80.

      As the title suggests, the author comments upon the
      De Casibus theme in Medieval works, and focuses his
      study upon *Edward II.* A good portion of this essay
      also touches upon *R2.*

*   Matte, Nancy Lightfoot. "The *Ars-Moriendi* in Selected
      Shakespearean History Plays." See 401.

*   Morrison, George Peter. "Shakespeare's Lancastrian
      Tetralogy in the Light of the Medieval Mystery Cycles:
      A Theory for Unity." See 402.

770. Maxwell, J. C. "*Richard II,* I, iii, 294-295." *SQ,*
      14(1963), 283.

      Maxwell indicates that Gregor Sarrazin was the first
      to note a Chaucerian echo from "The Wife of Bath's Tale"
      in the Shakespearean passage above. Maxwell corrects
      Freeman's note which credits Coghill for this discovery.

771. Nearing, Homer, Jr. "Julius Caesar and the Tower of
      London." *MLN,* 63(1948), 228-33.

      Shakespeare's reference to the tradition that Julius
      Caesar built the Tower of London (*R2,* V, i, and *R3* III,
      i) probably was derived from Lydgate's *Serpent* or
      Grafton's *Chronicles. The Parlement of the Three Ages*
      also refers to the tradition although it was not
      generally believed by most chroniclers.

772. Petronella, Vincent F. "Regal Duality and Everyman:
      Dante to Shakespeare." *HAB,* 30(1979), 131-46.

      The Medieval tendency of viewing the king as an
      "Everyman-figure" is traced from its roots in the
      concept of the king's two bodies, through Dante to
      Shakespeare. *R2* is a play about the transformation
      of Richard into Everyman.

773. Phialas, Peter G. "The Medieval in *Richard II.*"
      SQ, 12(1961), 305-310.

This essay rejects Tillyard's thesis that *R2* is
Shakespeare's picture of the Middle Ages, a picture
in which ceremony and pomp are of more value than an
event. Tillyard stresses propriety of sentiment and
elaborate rules of the game as Shakespeare's concept
of the Middle Ages. Phialas argues that the emphasis
on ceremony and inaction in Richard's England contrasts
with the vitality of the Middle Ages. The key to the
interpretation of the play is found in the words of
the dying Gaunt who indicates that Medieval England
had been a prosperous and dynamic land, whose rulers
had been loved at home and feared abroad. Their popularity was due in part to their military prowess,
a quality which Richard so pitifully lacks.

774.   ———. "*Richard II* and Shakespeare's Tragic Mode."
        TSLL, 5(1963), 344-55.

        R2 is a milepost in Shakespeare's progress toward the
        great tragedies in his later years. Along with the *De
        Casibus* theme of the earlier plays, Shakespeare links
        free will and moral behavior to advance the tragic
        experiences. Phialas also discusses the role of *De
        Casibus* tragedy in *Rom.* and *Lr.*

775.   Ribner, Irving. "The Political Problems in Shake-
        speare's Lancastrium Tetralogy." *SP,* 49(1952), 171-84.

        Concerning the Medieval, Ribner comments upon Richard
        as a symbol epitomizing the dying Medieval world, while
        Bolingbroke represents a way of life opposed to that of
        Richard by exhibiting the political philosophies of
        Machiavelli, Bruno, and Montaigne.

*   ———. "Morality Roots of the Tudor History Play."
        See 404.

776.   Sayles, G. O. "Richard II in 1381 and 1399." *EHR,*
        94(1979), 820-29.

        Of interest are the historical events surrounding
        Richard's surrender to Lancaster (1399) and the events
        of the Wat Tyler Rebellion (1381).

*   Stokes, James David. "Roots of the English History
        Play." See 408.

*   Stone, Charles Venable. "Dramas of Christian Time:
        Temporal Assumptions and Dramatic Form in the Medieval

Mystery Cycle, the Morality Play, and Shakespeare's
Second Tetralogy." See 313.

777. Thompson, R. Ann. "The 'two buckets' Image in *Richard
II* and 'The Isle of Gulls.'" *Archiv*, 213(1976), 108.

Thompson argues against Coghill's suggestion that
the two buckets image in *R2* derives from Chaucer's
"The Knight's Tale."

Richard III

* Bethell, S. L. *Shakespeare and the Popular Dramatic
Tradition*. See 29.

778. Clemen, Wolfgang H. "Tradition and Originality in
Shakespeare's *Richard III*." *SQ*, 5(1954), 247-57.

Clemen studies characterization, form, and structure
in *R3* and relates these ideas to Senecan and Medieval
concepts. Richard is a compound of the Senecan tyrant,
Machiavellian villain, and the Dissembler of the
morality play.

* Curtin, Madelyn Elaine Douglas. "Mistaking the Word
and Simple Syllogisms: Form and Function in Shakespeare's Wordplay." See 91.

* Dessen, Alan. "The Logic of Elizabethan Stage Violence:
Some Alarms and Excursions for Modern Critics,
Editors, and Directors." See 102.

779. Doebler, Bettie Anne. "'Despaire and Dye': The
Ultimate Temptation of Richard III." *ShakS*, 7(1974),
75-82.

Doebler shows the importance of the *ars-moriendi*
tradition in *R3*. The king who lives badly must, therefore, die badly. An iconic structure is given to scene
V, iii where Richard battles with the temptation of
despair.

780. French, A. L. "The World of *Richard III*." *ShakS*, 4
(1972), 25-39.

The morality play pattern does not apply to *R3*.
Instead of a cyclic or redemptive process there is
an atmosphere of uncertainty and unreality in the play.

781.   Fusillo, Robert James. "Tents on Bosworth Field."
       SQ, 6(1955), 193-94.

       There are too many problems arising from a literal way
       of staging the opposing tents in *R3* (V, iii). A
       probable solution would be the use of multiple staging,
       a stage practice descending from the mystery plays.

782.   Glover, A. S. B. "Shakespeare and Jewish Liturgy."
       TLS, 22 May 1953. p. 333.

       Glover notes a parallel between Richmond's prayer
       in *R3* and the Medieval canticle *Nunc Demittis*. The
       lines from the Medieval prayer are: "Save us, O Lord,
       while we are waking and guard us while we sleep, that
       we may watch with Christ; and rest in peace."

783.   Hapgood, Robert. "Three Eras in *Richard III*."
       SQ, 14(1963), 281-83.

       Hapgood reacts to Phialas' article "The Medieval in
       Richard III" by stating that Shakespeare's play makes
       distinctions between Medieval, Late Medieval and Ren-
       aissance times. According to Hapgood, Phialas goes
       too far in stressing the past as a thematic element in
       the play.

784.   Hughes, Daniel E. "The 'Worm of Conscience' in
       Richard III and *Macbeth*." *EJ*, 55(1971), 845-52.

       Commenting on the role of conscience in *R3* and *Mac.*,
       Hughes states that both Macbeth and Richard must be
       viewed as men who make their own moral decisions. They
       are not worked upon by fate nor are they to be regarded
       as agents worked upon by the Devil. Richard has, how-
       ever, some qualities similar to the Vice of the old
       moralities whose impish glee turns the moral world
       upside down. Hughes also believes that in contrast to
       Mac., *R3* is closer to the morality plays of the Middle
       Ages in being representational in its characters and
       in being didactic in its purposes.

*   Keilstrup, Lorraine M. "The Myth of Cain in the Early
       English Drama." See 185.

*   Matthews, Honor. *Character and Symbol in Shakespeare's
       Plays*. See 225.

*   Page, Susan Carolyn Ulichney. "The Emergence of the

Humanist Tragic Hero: A Study in the Dramatization of the Psychomachia in the Morality Plays and in Selected Plays of Shakespeare." See 255.

* Rosier, James Louis. "The Chain of Sin and Privation in Elizabethan Literature." See 279.

785. Rossiter, A. P. "The Structure of *Richard The III.*" *DUJ*, 31(1938), 44-75.

Rossiter illustrates that *R3* is Shakespeare's nearest approach to a political, morality play in the tradition of Bale's *Kynge Johan*.

786. Roth, Cecil. "Shakespeare and the Jewish Liturgy." *TSL*, 15 May 1953. p. 317.

Richmond's prayer in *R3* before going to sleep (V, iii, 112-114) is similar to the traditional Jewish night prayer. The Jewish prayer ends with the Medieval hymn *Adon Olan* which Roth speculates Shakespeare may have known.

787. Royster, J. F. "*Richard III*, IV, iv and the Three Marys of Medieval Drama." *MLN*, 25(1910), 173-74.

In this scene, Margaret of Anjou, Queen Elizabeth, and the Duchess of York lament their slain children and husbands. Royster finds a striking likeness between the Shakespearean passage and the *planctus* of the Three Marys before the tomb of Christ in the resurrection of the cycle plays. In each scene the women chant their sorrow for the dead in a lyric key, though no verbal similarities appear. Royster suggests a possible Medieval influence and refers to other Shakespearean plays which contain ideas from the earlier cycle plays.

* Schofield, William Henry. *Chivalry in English Literature.* See 291.

* Sheriff, William E. "Shakespeare's Use of the Native Comic Tradition in his Early English History Plays." See 407.

788. Spargo, John Webster. "Clarence in the Malmsey-Butt." *MLN*, 51(1936), 66-73.

Spargo discusses *R3* (I, iv, 158) where the murderers

stab Clarence and speak of drowning him in the malmsey-
butt. Earliest reference to the drowning of Clarence
is made by the writer of the chronicle *MS Cotton
Vitellius A* about 1480. Spargo determines that death
by drowning in an old wine barrel was a common method
of execution in the Middle Ages. The murderers'
stabbing of Clarence appears to be Shakespeare's own
addition to the story since all other references to
Clarence's death refer to his drowning. Malmsey wine
was popular in England, and Spargo notes that Chaucer's
"Shipman's Tale" mentions this type of wine.

*   Rossiter, A. P. *Woodstock, A Moral History*. See 280.
        Also, *Angel with Horns*. See 453.

789.   Taylor, George C. "The Relation of the English Corpus
        Christi Play to the Middle English Lyric." *MP*,
        5(1907), 1-38.

While developing the relationship of the *ubi sunt*
motif to the Towneley Shepherd plays, Taylor remarks
that Shakespeare uses the *ubi sunt* convention in *R3*
(IV, iv, 92-96).

Romeo and Juliet

*   Battenhouse, Roy W. *Shakespearean Tragedy: Its Art
        and Its Christian Premises*. See 426.

*   Bethell, S. L. *Shakespeare and the Popular Dramatic
        Tradition*. See 29.

790.   Cain, H. Edward. "*Romeo and Juliet:* A Reinterpreta-
        tion." *SAB*, 22(1947), 163-91.

Cain attempts to discredit those critics who interpret the play as a tragedy of fate or a tragedy involving the Medieval-type Fortune principle. He
emphasizes the tragic flaw of passion as it relates
to the characters' actions.

791.   Coghill, Nevill. "Introduction." *Romeo and Juliet,
        London Folio Society Edition*. London: Folio
        Society, 1950.

Shakespeare was closer to the "fresh fountain of
Medieval vision" in *Rom.* than in any other play. Coghill finds a number of similarities between Mercutio's
dream and the theory of dreams in *The Parlement of Foules*.

The author also comments that Shakespeare's use of
tragedy in this play is remarkably similar to that
found in Chaucer's *Troilus and Criseyde*. Shakespeare
adopts the plan of tragedy of Boethius and substitutes
stars for the goddess Fortune. The essay notes that
the nurse in Shakespeare's play offers Juliet the same
type of consolation that Pandarus gives Troilus--there
are many more lovers to choose from. In comparing
Juliet and Criseyde, Coghill finds Criseyde the weaker
of the two, though both succumb to the blows of Fortune.
Juliet's strength comes from the idea of holiness in
the bond of love, but Criseyde's weakness can be attributed to her not taking the bond of love seriously.

792. Culbert, Taylor. "A Note on *Romeo and Juliet* I, iii,
      89-90." *SQ*, 10(1959), 129-32.

      Culbert quotes from a passage in Chaucer's *House of
      Fame* (Robinson, 823-842) as a gloss upon the Shake-
      spearean passage noted above. He paraphrases Lady
      Capulet's speech to mean just as the fish thrives in
      the sea, so Juliet's natural station is in marriage.

*   Davidson, Clifford. "The Love Mythos in the Middle
      Ages and Renaissance." See 95.

793. Draper, J. W. "Shakespeare's 'Star-Crossed Lovers.'"
      RES, 15(1939), 16-34.

      Draper presents an astrological interpretation of
      Rom. by dealing with the planetary influences upon the
      characters' actions. In quoting W.C. Curry's *Chaucer
      and the Medieval Sciences*, Draper finds similarities
      between Medieval and Renaissance concepts of scientific
      and astrological beliefs. Draper further comments that
      some of Shakespeare's characters are like some of
      Chaucer's figures since they are apparently influenced
      by the stars and planets. The thrust of the essay is
      concerned with characters' actions in relation to the
      days of the week, the hours of the day, and the four
      basic humors.

794. Fergusson, F. "Romantic Love in Dante and Shakespeare."
      SR, 83(1975), 253-66.

      This essay compares Shakespeare's treatment of the
      love between Romeo and Juliet and Dante's presentation
      of the romance between Paolo and Francesca. Courtly
      love elements are emphasized while focusing upon the
      lovers.

795. Goldberg, M. A. "The Multiple Masks of Romeo: Toward
     a New Shakespearean Production." *AR*, 25(1968),
     405-26.

     A number of Romeo's speeches to Juliet are examined
     in light of the courtly love tradition. Romeo appears
     to be a slave to the rules of love as is seen in the
     balcony scene. Goldberg also adds that much of the
     conflict of the play derives from the conflation of
     courtly love in a serious sense and erotic and bawdy
     aspects of love.

796. Gray, J. C. "*Romeo and Juliet* and Some Renaissance
     Notions of Love, Time, and Death." *DR*, 48(1968),
     58-67.

     Gray interprets *Rom.* by referring to the Medieval
     ideas of goodness and sin. In a fallen world, good
     and bad are so inextricably intermixed that one cannot
     have one without the other. He does not deal with
     sources but suggests that the roots of the good and
     evil concepts go back to Augustine. The thrust of the
     essay is to show the ambivalent roles of love, time,
     and death.

  * Hawkins, Richard H. "Some Effects of Technique De-
     veloped in the Native English Drama on the Structure
     of Shakespeare's Plays." See 160.

797. Hays, Peter L. "The Dance of Love and Dance of Death
     in *Romeo and Juliet*." *DR*, 51(1971), 532-38.

     In *Rom.* (I, iv, 14) Romeo does not want to dance.
     Hays employs Medieval concepts (borrowed from Tillyard)
     of a chain, set of correspondences, and the dance to
     interpret Romeo's not dancing.

798. Lawlor, John. "*Romeo and Juliet*," pp. 123-43 in
     Early Shakespeare. London: Edward Arnold Pub., 1961.

     Shakespeare is working in the tradition of Medieval
     tragedy in *Rom.* and *R2*. The Fortune concept of tragedy
     is traditionally understood in terms of its working
     rather than its final effect. Lawlor observes that the
     end of Medieval tragedy is to have the spectator look
     beyond a limited time of "inexplicable suffering to a
     greater happiness beyond time's reach." In examining
     the tragic concept in Dante and Chaucer, Lawlor believes
     that the final experience of Medieval-type tragedy
     "corresponds to the Katharsis of nemesis-type tragedy."

As such Medieval tragedy as well as that found in *Rom.* is not profoundly pessimistic. The ending of *Rom.* is a re-ordering of life and a type of regeneration which experiences "beauty too rich for use, for earth too dear." Shakespeare has not broken with the Medieval tradition but rather reaffirmed a distinctive quality of that type of tragedy.

* ——. *The Tragic Sense in Shakespeare.* See 448.

* Lord, John B. "Sources of the Technique of Comic Scenes in Shakespearean Tragedy." See 449.

799. Maxwell, J. C. "Chaucer in the Queen Mab Speech." *N&Q*, 205(1960), 16.

Shakespeare's *Rom.* (I, iv, 70-88) is based upon Chaucer's *The Parlement of Foules*, 99-105. Maxwell also disagrees with Marie Podgett's article dealing with Claudius' influence on Shakespeare's *MM* (III, i, 125-127). He argues that Shakespeare went to Chaucer as his source for the above mentioned passage.

* Patterson, Frank Allen. "Shakespeare and the Medieval Lyric." See 262.

* Presson, Robert K. "Some Traditional Instances of Setting in Shakespeare's Plays." See 382.

800. Siegel, Paul N. "Christianity and the Religion of Love in *Romeo and Juliet*." *SQ*, 12(1961), 371-92.

The two traditional interpretations of the play are inadequate: that the play is a drama of fate; that the lovers should be seen as guilty sinners. Only an interpretation which deals with the religion of love which persisted from the Middle Ages can be wholly satisfying. From the Medieval world, Shakespeare borrowed the concept that sexual love is a manifestation of the cosmic love of God which holds together the universe in a chain of love and imposes order on it. In Shakespearean drama as in Chaucer's "The Knight's Tale," divine love providentially works in elevating human love. Siegel examines the tenets of the religion of love and the paradise of lover's delight and relates these concepts to *Rom.* and concludes that Shakespeare worked in the courtly love tradition in which the praise of sexual love is a manifestation of God's creative energy.

801. Soellner, Rolf. "Shakespeare and the 'Consolatio.'"
      N&Q, 1(1954), 108-09.

      Friar Lawrence's words to Romeo (III, iii, 54) should
      not be attributed to Lyly's *Euphues* but rather to
      Erasmus' *De Conscribendis Epistolis*, a work derived
      from Boethius and used for rhetorical study in
      grammar school.

*   Spencer, Theodore. *Death and Elizabethan Tragedy*.
      See 306.

802. Walley, Harold. "Shakespeare's Debt to Marlowe in
      Romeo and Juliet." *PQ*, 21(1942), 257-67.

      Part of this essay compares Arthur Brooke's poem to
      Shakespeare's *Rom*. Walley points out that Brooke's poem
      follows the tradition of the tragic tale and is "med-
      ieval in its convention, its lamentations, and its
      moralizing." Shakespeare's play, however, is conceived
      "in the heady spirit of the pagan Renaissance."

803. Williams, Philip. "The Rosemary Theme in *Romeo and
      Juliet*." *MLN*, 68(1953), 400-03.

      Williams notes a possible Shakespearean borrowing
      from connotations associated with Rosemary, a flower
      which represents both life and death. The imagery is
      traced throughout the play and its paradoxical associ-
      ations are shown.

*   Vyvyan, John. *Shakespeare and the Rose of Love: A
      Study of the Early Plays in Relation to the Medieval
      Philosophy of Love*. See 390.

804. Zbierski, Henryk. "Possible Echoes of Boccaccio's
      Decameron in the Balcony Scene of *Romeo and Juliet*."
      SAP, 3(1970), 131-38.

      Wordplay between Romeo and Juliet suggests the in-
      fluence of the *amour courtois* convention. Further,
      Shakespeare's use of the bird imagery (nightingale)
      has bawdy and ribald connotations which were borrowed
      from the *Decameron*, particularly the tale of *Novella
      Quarto, Giornata Quinta*.

                              Sonnets

*   Lacey, Stephen Wallace. "Structures for Awareness
      in Dante and Shakespeare." See 205.

805. Landry, Hilton. *Interpretations in Shakespeare's Sonnets*. Berkeley: U. of California Pr., 1963. 185 pp.

    This book contains scattered comments on Medieval influences on the sonnets. Concerning Sonnet 94, Landry glosses the words "nature's riches" to mean gifts of nature in the Medieval sense--"endowments of body and soul or mind" as opposed to the gifts of Fortune. For further clarification of nature, fortune, and grace, Landry refers to Chaucer's "The Parson's Tale," II, 450 ff; "The Merchant's Tale," II, 1311 ff; and "The Physician's Tale," II, 19-29; 293 ff.

806. Hubler, Edward. *The Sense of Shakespeare's Sonnets*. New York: Hill and Wang, 1952. 169 pp.

    Chapter Three discusses the influence of *The Romance of the Rose* upon Shakespeare's conception of love. Concepts of plentitude in *The Romance of the Rose* are the same as those in the sonnets.

807. Hussey, Richard. "Shakespeare and Gower." *N&Q*, 180 (1941), 386.

    Hussey notes a similarity between Shakespeare's sonnet 64 and two places in Gower's *Vox Clamantis*. The Shakespearean line reads, "When I have seen such interchange of state,/Or state itself confounded to decay."

808. Ord, H. *Chaucer and the Rival Poet in Shakespeare's Sonnets*. 2 nd ed., rpt. New York: AMS Pr., 1973. 63 pp.

    Ord believes that Shakespeare was influenced by Chaucer and *The Roman de la Rose*. While focusing upon the sonnets, Ord points out a number of verbal similarities, themes, treatment of themes, and allusions which are found in Chaucer's works and *The Roman de la Rose*.

809. Pirkhofer, Anton M. " A Pretty Pleasing Pucket--on the Use of Alliteration in Shakespeare's Sonnets." *SQ*, 14(1963), 3-14.

    Shakespeare's extensive use of alliteration in the sonnets is traced to the Anglo-Saxon tradition. The essay suggests that the "Northern and Scottish alliteration romances" may have consciously or unconsciously influenced Shakespeare.

810. Steadman, John M. "'Like Two Spirits': Shakespeare and
      Ficino." *SQ*, 10(1959), 244-46.

      Steadman believes that the Platonic idea of two loves
      and the Medieval conception of good and evil spirits
      contending for man's soul are the traditions used by
      Shakespeare in Sonnet 144. Steadman also shows other
      works in which these traditions are used. *LLL*, Ficinio's
      Commentary on Plato's Symposium, and Burton's *The
      Anatomy of Melancholy*.

*   Stevenson, David L. *The Love-Game Comedy*. See 312.

                   The Taming of the Shrew

811. Bean, John C. "Comic Structure and the Humanizing of
      Kate in *The Taming of the Shrew*," pp. 65-78 in *The
      Woman's Part*. eds. Carolyn Lenz, Gayle Green, and
      Carol Neely. Urbana: U. of Illinois Pr., 1980.

      This essay shows Kate emerging as a humanized heroine;
      thus the play reveals a relationship between the
      sophistication of comic structure and the liberation
      of women away from Medieval notions of male autocracy.

812. Bergeron, David M. "The Wife of Bath and Shakespeare's
      The Taming of the Shrew." *UR*, 35(1969), 279-86.

      Bergeron shows a number of parallels between the
      Wife of Bath and Katharine. Shakespeare's heroine
      develops into the Griselda type; and as the shrew in
      the play she has a certain relationship to the "loathly
      lady" in the tale told by the Wife of Bath.

813. Brooks, Charles. "Shakespeare's Romantic Shrews."
      SQ, 11(1960), 351-56.

      In discussing the role of the shrew in Shakespeare's
      plays, Brooks makes a number of comparisons to Chaucer's
      "The Wife of Bath's Tale," "The Clerk's Tale," and
      "The Franklin's Tale." The author believes that Shake-
      speare finds marriage a bargain in which the husband
      works for the wife, and she in turn serves him faith-
      fully. The farcical action in *Shr.* and *Err.* is de-
      pendent upon the shrew's relation to the marriage
      bargain.

814. Brunvand, Jan Harold. "The Folktale Origin of *The
      Taming of the Shrew*." *SQ*, 17(1966), 345-59.

In referring frequently to Medieval and early Renaissance legends which may have influenced Shakespeare
in the writing of *Shr.*, Brunvand argues that Shakespeare's subplot must have ultimately come from oral
tradition. There is a similarity between Shakespeare's
play and Type 901 tale, a story in which the husband
uses severe punishment on a cat in order to frighten
his wife. The origins of this tale are found in
fourteenth-century literature. Shakespeare used the
"horse-killed" versions of the tale for his play.

*   Coghill, Nevill. "The Basis of Shakespearean Comedy:
     A Study of Medieval Affinities." See 369.

*   Courthope, W. J. *A History of English Poetry: The
     Development and Decline of the Poetic Drama.* See 80.

*   Galway, Margaret. "Flyting in Shakespeare's Comedies."
     See 373.

815.   Hosley, Richard. "Sources and Analogues of *The Taming
     of the Shrew." HLQ,* 27(1964), 289-308.

In reviewing scholarship concerning the sources and
analogues for *Shr.*, Hosley comments upon a possible
influence of *El Conde Lucanor* (1335) and *The Book of
the Knight of La Tour-Landry,* translated by Caxton in
1484.

816.   Houk, Robert. "Shakespeare's Heroic Shrew." *SAB,*
     18(1943), 121-32; 175-86.

Houk disagrees with those critics who interpret
Katharine's behavior in terms of the humor concept.
On the contrary, Kate is a descendant of the shrew
of Medieval literature.

817.   Ingram, Angela. "No More Forced Marriages, or How a
     Feminist Should Not Put Her Hand Under the Foot of
     the Immortal Bard." *SCB,* 40(Fall 1980), 112.

Ingram discusses Shakespeare's *Shr.* in light of the
shrew of Medieval and Renaissance plays.

818.   Jayne, Sears. "The Dreaming of the Shrew." *SQ,* 18
     (1966), 41-56.

There are a number of late Medieval influences in the
play. The theme of the shrewish wife is a deliberate

inversion of the Biblical dictum that a man shall rule
over his wife. The fist-fight of Noah and his wife,
a popular scene in Medieval drama, is an earlier handling of the shrew theme. The wooing of the maid and
the troubles of the drunken tinker are also subjects
of earlier plays. Shakespeare meant his play to be
associated with the dream convention of Medieval
literature.

*   Owst, G. R. *Literature and Pulpit in Medieval England.*
        See 254.

819.   Ribner, Irving. "The Morality of Farce: *The Taming
        of the Shrew.*" *EAEL*, 15(1967), 56-70.

        The Bianca-Lucentio subplot is fully within the
        courtly love tradition of the Middle Ages, while the
        Petruchio-Kate relationship offers an opposing point
        of view also derived from Medieval literature, the
        anti-feminist movement.

*   Russell, William M. "Courtly Love in Shakespeare's
        Romantic Comedies." See 384.

820.   Shroeder, John W. "A New Analogue and Possible Source
        for *The Taming of the Shrew.*" *SQ*, 10(1959), 251-55.

        The tale of Queen Vastis given in Caxton's trans-
        lation of the *Book of the Knight of La Tour-Landry*
        (1484) is Shakespeare's source for *Shr.* The Jutland
        tale is not the source for the play, for it omits
        incidents in the plot which are found in the tale of
        Queen Vastis. The postprandial setting for the
        summoning of the wives and the confinement and star-
        vation of the shrew are found in the tale of Queen
        Vastis. Shroeder also discounts the theory of the
        lost source for the play.

821.   Soellner, Rolf. "The Troubled Fountain: Erasmus
        Formulates a Shakespearean Simile." *JEGP*, 55(1956),
        70-74.

        Shakespeare may have received the image of the muddy
        fountain (*Shr.*, V, ii, 142-45 and *Tro.*, III, iii, 310-
        15) from Erasmus' *De Parabolis Sive Similibus*, a
        collection of essays dealing with rhetorical devices
        which were used by school boys in the Renaissance.
        A number of these rhetorical devices come from Medieval
        source material.

822. Thorne, William Barry. "Folk Elements in *The Taming of the Shrew*." *QQ*, 75(1968), 482-96.

Much of the essay is concerned with the induction scene as reflecting the influence of Medieval folk-players. Furthermore, the induction (I, 83-87) is remarkably similar to the traditional mummers' wooing play. The metaphors, characters, and the plot of the play owe much to folk-drama, particularly seasonal rituals, folk festivals, and Saturnalian holidays.

823. Tillyard, E. M. W. "The Fairy-Tale Element in *The Taming of the Shrew*, pp. 110-14 in *Shakespeare 1564-1964: A Collection of Modern Essays by Various Hands*. ed. Edward A. Bloom, Providence Rhode Island: Brown U. Pr., 1964.

The Petruchio-Katharina story not only contains themes common to the fabliau but also contains fairy tale elements seen in a number of stories, particularly the story of King Thrushbeard. Tillyard emphasizes the proud daughter who has to be educated and who later becomes married.

824. Tolman, Albert H. "Shakespeare's Part in *The Taming of the Shrew*." *PMLA*, 5(1890), 202-77.

Of interest are Tolman's remarks concerning source material that Shakespeare possibly used. Tolman refers to Caxton's *The Book of the Knight of La Tour-Landry* in regard to the wager scene in *Shr*. He also comments that the supremacy of a husband over a wife and its opposite was the basis of many popular tales in the Middle Ages.

825. West, Michael. "The Folk Background of Petruchio's Wooing Dance: Male Supremacy in *The Taming of the Shrew*." *ShakS*, 7(1974), 65-74.

In examining the folk background for *Shr.*, West demonstrates that the Petruchio-Kate relationship is not a model for the subjugation of women. Much of the folk-lore background points to erotic contexts, and the play is suffused with a sense that a spirited woman like Kate makes the best wife.

The Tempest

*   Bergeron, David M. *English Civic Pageantry 1558-1642*. See 27.

826.   Bundy, Murray W. "The Allegory in *The Tempest.*" *RS*,
        32(1964), 189-206.

        Tmp. is in the tradition of the morality in which
        struggles of virtues and vices were often presented
        in terms of Reason, Will, and the Imagination. Bundy
        relates Medieval and Renaissance psychology to the
        characters' actions as a means to explain their
        behavior. Thus, Caliban symbolizes the vegetative soul,
        while Ariel is a symbol of the will.

827.   Cawley, Robert Calslin. "Shakespeare's Use of the
        Voyagers in *The Tempest.*" *PMLA*, 41(1926), 688-726.

        In the section entitled "Monsters" (721-726), Cawley
        suggests that Shakespeare's description of monsters
        in *Tmp.* (II, ii) has a parallel in *Batman Upon Bartholo-
        mew* (p. 224), a Medieval work translated by Stephen
        Batman in 1582.

*   Coghill, Nevill. "The Basis of Shakespearean Comedy:
        A Study in Medieval Affinities." See 369.

828.   Collins, J. Churton. "Poetry and Symbolism: A Study
        of *The Tempest.*" *ContempR*, 93(1908), 65-83.

        Collins discusses Dante's four-fold interpretation of
        literature and speculates that the *Tmp.* should be
        understood in an allegorical sense depicting Christian
        sentiment and beliefs.

*   Coursen, Herbert R., Jr. *Christian Ritual and the
        World of Shakespeare's Tragedies.* See 432.

829.   Cranefield, Paul F. and Walter Federn. "A Possible
        Source of a Passage in *The Tempest. SQ*, 14(1963),
        90-92.

        Boemus (Aubanus) who lived in late Medieval times
        wrote *The Manner, Lawes and Customs of All Nations*,
        a work Shakespeare perhaps used for the "mountaineers
        ... wallets of flesh" in *Tmp.* (III, iii, 43-46).

830.   Felperin, Howard. "Shakespeare's Miracle Play." *SQ*,
        18(1967), 363-74.

        Shakespeare cultivated the archaic Medieval world
        deliberately. Shakespeare's moral symbols are in part
        derived from Medieval interludes, while specific lines
        (III, ii, 27) call to mind Renaissance woodcuts which

represent the *danse macabre*. Shakespeare adopted the
allegorical method from the religious drama of the
Middle Ages and his moral and Christian philosophy was
becoming increasingly dogmatic. See G. Wilson Knight
The Crown of Life (pp. 22-23) in support for Shakespeare's growth toward an unalterable world moral
order.

831. Goldsmith, R. H. "The Wild Man on the English Stage."
     MLR, 53(1958), 481-91.

     This essay traces the wild man of the English stage
     to the literature of the Middle Ages and suggests that
     the wild man originated with folk ritual. Froissart's
     Chronicles shows that by 1392 the wild man was depicted
     in literature, and Shakespeare's Caliban is a "variant
     of the Medieval wodemose." Like his Medieval fore-
     bearers, Caliban is deformed and lecherous.

832. Goodley, Nancy Carter. "Thy Kingdom Come: The
     Eschatological Version of *The Tempest*." pp. 238-46
     in *Religion in Life*. Nashville, Tenn.: 45(1976).

     "The play leads the audience through the steps of
     memory, repentance, and forgiveness, like the holy
     sacrament." The themes of justice, mercy, and for-
     giveness have elements "derived from ... the Lord's
     Prayer and Holy Communion."

833. Kermode, Frank. "Introduction," *The Tempest, Arden
     Shakespeare Edition*. London: Methuen and Co., Ltd.,
     1958.

     Kermode has a number of comments on the wild man of
     the Middle Ages and Caliban. Neither can control his
     sexual instincts; both are emblems of primitive sex-
     uality, and their behavior contrasts with that of the
     courtly love tradition. The knight of Medieval lit-
     erature practiced a restrained appetite for the sake
     of his lover and civilized society. The Caliban-Ferd-
     inand situation echoes the theme of courtly love and
     primitive sexuality.

834. Latham, Jacqueline E. M. "The Magic Banquet in *The
     Tempest*." *ShakS*, 12(1979), 215-27.

     Lathan reconstructs the awareness that Shakespeare's
     audience had of the magic banquet scene. The scene
     is ambiguous though "likely to be more evil than good."

Lathan cites details from folktale and emblem literature
which depict banquets.

835. Madsen, William G. "The Destiny of Man in *The Tempest*."
      EMQ, 20(1964), 175-82.

      Madsen studies the play from the point of view of
      variations on the *felix culpa* theme. Gonzalo uses the
      convention when he pronounces the benediction on
      Ferdinand and Miranda (V, i).

836. Markland, Murray F. "The Order of 'The Knight's Tale'
      and *The Tempest*." *RS*, 33(1965), 1-10.

      Markland finds no specific Medieval influence upon
      Shakespeare, but he contends that by comparing and
      contrasting Chaucer's tale with Shakespeare's play
      we come to understand each writer better. "The Knight's
      Tale" and *Tmp*. are comparable in that their "artistic
      order reflects the philosophical order perceived by
      their authors." The action of both works is univer-
      salized by being cut off from time. Both stories use
      supernatural events; each has a character who attempts
      to control action and determines the fate of others.
      A point of contrast is that Theseus punishes Creon
      immediately, but Prospero suffers in exile. Markland
      concludes that Chaucer's view of God and the scheme of
      things is fixed and single, while Shakespeare's world
      is not orderly, proportioned, and reducible to truth-
      ful propositions. In the Medieval world, man is more
      passive; and Divinity asserts itself. In the Renaissance
      man must act in order to be responsible and his relation-
      ship to God has been redefined.

837. Palomo, Dolores Josephine. "The Syntax of Revenge: A
      Structuralist Reading of English Revenge Drama."
      DAI, 33(1973), 732-A (S.U.N.Y., Buffalo).

      The *Tmp*. is the consumate revenge play. Revenge
      tragedy was successful because of the transposition of
      world ideologies to family-state analogy, a device
      commonplace to Medieval political rhetoric.

838. Schuman, Samuel. "Man, Magician, Poet, God--An Image
      in Medieval, Renaissance, and Modern Literature."
      Cithara, 19(May 1980), 40-54.

      The author argues that there are verbal echoes and
      thematic resemblances between Chaucer's "The Franklin's
      Tale" and Shakespeare's *Tmp*.

839. Still, Colin. *Shakespeare's Mystery Play*. London:
     Cecil Palmer, 1921. 248 pp.

     Tmp. is of the "same class of religious drama as the
     Medieval mysteries, miracles, and moralities." The
     play is an allegory with the actions and experiences in
     the drama relating to man's quest for redemption.
     Still discusses the "initiation" and its various rituals
     and observances and has individual chapters on the
     "fall" and "ascent."

840. Thompson, R. Ann. "'Our revels now are ended': A
     Possible Allusion to 'The Franklin's Tale.'" *Archiv*,
     121(1975), 317.

     Prospero's words (IV, i) in the *Tmp.* possibly echo
     words in Chaucer's tale. The context and actual words
     are similar.

Timon of Athens

841. Bergeron, David M. "*Timon of Athens* and Morality Drama."
     CLAJ, 10(1967), 181-88.

     Bergeron compares *Tim.* and *Everyman* in regard to
     character and structural similarities. The conver-
     sation between the painter and poet in Shakespeare's
     play resembles the introductory speech by the messenger
     in *Everyman*. The role of Flavius is comparable to that
     played by Death in the morality play. In addition,
     both Timon and Everyman have a similar fate, for they
     begin in apparent ease and progress toward trouble.
     Both seek comfort from their friends. Everyman comes
     to a knowledge of salvation, while Timon, in contrast,
     becomes cynical and disillusioned.

842. Collins, A. S. "*Timon of Athens*: A Reconsideration."
     RES, 22(1946), 96-108.

     The drama is a true "morality play" in the straight
     sense." The key to the morality is found in the three
     strangers in Act III, scene ii who indicate that the
     play is in the morality tradition. Collins points out
     that the characters in the play serve as abstractions
     of moral qualities. Timon, for example, represents
     "Ideal Bounty" and "Friendship" struggling in a de-
     generate state. Juxtaposed to Timon is Alcibades who
     represents realism, the only force which can bring
     harmony and order to the chaotic state.

843.   Draper, John W. "The Theme of *Timon of Athens*."
       MLR, 29(1934), 20-31.

       Draper interprets the play in terms of the waning
       feudal classes and the rising merchant class. He finds
       that the play deals with the departed values of chivalry
       as opposed to the materialism of the Renaissance. At
       the heart of the play is the theme of usury which de-
       stroyed the old order and enriched the new classes.
       The theme of usury and feudal concepts is shown in
       both Medieval and Renaissance works.

844.   Draper, R. P. "*Timon of Athens*." *SQ*, 7(1957),
       195-200.

       Of interest is Draper's remark that Timon is a larger-
       than-life figure who represents a social class which
       came to ruin in Shakespeare's day. R.P. Draper's
       comments parallel those of John Draper regarding the
       passing of the feudal aristocracy.

845.   Farnham, Willard. "*Timon of Athens*," pp. 121-37 in
       Shakespeare: the Tragedies. ed. Clifford Leech.
       Chicago: U. of Chicago Pr., 1965.

       This essay is a reprint of a section of Farnham's
       book *The Medieval Heritage of Elizabethan Drama*.

846.   Ferrara, Fernando. "*Timon of Athens*," pp. 161-79 in
       Critical Dimensions, ed. by Mario Curreli and Alberto
       Martino. Cuneo: SASTE, 1978. 560 pp.

       Ferrara gives a reading of *Tim.* as an "estates
       morality." The play is a social satire in which the
       crisis facing Timon reflects the crisis of the
       aristocracy in the Elizabethan Age.

847.   Knights, L. C. "*Timon of Athens*," pp. 1-17 in *The
       Morality of Art*. ed. D.W. Jefferson. London:
       Routledge and Kegan Paul, 1969.

       Tim. is closely aligned to the morality play tradition
       and is a satire on the power of money. Timon's self-
       hatred and self-contempt, however, is the heart of
       the play.

848.   Lancashire, Anne. "*Timon of Athens:* Shakespeare's
       Dr. Faustus." *SQ*, 21(1970), 35-44.

       The morality play pattern is reversed in *Tim.* since
       the destruction of Timon is shown rather than his sal-

vation . The unfinished state of the play is both a
logical and necessary aspect of morality drama.

849. Landman, Sidney I. "The Tragic Mode of *Timon of Athens*
and *Coriolanus*." *DAI*, 27(1967), 4223-A (Vanderbilt).

Chapter Three traces the development of Medieval
tragedy, beginning with the Roman worship of the goddess
Fortune. Landman studies Boccaccio and Lydgate and the
influence of Medieval Christianity, particularly as it
is expressed in religious drama. The final two chapters
analyze *Tim.* and *Cor.* in respect to the above discussion.
In addition, the influence of the stock character in
Medieval drama is pointed out.

850. Lerner, Laurence. "Literature and Money." *E&S*,
28(1975), 106-22.

Lerner discusses the theme of money in *Tim.* and *Err.*
and shows similarities to Chaucer's treatment of money
in "The Pardoner's Tale."

851. Levitsky, Ruth. "Shakespeare's Magnyfycence and an
Embryonic Lear." *ShakS*, 11(1978), 107-21.

Tim. is viewed as a secular morality similar to
Skelton's *Magnyfycence*. Magnificence is equated with
liberality which resists temptation and endures adversity. Shakespeare depicts a type of "pagan morality"
with his characters representing a number of philosophical positions.

852. Maher, Michael Kevin. "Shakespeare's *Timon of Athens*
and Elizabethan Prodigal-Son Plays." *DAI*, 35(1975),
5353-A (Georgia).

Timon is not a tragic hero because *Tim.* is not a
tragedy. The play is didactic and is patterned after
morality plays.

853. Pettet, E. C. "*Timon of Athens*: The Disruption of
Feudal Morality." *RES*, 33(1947), 323-36.

Shakespeare deals with the Medieval concepts of
bounty, open-handed generosity, and mutual service
in *Tim.* and *MV*. Pettet stresses that "usury and the
embryonic forms of capitalism were shattering the
fabric of Medieval ideas and institutions." The Medieval concept appears to win out in *MV*, but in *Tim.*
Shakespeare again pursues the concepts of usury and

capitalism with the purpose of destroying the old world order of feudal morality. Pettet relates *Tim.* to the morality play but attempts to make the play more relevant to Shakespeare's time.

*   Ribner, Irving. *Patterns of Shakespearean Tragedy.*
        See 452.

854.   Walker, Lewis. "Fortune and Friendship in *Timon of Athens.*" *TSLL*, 18(1977), 577-600.

        Walker presents the Medieval background of fortune as a Harlot and argues that the image is "of great importance in determining what happens in the play." Allegorical and naturalistic elements (often disturbing to the modern reader) are demonstrated constantly in the dramatic action.

855.   ———. "*Timon of Athens* and the Morality Tradition." *ShakS*, 12(1979), 159-77.

        Walker cites details from *The Castle of Perseverance, Wisdom Who is Christ, Mundus et Infans,* and *Mankind* to show parallels between *Tim.* and the moralities. Some common themes are worldliness, a moralizing counselor, and compatriots representing various vices.

Titus Andronicus

856.   Baker, Howard. *Induction to Tragedy.* Baton Rouge: Louisiana State U. Pr., 1939. 220 pp.

        Of interest is Chapter Four "Transformations of Medieval Structure: *Titus Andronicus* and Shakespearean Practice." English tragedy "developed from Medieval metrical tragedy" which is closely related to the Wheel of Fortune and *De Casibus* tragedies. Baker comments upon the extensive action of metrical romances and the novella and its relationship to Elizabethan tragedy and further relates dramatic expositions to a "Gothic principle adapted from the older drama, from mystery, and interlude, into the formal pattern of Medieval tragedy."

857.   Granger, Frank. "Shakespeare and the Legend of Andronicus." *TLS*, 2 April, 1920. p. 213.

        Granger compares Shakespeare's Titus with a historical, Byzantine figure called Andronicus Commenus who is viewed in Medieval and Renaissance works as an example

of human fortune. Latin works were available to Shakespeare which gave an account of the historical Andronicus.

858.   Harvey, Nancy L. *"Titus Andronicus* and the *Shearmen
       and Taylor's Play."* *PQ*, 22(1969), 27-31.

       A possible source for *Tit.* is the scene dealing with
       the Slaughter of the Innocents in the *Shearmen and
       Taylor's Play* of the Coventry mystery cycle. Harvey
       lists eight verbal similarities between the two plays.

859.   Hastings, William T. "The Hardboiled Shakespeare."
       SAB, 17(1942), 114-25.

       Tit. fails to be a successful play because of the
       blending of the secular abstractions of the English
       moral plays and the type of figures of classical comedy
       and tragedy. In addition, Hastings comments on the
       survival of the Medieval debate in *Ven.* in terms of
       love and lust.

*   Jones, Emrys. *The Origins of Shakespeare.* See 179.

*   Keilstrup, Lorraine M. "The Myth of Cain in the Early
       English Drama." See 185.

*   Lacey, Stephen Wallace. "Structures for Awareness in
       Dante and Shakespeare." See 205.

860.   Price, H. T. "The Authorship of *Titus Andronicus.*"
       JEGP, 42(1943), 55-81.

       The thrust of the essay argues that Shakespeare is
       the author of *Tit.*, but in discussing Aaron's character,
       Price notes that he is the child of the English stage
       tradition. By having Aaron mount a ladder to be hanged,
       Shakespeare is using techniques of drama which go back
       to Medieval times. Moreover, Aaron resembles the villain
       of the Medieval mysteries in his temperament and color.

861.   ————. "The Yew Tree in *Titus Andronicus.*"
       N&Q, 208(1963), 98-99.

       Price explains how the yew tree could have killed
       Tamora (II, iii, 108) by referring to *Batman Upon
       Bartholomew.* A section of this work describes how
       poisonous vapors of the yew tree make people sick.

*   Ribner, Irving. *Patterns of Shakespearean Tragedy.*
       See 452.

*   Rosier, James Louis. "The Chain of Sin and Privation
        in Elizabethan Literature." See 279.

*   Spivak, Bernard. *Shakespeare and the Allegory of Evil.*
        See 456.

Troilus and Cressida

862.   Aggeler, Geoffrey D. "Madness in Reason: A Paradoxical
        Kinship in *Troilus and Cressida. WascanaR,* 4(1969),
        39-57.

        In *Tro.* Shakespeare exposes irrational chivalric
        idealism and romanticism. Further, he satirizes neo-
        stoicism and Machiavellian pragmatism. *Tro.* is a
        tragedy which affirms positive values despite the
        awareness of man's depravity.

863.   Arnold, Aerol. "The Hector-Andromache Scene in Shake-
        speare's *Troilus and Cressida." MLQ,* 14(1953), 335-40.

        Arnold reacts to John Tatlock's remark in his article
        "The Siege of Troy ..." that Act V, Scene iii of *Tro.*
        was Shakespeare's own addition to the play. Arnold
        finds Tatlock in error and argues that the scene is
        Lydgate's *Siege of Troy* and Caxton's *Recuyell of the
        Histories of Troye.*

864.   Asp, Carolyn. "Th' Expense of Spirit is a Waste of
        Shame." *SQ,* 22(1971), 345-57.

        Shakespeare attacks the convention of courtly love in
        Tro. and shows that the forms of courtly behavior are
        contrary to a realistic, moral, and rational view of
        life.

865.   Benson, Morris. *Renaissance Archetypes, the Long
        Shadows.* London: Coleman Pub. Co., 1977. 180 pp.

        Of interest is the section (1-40) which concerns
        Chaucer's courtly love myth. Shakespeare changed the
        tone of *Tro.* to a type of ironic realism.

*   Boas, F. S. *Queen Elizabeth in Drama and Related Studies.*
        See 38.

866.   ———. "Aspects of Classical Legend and History in
        Shakespeare." *PBA,* 29(1943), 107-32.

        Boas briefly comments upon the Medieval aspects of

Tro. such as courtly love ideas and the Medieval handling of the Greek and Trojan leaders. Thersites is a character of whom "there is little question of the Medieval influence." In addition, Shakespeare's Thersites is similar to the character Ribaldry in Medieval drama.

867. Bradbrook, M. C. "What Shakespeare Did to Chaucer's *Troilus and Criseyde.*" *SQ,* 9(1958), 311-19.

Behind Shakespeare's depiction of the siege, there are the works of Homer, Lydgate, and Caxton, while the source for the story of *Tro.* is Chaucer and Henryson. Shakespeare deflated Chaucer's heroic romance. Other changes relate to compression and inversion. Chaucer's books are represented by one or two scenes in Shakespeare's play. Further, Chaucer's Troilus is fully in the courtly love tradition, while Shakespeare's Troilus acts more like an Elizabethan soldier. Chaucer's Criseyde has the graces of a lady of a romance court, while Shakespeare's lady is raw and brutal. Chaucer's Pandare brings the two lovers together in the service of love, while Shakespeare's Pandarus is viewed more as a procurer.

868. Boatner, Janet W. "Criseyde's Character in the Major Writers from Benoit through Dryden: The Changes and Their Significance." *DAI,* 31(1971), 4705-A (Wisconsin).

In Benoit, Boccaccio, Chaucer, Henryson, Shakespeare, and Dryden, Criseyde is the object of anti-feminist satire, the cruel mistress of the courtly love convention and a sincere repentant sinner. Criseyde is viewed as shallow and silly.

869. Bonjour, Adrien. "Hector and the One in Sumptuous Armour." *ES,* 75(1964), 104-08.

Hector is a victim of his own chivalric code, a code of living which is at odds with the scheme of things. He brings on his own death and dies a "verray parfit gentil Knight."

870. Brooke, Tucker. "Shakespeare's Study in Culture and Anarachy." *YR,* 17(1928), 571-77.

Brooke is concerned with *Tro.* particularly in regard to Chaucer's and Caxton's contributions to the themes of "the decaying feudal nobility" and the "delicacy of life." Shakespeare's Cressida like Chaucer's portrays

a delicate sincerity which is juxtaposed to the cruel
world about her. Shakespeare's intention in *Tro.* is
to "anatomize England of dying Elizabeth." Decadent
chivalry is juxtaposed to the world of the cavalier
and puritan.

871.   ――――. "Shakespeare's Study in Culture and Anarchy,"
        pp. 71-77 in *Essays on Shakespeare and Other
        Elizabethans*. New Haven: Yale U. Pr., 1948.

        See previous entry.

872.   Bullough, G. "The Lost Troilus and Cressida." *E&S*,
        17(1964), 24-40.

        Bullough reviews in detail scene descriptions and
        character descriptions in the various accounts of the
        Troy material――Caxton's Lydgate's, Homer's, and Chaucer's.
        Further discussion is given to the Troy account (British
        Museum, 10.449).

873.   Campbell, Oliver W. *Troilus and Cressida:* A
        Justification." *LM*, 4(1921), 48-59.

        Shakespeare's Troilus like Lydgate's in *The Book of
        Troy* takes "victory as he may" and finds mercy a vice
        in war. In both works Troilus believes that mercy
        "better fits a lion than a man."

874.   Campbell, Oscar T. *Comicall Satyre and Shakespeare's
        Troilus and Cressida*. San Marino: Adcraft Pr.,
        1938. 234 pp.

        Campbell reviews the scholarship concerning *Tro.* and
        refers to Boas, Tatlock, Rollins, and Lawrence who
        comment upon the Medieval background of the play. Camp-
        bell argues that while Shakespeare used Medieval ideas
        in the play, his method of playwriting bears a close
        resemblance to Jonsonian comedy in that the folly and
        vice of men are held up to ridicule and derision. In
        addition, Campbell associates Elizabethan military
        expeditions of the time to Medieval chivalric codes
        and knightly honor. The Medieval *fini amour* reflects
        the manners of Elizabeth and her court. The Medieval
        aspects of the play serve more than a decorative pur-
        pose and are combined so as to point out the changing
        social conditions of the time.

875.   Chapman, Anthony U. "The Influences of Shakespeare's
        Sources on the Dramaturgy of *Troilus and Cressida*."
        DAI, 36(1975), 1520-A(Kent State).

Tro. was unsuccessful in many ways because Shakespeare followed Chaucer's and Caxton's versions too
closely. Chaucer's Medieval love conventions are
different from the ones in the Elizabethan period.
Chapman argues that Shakespeare places his "greatest
reliance upon Chaucer and Caxton in composing the
falling action and the catastrophe."

*   Charlton, H. B. "The Dark Comedies." See 368.

876.   Cook, Albert S. "The Character of Criseyde." *PMLA*,
      22(1907), 531-47.

Cook studies the character of Criseyde in the works
of Boccaccio, Chaucer, and Shakespeare. Boccaccio
portrays Criseyde lasciviously, Chaucer piteously,
and Shakespeare lustily.

877.   De Selincourt, E. *"Troilus and Cressida,"* pp. 78-105
      in *Oxford Lectures on Poetry*. 2nd ed., rpt. Freeport,
      New York: Books for Libraries Pr., 1967.

This essay compares Shakespeare's and Chaucer's story
about Troilus and points out how each author treated
various ideas. Shakespeare's love story is secondary,
while Chaucer's main concern is the love element.
De Selincourt suggests that Shakespeare's different
treatment of the love story may be due to his ignorance
of the Medieval court of love or it may also be
attributed to following the Henryson tradition. The
author also comments upon Troilus' disillusionment with
chivalry and Hector's "vice of mercy" as mere fool's
play.

*   Dessen, Alan. *Elizabethan Drama and the Viewer's
      Eye*. See 100.

878.   Deutschberger, Paul. "Shakespeare on Degree: A Study
      in Backgrounds." *SAB*, 17(1942), 200-07.

Ulysses' speech (*Tro.* I, iii.) draws upon the Medieval
heritage which survived in the sixteenth century. Similar ideas are found in the works of Dante and Boethius.

879.   Drayton, W. B. "Shakespeare's *Troilus and Cressida*
      Yet Deeper in Its Tradition," pp. 127-56 in *Parrot
      Presentation Volume*. ed. Hardin Craig. New York:
      Russell and Russell, 1935.

This detailed study shows Shakespeare's debt to
Caxton and Lydgate for the events and episodes surrounding

the Troy story. The opening section brings the scholarship together which relates Shakespeare to his Medieval
predecessors. From Lydgate Shakespeare derived concepts
of chivalry which form a dialectic. Achilles, for
example, illustrates "pride clashing with chivalry."

880. Harrier, Richard G. "Troilus Divided," pp. 142-56
      in *Studies in the English Renaissance Drama*. ed.
      Josephine W. Bennett. New York: New York U. Pr., 1959.

      Harrier's concerns are mainly the themes of honor,
      reason, and chivalry as seen throughout the play.
      Thersites assumes a chivalric attitude in order to
      cover his basic animality. Troilus' flawless concern
      for Cressida and Helen is an outmoded chivalric code
      which opposes reason and brings his own destruction.

881. Herdman, H. H. Jr. "The *Troilus and Cressida* of Chaucer
      and of Shakespeare." *SR*, 7(April 1899), 161-81.

      The discussion of the conditions and cirumstances
      under which Chaucer and Shakespeare wrote is of interest.
      Herdman believes this aspect contributes to the emphasis
      each author has placed upon the Troy legend. Shake-
      speare and Chaucer agree upon plot structure and the
      character of Troilus. However, their treatment of
      Cressida's character and the character of Pandarus
      "differ greatly."

882. Kaula, David. "The Moral Vision of Shakespeare's
      Troilus and Cressida." *DAI*, 16(1956), 2150-52
      (Indiana).

      The underlying moral perspective of *Tro.* is an
      orthodox Christian one. In the combined community of
      his Greeks and Trojans, Shakespeare "presents what may
      be described as a post-Medieval vision of the Augustine
      earthly city." Other sections of this study compare
      Chaucer's and Shakespeare's treatment of character and
      theme.

883. ————. "Mad Idolatry in Shakespeare's *Troilus and
      Cressida*." *TSLL*, 15(1973), 25-38.

      The language of the "mad idolatry" theme suggests that
      Tro. is in part a morality play. Kaula finds parallels
      between the language used in moralities and Shakespeare's
      play.

884. Kimbrough, Robert. "The Origins of *Troilus and Cressida*."
      PMLA, 77(1962), 194-99.

See entry below.

885. ————. *Shakespeare's Troilus and Cressida and Its
       Setting*. Cambridge: Harvard U. Pr., 1964. 208 pp.

   Chapters Two and Three discuss the theatrical and
   literary origins of Shakespeare's *Tro*. Shakespeare's
   sources for his play "probably were Caxton, Chaucer,
   and Homer." The discussion primarily deals with the
   character of Troilus, Pandarus, and Cressida.

886. Knights, L. C. *"Troilus and Cressida."* *TLS*,
       2 June 1932. p. 408.

   Tro. is a morality play in direct line of descent
   "from Medieval and early Tudor mystery and morality
   plays." Pandarus is presented in the first scene as
   a conventional character such as Herod or the Vice.
   Troilus and Cressida are themselves personifications
   of faith and inconstancy. The sententious lines and
   the debates among the Greeks and Trojans on order,
   love, and value relate to the morality play.

887. Lawrence, William Witherle. *"Troilus and Cressida,"*
       pp. 137-211 in *Shakespearean Studies*. New York:
       Columbia U. Pr., 1916.

   The chief difficulty with *Tro.* lies in the sensual
   treatment of Cressida, the cynicism associated with
   Pandarus, and the disagreeable portrayal of the Greek
   camp. A study of Shakespeare's sources reveals that the
   dramatist was bound by the historical handling of the
   themes mentioned. Indeed, Shakespeare's hands were
   tied in this manner. The treatment of the love story
   of Troilus and Cressida follows Chaucer. For details
   concerning the Greek and Trojan camps, Shakespeare is
   indebted to Caxton who portrayed the Greeks in a
   pejorative way.

888. Levenson, Jill L. "Shakespeare's *Troilus and Cressida*
       and the Monumental Tradition in Tapestries and
       Literature." *RenD*, 7(1976), 43-84.

   Medieval and Renaissance tapestries that depict the
   Trojan legend as splendid and opulent are discussed.
   The author concludes that Shakespeare's play is not
   in this tradition since rather reductive elements of
   love and war are depicted. Shakespeare's sources
   for his play come from the literature of the Middle
   Ages.

889.   Lombardo, Agostino. "*Sul Troilus and Cressida*," pp.
       135-59 in *Critical Dimensions*, ed. by Mario Curreli
       and Alberto Martino. Cuneo: SASTE, 1978.

       Lombardo reads *Tro.* as an elegy on the end of the
       Medieval world picture. Shakespeare attempted to
       symthesize Medieval and Renaissance conceptions and
       produced a new theatrical language which is clearly
       seen in the later tragedies.

890.   Longo, Joseph A. "A propos the Love Plot in Chaucer's
       Troilus and Creseyde and Shakespeare's *Troilus and
       Cressida*." *CahiersE*, 11(1977), 1-15.

       Longo argues that Shakespeare borrowed Chaucer's
       treatment of the love story as well as thematic issues
       to create the atmosphere in *Tro.*

891.   Meyer, George Wilbur. "Order out of Chaos in Shake-
       speare's *Troilus and Cressida*." *TSE*, 4(1954),
       45-56.

       This essay is valuable for its listing and reviewing
       of criticism concerning *Tro.* Medieval sources are
       briefly discussed (Lydgate, Chaucer, and Caxton).
       Meyer interprets the play as a treatise on moral and
       political confusion.

*   Miskimin, Alice S. *The Renaissance Chaucer*. See 238.

*   Mohl, Ruth. *The Three Estates in Medieval and
       Renaissance Literature*. See 239.

892.   Morris, B. "The Tragic Structure of *Troilus and
       Cressida*." *SQ*, 10(1959), 481-91.

       Morris believes that the many features which Shake-
       speare inherited in the Troilus story make the drama
       difficult to perceive as tragedy. It appears that
       Shakespeare is furthering the denigration of the story
       by presenting a moral world in which evil is unrelieved.

893.   Muir, Kenneth. "*Troilus and Cressida*." *ShS*, 8(1955),
       28-39.

       Muir reviews various criticisms of *Tro.* and interprets
       the drama as a dramatic statement of the power of time.
       He compares Shakespeare's play to Chaucer's and finds
       that Chaucer distances Cressida's surrender to Diomed
       which plays down her inconstancy while Shakespeare shows

her as a whore and Pandarus as the archetypal pimp.
Like others before him, Muir determines that this story
was so dramatized before Shakespeare that he could do
nothing but follow the stories in existence.

894. ————. *Shakespeare's Sources: I, Comedies and
      Tragedies*. London: Methuen and Co., Ltd., 1957.
      267 pp.

      Muir credits Chaucer's *Troilus and Criseyde* for the
      main source of Shakespeare's play and presents addition-
      al comments upon Shakespeare's borrowing from Caxton,
      Henryson, and Lydgate.

895. Nass, Barry Nathan. "The Troy Legend in Shakespearean
      Drama." *DAI*, 39(1979), 5530-A (Princeton).

      Chapter One explores the Troy legend from Homer to
      Henryson with reference to specific themes and attitudes
      that affected Shakespeare's conception of the myth.
      Primary emphasis is upon Shakespeare's play but other
      literature is mentioned that deals with the Troy legend.

896. Oates, J. C. "The Ambiguity of *Troilus and Cressida*."
      SQ, 17(1966), 141-50.

      Concerning the Medieval element in *Tro.*, Oates remarks
      that Shakespeare's Troilus must die because his death is
      his only allowed rejection of the world. Chaucer's
      Troilus ascended to the eighth sphere and saw the
      absurdity of his former idolatry. Shakespeare's
      Toilus cannot believe that his suffering on earth and
      the criminality of earth's people are not important,
      while Chaucer's Troilus sees the vanity of the human
      condition.

897. Owens, Roger. "The Seven Deadly Sins in the Prologue
      to *Troilus and Cressida*." *SJW*, 116(1980), 85-92.

      The prologue serves to "outline the moral failings
      which will be the concern of the remainder of the play.
      The presence of the Seven Deadly Sins, then, points to
      the need for a reassertion of the basic virtues which
      allow the selflessness of human sharing."

898. Palmer, Kenneth. *Arden Edition of Troilus and Cressida*.
      London: Methuen 1980. 337 pp.

      For a discussion of Chaucer's influence on Shakespeare's
      Tro. see pages 23-26. Shakespeare drew heavily upon

Chaucer for the love action in the play. Palmer also discusses Caxton and Lydgate and their contribution to Shakespeare's play. See pages 26–30.

*   Patchell, Mary F. *The Palmerin Romances in Elizabethan Prose Fiction.* See 261.

899.   Pearce, T. M. "'Another Knot, Five-Finger-Tied!' Shakespeare's *Troilus and Cressida,* V, ii, 157." *N&Q,* 7(1953), 18–19.

This is a source study which points to the homily of the Parson in Chaucer's *The Canterbury Tales* for Troilus' phrase "another knot, five-finger-tied." The phrase is linked to concepts of lechery.

*   Pettet, E. C. *Shakespeare and the Romance Tradition.* See 381.

*   Phillias, James E. *The State in Shakespeare's Greek and Roman Plays.* See 263.

900.   Presson, Robert K. "The Structural Use of a Traditional Theme in *Troilus and Cressida.*" *PQ,* 31(1952), 180–88.

Of interest is Shakespeare's characterization of Troilus in contrast to Chaucer's. Shakespeare's Troilus has sensual doting which seals his eyes. Chaucer's Troilus is a courtly lover while Shakespeare's Troilus is an example of passion overpowering reason.

901.   ————. *Shakespeare's Troilus and Cressida and the Legends of Troy.* Madison: U. of Wisconsin Pr., 1953. 165 pp.

This study emphasizes Shakespeare's debt to previous writers for the siege plot and the love story. Presson's method is to take particular scenes such as the dissension of the Greek army and to see this scene from the point of view of all writers mentioning it. In this way, Presson determines Shakespeare's debt to Chapman, Caxton, Chaucer, and others. Chapman's account is the basis for the siege plot, whereas the love story shows a debt to Caxton, Chaucer, and others.

902.   Rollins, H. E. "The Troilus and Cressida Story from Chaucer to Shakespeare." *PMLA,* 32(1917), 383–429.

Rollins compares Chaucer's version of this story to Shakespeare's and points out that Chaucer had sympathy

for Pandarus, Troilus, and Criseyde while Shakespeare's
presentation of these characters portrays their lust
and sensuousness. Rollins argues that history and
tradition had so established the characters that
Shakespeare could not portray them otherwise.

903. Root, R. K. "Shakespeare Misreads Chaucer." *MLN*,
38(1933), 346-48.

In Act V of *Tro.*, Shakespeare notes that Troilus
climbed the Trojan wall looking for Cressida with the
full moon shining. Root examines Chaucer's *Troilus
and Criseyde* and finds Chaucer made a point of having
the moon invisible while Troilus was looking for
Criseyde. Shakespeare uses a full moon as a romantic
setting, while Chaucer uses the signs of the moon as a
way of measuring the days.

* Schofield, William Henry. *Chivalry in English
Literature*. See 291.

* Siegel, Paul N. *Shakespearean Tragedy and the
Elizabethan Compromise*. See 294.

* Stevenson, David L. *The Love-Game Comedy*. See 312.

904. Tatlock, John P. "The Siege of Troy in Elizabethan
Literature, Especially in Shakespeare and Heywood."
PMLA, 30(1915), 673-770.

Tatlock refers to Henryson's *Testament of Cresseid*,
Chaucer's *Troilus and Criseyde*, and Caxton's account
of the siege of Troy while comparing Shakespeare's
and Heywood's version of the story. In the prologue
Shakespeare borrowed some from Chaucer, while the fifth
act, scene five, shows evidence of his having used
Caxton.

905. ————. "The Chief Problem of Shakespeare." *SR*,
24(1916), 129-147.

Tatlock compares Shakespeare's *Tro.* with its Medieval
and Renaissance sources in an attempt to answer the
question as to why he treated Cressida with scorn.
Tatlock suggests that the playwright dealt with a popular subject that was so familiar that it was largely
unmalleable. Thus, while Shakespeare used Medieval
accounts of the story, he rejected them and characterized
Troilus in a Renaissance manner.

906.   Taylor, George. "Shakespeare's Attitude Toward Love
        and Honor in *Troilus and Cressida*." *PMLA*, 45(1930),
        781-86.

        Taylor questions the critical comments of Tatlock,
        Lawrence, and Rollins who hold that Shakespeare was
        bound by tradition in presenting most of the material
        in the play. Shakespeare's cynical attitude toward
        love and honor is not the result of his source material
        but resulted from his analysis of the ideals of heroism
        and romance. Love and honor are treated cynically
        throughout the Shakespearean canon. Tatlock refers
        to love and honor in *Ant.* and *Oth.* and suggests that
        it was part of Shakespeare's technique to question the
        concepts related to virtue, honor, and love.

907.   Thompson, Ann. *"Troilus and Criseyde* and *Romeo and
        Juliet*." *YES*, 6(1976), 26-37.

        Thompson argues that Chaucer's poem was "very much in
        Shakespeare's mind." She shows a number of parallels
        and discusses common themes and their treatment by
        both authors.

*   ————. *Shakespeare's Chaucer: A Study in Literary
        Origins*. See 321.

908.   Thompson, Karl F. *"Troilus and Cressida:* the
        Incomplete Achilles." *CE*, 27(1965), 532-36.

        Shakespeare adopts the Medieval themes of love and
        honor and courtly love in *Tro.* The playwright does not
        deal consistently "either in fun or seriousness with
        the courtly love tradition."

*   Toole, William B. *Shakespeare's Problem Plays.* See 329.

909.   Ure, Peter. "Addition: *Troilus and Cressida* IV, v,
        141." *N&Q*, 211(1966), 135.

        "I came to kill thee, cousin, and bear hence a great
        addition earned in thy death." "Addition" is used in a
        heraldic sense and refers to marks of honor. Ure
        comments that this heraldic reference and others in the
        play indicate that Shakespeare is working with various
        aspects of chivalry throughout the play.

Twelfth Night

*   Curtin, Madelyn Elaine Douglas. "Mistaking the Word and

and Simple Syllogisms: Form and Function in Shakespeare's Wordplay." See 91.

* Dessen, Alan. *Elizabethan Drama and the Viewer's Eye*. See 100.

* Hassel, R. Chris, Jr. *Faith and Folly in Shakespeare's Romantic Comedies*. See 376.

910. Lewalski, Barbara. "Thematic Patterns in *Twelfth Night*." *ShakS*, 1(1965), 168-81.

The allegory in the play is in some ways similar to the Christian typology of the Middle Ages, a method whereby historical events or personages from the Old Testament and certain classical fictions were seen to point to aspects of the Gospel story without losing historical or fictional reality. In many ways, the author's reading resembles Barber's concept of certain festivities and pagan saturnalia. Maria represents wit and cleverness, while Belch, Aguecheek and Fabian represent merriment, song, and revelry. Illyria is associated with the place of good will, restoration, and peace. Viola and Sebastian represent the restorative process.

* Pettet, E. C. *Shakespeare and the Romance Tradition*. See 381.

* Russell, William M. "Courtly Love in Shakespeare's Romantic Comedies." See 384.

* Thompson, K. M. "Shakespeare's Romantic Comedies." See 387.

Two Gentlemen of Verona

* Charlton, H. B. *Shakespearean Comedy*. See 367.

* Curtin, Madelyn Elaine Douglas. "Mistaking the Word and Simple Syllogisms: Form and Function in Shakespeare's Wordplay." See 91.

911. Jones, Connie Holt. "Shakespeare and the Problem of Forgiveness: The Diversity Between Mercy and Vain Pity in *Two Gentlemen of Verona, Measure for Measure,* and *The Tempest*." *DAI*, 36(1975), 903-04-A (Alabama).

TGV, MM, and *Tmp.* show a pattern of forgiveness de-

pendent upon the conflict between the classical concept
of vain pity and the Christian concept of charity.

*   Pettet, E. C. *Shakespeare and the Romance Tradition.*
        See 381.

912.   Sargent, Ralph M. "Sir Thomas Elyot and the Integrity
        of *Two Gentlemen of Verona.*" *PMLA*, 65(1950),
        1166-80.

        The confusion over the critics' assessment of *TGV*
        can partially be abated if we recognize the conventions
        of romantic love Shakespeare was using. The religion
        of love, an inheritance of the Middle Ages, was changed
        by Shakespeare into the Christian ideal of marriage.
        In addition, the Medieval conception of the sworn brother
        idea plays an important role in the play. By using
        these two conventions, Shakespeare has his characters
        involved in the problem of loyalty to both ideals, and
        the conflict and reconciliation of these principles is
        the basis of the play.

913.   Taylor, John Alfred. "Rogues in Arden: A Study of
        Elizabethan Newgate Pastoral." *DAI*, 29(1969),
        3158-A (Berkeley).

        Chapters, Three, Four, and Five focus upon the Robin
        Hood legends in ballads, folk drama, and folk festivals.
        Other sections concern the survival of Medieval fool
        satire and its influence upon *TGV*.

*   Thompson, K. M. "Shakespeare's Romantic Comedies."
        See 387.

*   Vyvyan, John. *Shakespeare and the Rose of Love: A
        Study of the Early Plays in Relation to the Medieval
        Philosophy of Love.* See 390.

                        Two Noble Kinsmen

914.   Bertram, Paul. *Shakespeare and The Two Noble Kinsmen.*
        New Brunswick: Rutgers U. Pr., 1965. 306 pp.

        See Chapter Six "The Composition of the Play" for a
        detailed discussion of Chaucer's "The Knight's Tale"
        and Shakespeare's *TNK*. "Verbal parallels," dramatic
        construction, and character depiction are emphasized.

*   Thompson, Ann. *Shakespeare's Chaucer: A Study in
        Literary Origins.* See 321.

Venus and Adonis

915. Allen, Don Cameron. "On *Venus and Adonis*," pp. 100-11
in *Elizabethan and Jacobean Studies Presented to
Frank Percy Wilson*. ed. Herbert Davis and Helen
Gardner. Oxford: The Clarendon Pr., 1959.

Allen interprets *Ven.* in light of both classical and
Medieval concepts. The larger scheme of the hunt
controls the first four stanzas of the poem, and the
symbols entailed evolve from the Middle Ages. He
discusses the hunt in Medieval literature and relates
it to knighthood and the forming of a gentleman. Then
he comments on the "love hunt," the work of those who
will become heroes. The poem can be read as a satire
on courtly love or as a burning indictment of lust.

916. Brown, Carleton. "Shakespeare and the Horse."
Library, 3(1912), 152-80.

Brown lists classical and Medieval literature which
deals with horses and comments upon possible Shakespearean borrowings from these sources for *Ven.* He
sees a general influence from Medieval romances.

917. Bush, Douglas. "Shakespeare: *Venus and Adonis* and
'The Rape of Lucrece,'" pp. 139-55 in *Mythology and
the Renaissance Tradition*. Minneapolis: The U. of
Minnesota Pr., 1932.

Bush finds the classical tradition to be very strong
in *Ven.*, yet Shakespeare was influenced by the "apostrophe to Death, which is thoroughly of the Renaissance
and also thoroughly Medieval." Bush has references and
comparisons to the *Philomena*. Concerning "Lucrece"
Bush remarks that it is "thoroughly in the Medieval
tradition." Shakespeare's technique is nearer to
Chaucer's than to Ovid's. Tarquin's threat to kill
one of Lucrece's slaves and the carrying of her body
to Rome are details which indicate that Shakespeare
was thoroughly acquainted with Chaucer's *Legend of
Good Women*. Bush observes that "the brief reflections
in Chaucer on Tarquin's violation of chivalry might
have suggested a text for the long debate in
Shakespeare."

918. Dickey, Franklin M. "Attitudes Toward Love in *Venus
and Adonis* and 'The Rape of Lucrece,'" pp. 46-62 in
Not Wisely But Too Well. San Marino: The Huntington
Library, 1957.

Dickey relates *Ven.* to the Ovidian love tradition and
to the allegorical mode of the Middle Ages. Images of
lust, gluttony, passion, strength, and power are
associated with Venus to such an extent that they can
be treated allegorically. Images of innocence and love
are associated with Adonis. Dickey reads "Lucrece" as
an *exemplum* illustrating the fall from grace and notes
that it is in the same tradition as Lydgate's *Fall of
Princes*. He also shows that the imagery in "Lucrece"
is typically Medieval going back to allegory like *The
Soul's Ward* or to the morality plays like *The Castle
of Perseverance*.

919.   Hatto, A. T. *"Venus and Adonis*--and the Boar." *MLR,*
       41(1946), 353-61.

Hatto "detects a faint lingering mist of Medieval
courtliness" in *Ven.* despite its classical theme. He
traces the symbol of the noble boar to the works of
Chaucer, Boccaccio, Thomas of Britain, and Gottfried
von Strassburg. "The boar in the Middle Ages stood
out essentially as a symbol of overbearing masculinity
in love and war, with unmistakable and long-standing
associations of nobility." Venus is thus jealous of
the boar's ability to attract Adonis.

920.   Miller, Robert P. "The Myth of Mar's Hot Minion in
       Venus and Adonis." ELH, 26(1959), 470-81.

Miller insists upon the moral message of *Ven.* and
shows the artistry of Shakespeare's irony in the poem.
He documents classical, Medieval, and Renaissance sources
for the poem and argues that a moral tale is hidden
beneath the allegory which involves a standard Medieval
pattern sometimes referred to as the horse-and-rider
convention. The substance of the poem is the spirit
contending with the flesh, and reason against
sensuality.

921.   Rebhorn, Wayne A. "Mother Venus: Temptations in
       Shakespeare's *Venus and Adonis." ShakS,* 11(1978),
       1-19.

In this study particular attention is given to the
courtly love tradition. A number of Chaucer's works
are surveyed as well as the poems of Skelton in
establishing the background of the courtly love
convention.

922. Rollins, Hyder. "The Sources of *Venus and Adonis* and "Lucrece," pp. 390-405; 416-39 in *New Variorum Edition of Shakespeare, The Poems*. Philadelphia: J.B. Lippincott Co., 1938.

Rollins presents a summary of scholarship concerning Shakespeare's source material. Critics argue primarily against the native tradition for *Ven.* But many such as Craig see Chaucer's *Legend of Good Women* influencing "Lucrece."

923. Wade, James Edgar. "Medieval Rhetoric in Shakespeare." Diss., U. of Saint Louis, 1942.

The rhetoric in Elizabethan England developed largely from the Middle Ages which modified the rhetoric of Cicero and Quintillian by merging rhetoric and poetic within the third division of rhetoric: *elocutio*, a study of style from the point of view of figures of speech. Wade examines *Ven.* and "Lucrece" in terms of Medieval rhetoric and determines that Shakespeare was greatly influenced by the native tradition.

924. Wyndham, George. "The Poems of Shakespeare," pp. 237-388 in *Essays in Romantic Literature*. ed. Charles Whibley. London: Macmillan and Co., Ltd., 1919.

Shakespeare's style and diction in *Ven.* stem from Ovid and from Medieval rhetoric which Wyndham calls "liquidity of diction." The author shows that Shakespeare's imagery and diction owe a debt to his Medieval predecessors.

The Winter's Tale

925. Bryant, J. A. "Shakespeare's Allegory: *The Winter's Tale*." *SR*, 63(1955), 202-222.

The four fold allegorical interpretation of literature (letter, allegory, trope, and anagoge) so common to Medieval writings may be appropriately related to the *WT*. Bryant comments upon Dante's and Aquinas' ideas regarding allegorical interpretation and modifies their views in his discussion of the play. *WT* is similar in some ways to the vernacular plays of the fourteenth-century cycles in that both can be related to the four-fold method of interpretation. Scenes from *WT* depict the story of Christ's birth, death, and resurrection.

*   ————. *Hippolyta's View: Some Christian Aspects of
         Shakespeare's Plays.* See 50.

*   Cooper, Helen. *Pastoral: Medieval into Renaissance.*
         See 76.

*   Hawkins, Richard H. "Some Effects of Technique De-
         veloped in the Native Drama on the Structure of
         Shakespeare's Plays. See 160.

*   Hengerer, Joyce H. "The Theme of the Slandered Woman
         in Shakespeare." See 162.

926.   Hoeniger, F. David. "The Meaning of *The Winter's Tale*."
         UTQ, 20(1950), 11-26.

         Hoeniger discusses the surface meaning of the drama
         in order to show its limitations and reviews Dante and
         the Medieval tradition of allegory. Shakespeare's use
         of allegory is similar to that of Medieval writers.
         Four themes which are treated allegorically are: the
         identity between parents and children; the rebirth of
         nature; the progression of man from youth, old age, and
         to death with a corresponding emphasis upon innocence,
         sin, and redemption; finally, the relationship of art
         to nature and the creative imagination.

*   Hunter, Robert Grams. *Shakespeare and the Comedy of
         Forgiveness.* See 377.

927.   Maveety, Stanley R. "Hermione, A Dangerous Ornament."
         SQ, 14(1963), 485-86.

         Leonte's mentioning of a 'dagger muzzled' in *WT*
         (I, v, 153-58) may well echo the dagger mentioned in
         Chaucer's "The Merchant's Tale."

928.   ————. "High Style, Strange Words, and the Answer
         to an Old Problem." *ELN*, 5(1968), 159-63.

         Maveety comments that Francis Sabie's *The Fisherman's
         Tale* was a source for Robert Greene's *Pandosto;* and
         although Shakespeare probably used *Pandosto* for *WT*,
         he may have also borrowed from Sabie's work. Maveety
         then notes that Sabie's narrative is set in a framework
         reminiscent of the Medieval dream allegory. He then
         shows the influence of this dream allegory upon Shake-
         speare.

929. Meldrum, Ronald M. "Dramatic Intention in *The Winter's Tale.*" *BCAH*, 19(1969), 52-60.

> Meldrum reviews and classifies past criticism of *WT* and basically agrees with those who interpret the play in a Christian allegorical manner. The school of Frye, Wincor, Leavis, and James emphasize the nature myth as central to the meaning of the play. Tillyard, Spencer, Knight, Bethell, and Traversi interpret the play in light of Christian myth. The Medieval school (Coghill, Hoeniger, and Bryant) use the allegorical method that was familiar to early church fathers.

* Salinger, Leo. *Shakespeare and the Tradition of Comedy.* See 385.

930. Scott, William. "Seasons and Flowers in *The Winter's Tale.*" *SQ*, 14(1963), 411-17.

> Scott applies the surviving Medieval tradition of the seasons with the analogy of the courses of the year to a man's life. February is early childhood; June is the prime of life; in October a man should make his peace with God; and in January man faces death. The above ideas are shown in relation to the major characters in *WT*. Scott also comments upon the Medieval survival of herbs and floral symbols as they relate to the play.

931. Thorne, W. B. "Things Newborn: A Study of the Rebirth Motif in *The Winter's Tale.*" *HAB*, 19(1968), 34-43.

> Shakespeare adapts the winter-spring convention of Medieval poetry and works with concepts of birth and death, youth and age, and goodness and evil. Paulina emerges as a morality personification for the king.

932. Traversi, Derek. *Shakespeare: The Last Phase.* New York: Harcourt, Brace and Co., 1955. 272 pp.

> Traversi's interpretation of *WT* (105-92) is based upon the salvation theme of the earlier Christian cycle plays. The imagery of flowers, seasons, love, and death is deliberately used by Shakespeare to indicate patterns of redemption, grace, repentance, and reconciliation.

* Vyvyan, John. *The Shakespearean Ethic.* See 333.

* ————. *Shakespeare and the Rose of Love: A Study of*

*the Early Plays in Relation to the Medieval Philosophy
of Love.* See 390.

933. Wilson, Harold S. "'Nature and Art' in *Winter's Tale*."
        SAB, 18(1943), 114-20.

In the words cited above, Shakespeare refers to
grafting a gentle scion upon wild stock in order to
improve nature. Wilson refers to Medieval and Renaissance writings to show the thought expressed by
Shakespeare was not original. Wilson also concludes
that Shakespeare's horticultural illustrations were
familiar Renaissance discussions long before Shakespeare's birth.

AUTHOR INDEX